The Java™ FAQ

The Java™ Series

Lisa Friendly, Series Editor
Bill Joy, Technical Advisor

The Java™ Programming Language
Ken Arnold and James Gosling
0-201-63455-4

Java™ Language Specification
James Gosling, Bill Joy, and Guy Steele
0-201-63451-1

The Java™ Virtual Machine Specification
Tim Linhold and Frank Yellin
0-201-63452-X

The Java™ Application Programming Interface, Volume 1: Core Packages
James Gosling, Frank Yellin, and the Java Team
0-201-63453-8

The Java™ Application Programming Interface, Volume 2: Window Toolkit & Applets
James Gosling, Frank Yellin, and the Java Team
0-201-63459-7

The Java™ Tutorial: Object-Oriented Programming for the Internet
Mary Campione and Kathy Walrath
0-201-63454-6

The Java™ Class Libraries: An Annotated Reference
Patrick Chan and Rosanna Lee
0-201-63458-9

Concurrent Programming in Java™ : Design Principles and Patterns
Doug Lea
0-201-69581-2

JDBC Database Access with Java™ : A Tutorial and Annotated Reference
Graham Hamilton, Rick Cattell, and Maydene Fisher
0-201-30995-5

The Java™ FAQ

Jonni Kanerva

ADDISON-WESLEY

An imprint of Addison Wesley Longman, Inc.
Reading, Massachusetts • Harlow, England • Menlo Park, California
Berkeley, California • Don Mills, Ontario • Sydney
Bonn • Amsterdam • Tokyo • Mexico City

The publisher offers discounts on this book when ordered in quantity for special sales.
For more information, please contact:

> Corporate & Professional Publishing Group
> Addison-Wesley Publishing Company
> One Jacob Way
> Reading, Massachusetts 01867

Text printed on recycled and acid-free paper

ISBN 0-201-63456-2

1 2 3 4 5 6 7 8 9 -MA- 0100999897
First printing, July 1997

Table of Contents

Preface . . . . **vii**

1   Classes, Interfaces, and Packages **1**

Objects, Classes, and Methods. 1
Subclassing, Overloading, and Overriding 13
Interfaces and Abstract Classes 25
Packages and Access Modifiers. .33

2   Java Language **41**

Constants and Expressions. 41
Variables and Methods 53
Arrays. 65
Exceptions 68

3   Virtual Machine **77**

4   Applets **91**

Applets versus Applications 91
Installing Applets. 95
Applet User Interface. 103
Applet Program Structure 107
Applet Communication 111
Miscellaneous 114

5   Abstract Window Toolkit **117**

Components, Containers, and Peers. 117
Windows, Frames, and Dialogs .127
Miscellaneous 131

6   Events—JDK 1.0.2 .... **135**

7   Events—JDK 1.1 .... **151**

Event Classes, Listeners, and Methods 151
Semantic Events.................................161
Low-level Events 167

8   Drawing **173**

Drawing AWT Components 173
Loading and Drawing Images 179
Images—JDK 1.0.2 192
Images—JDK 1.1................................195

9   Threads.................................... **201**

Creating and Controlling Threads 201
Thread Interactions 208
User Threads versus System Threads 222

10 Input, Output, and Network..................... **225**

Basic Input and Output 225
URL Connections...............................235
Internet Addresses 244
Sockets......................................245

11 Miscellaneous.............................. **255**

Classes in **java.lang** and **java.util** 255
Audio 261
Miscellaneous 265

Index.................................. **271**

Preface

Java™ technology has achieved remarkably widespread use in a very short time. The broad acceptance of Java reflects Java's technical strengths and feature set: platform-neutrality, dynamism, object-orientation, garbage collection, security, concurrency, robustness, and Internet savvy. The Java language has established itself as a mature, general-purpose programming language, and the standard Java class libraries provide an ever-broadening platform supporting a wide spectrum of application development.

Nevertheless, the speed and passion with which many developers have adopted Java shows that more than just technical soundness is at work. Java is *fun to use* and *practical*. It removes tedious and error-prone parts of application development such as memory management and cross-platform porting. It allows the developer to focus more energy on program design and functionality. The language is also comparatively easy to learn, thanks to a strong principle that guided the creation of Java: "Keep it simple!" An important corollary to this principle is: "Keep it learnable!" Java is not only fun to use but also fun to learn.

This book is a tool for developers learning to use Java. Its primary goals are unabashedly pragmatic:

- to provide easy access to highly relevant information
- to avert or debug common misunderstandings and errors
- to give you the information you need in a form you can use

The Java FAQ is not a fully detailed treatise on Java technology—for this, see *The Java Language Specification*, *The Java Virtual Machine Specification*, or one of the API reference books in the Java Series. Nor is it a carefully guided, sequenced exposition of Java—for this, see *The Java Programming Language* or *The Java Tutorial*.

This book, by means of its frequently asked-question (FAQ) format, takes direct advantage of a teacher's two favorite tools, questions and examples. Questions specify an informational need: if you can spell out what information you are missing, you are more than halfway towards attaining it. A question sets the context for linking new information into existing knowledge; it establishes the *relevance* (or usefulness) of the information.

Examples, likewise, give a penetrating edge to information. A specific example is usually easier to grasp than the general idea it illustrates. Sample code, moreover, is an especially useful form of example, since it can often be built into larger, working programs.

What qualifies as a frequently asked question? The primary source of questions for this book was the e-mail traffic at the java@java.sun.com address. This e-mail address was the default technical support pipeline for Java technology, especially in the formative period when Java and HotJava were progressing from a 1.0 alpha release, to beta, and finally to FCS (First Customer Ship). Although the term *frequently asked questions* suggests a collection of the most common questions (plus answers), this book has a slightly different target: *frequently ask-worthy questions*, that is, the questions you need to have answered in order to learn Java quickly and use it effectively. *The Java FAQ* aims for the question behind the question: the more general information gap or misunderstanding that, when filled or corrected, can answer a host of more specific questions.

When you ask a question, it is important to know if your question has been answered. Thus, this book follows the admirable example set by *The C++ FAQs* (by Cline and Lomow, Addison-Wesley, 1995) of providing a highlighted short answer immediately following each question. This gives the answer in a nutshell, and the rest of the answer then explains and exemplifies the nutshell answer.

Many answers end in a pointer in the form of a partial URL (Uniform Resource Locator), such as *GrabPixelsExample.html*. These pointers refer to web pages containing sample code, applets, or other example material related to the answer. You can access these web pages by following links starting from the Java Series home page at the JavaSoft web site: `http://java.sun.com/Series`.

Each question–answer pair is intended to stand on its own as far as possible, but numerous cross references are included to indicate connections or dependencies in the material. You can dive into the middle of the book and follow leads from there, or you can start at the beginning and read straight through.

The Java FAQ covers the Java language, the Java Virtual Machine, and the standard classes in the following packages: `java.lang`, `java.applet`, `java.awt`, `java.awt.image`, `java.awt.event`, `java.io`, `java.net`, and `java.util`. This is essentially the contents of Sun's Java Devloper's Kit (JDK) 1.0 release together with updated information for the JDK 1.1 release. Information and sample code specific to one or another release is flagged explicitly throughout the book: "JDK 1.0.2" for the version most widely deployed during the span of this book's writing and "JDK 1.1" for the family of releases from JavaSoft in the first half of 1997 (JDK 1.1, 1.1.1, and 1.1.2). Packages representing wholly new functionality added in the JDK 1.1, such as `java.rmi`, `java.beans`, and `java.security`, are not covered.

This book would not have been possible but for the professional and personal assistance of many fine people at JavaSoft and elsewhere. Lisa Friendly first conceived of the book and encouraged me to take it on. Her patient yet persistent care as series editor helped me stick out this large project to the end. Carla Schroer graciously allowed me to take on the commitment despite other duties that were already claiming more than 100 percent of my time. Mary Aline's detailed edits of several early draft chapters reminded me to keep the writing clear, simple, and pleasantly grammatical. Mary Campione, Eric Chu, Jazmin Ellis, Doug Kramer, Nancy Lee, Rick Levenson, Marvin Ma, Ron Mandel, Freeman Murray, Scott Rautmann, Richard Scorer, Greg Voss, and Kathy Walrath added that nice human touch to my work environment, improving the quality of both my work time and my break time. For technical assistance with wide-ranging material, I am indebted to Tom Ball, Dave Brown, Patrick Chan, Dave Connelly, Jeff Dinkins, Pavani Diwanji, Amy Fowler, Jim Graham, Jeannette Hung, Herb Jellinek, Tim Lindholm, Marianne Mueller, Tim Prinzing, John Rose, Georges Saab, Nakul Saraiya, Sami Shaio, Arthur van Hoff, Chris Warth, and Frank Yellin. It was a delight to work with and learn from such a talented group of engineers. At Addison Wesley, Mike Hendrickson, Katie Duffy, Marina Lang, and Simone Payment made the difficult process of book development as sane as possible. Their good humor, hard work, and courteous professionalism go beyond the call of duty. Addison Wesley's manuscript reviewers and proofreaders considerably improved the book by their detailed comments and constructive criticism. In the later stages of the game, Vicki Hochstedler helped me navigate the joys and agonies of putting the book into final format, and Rosemary Simpson pulled together a painstaking and powerful index.

Above all, I am indebted to my family, who understand the demands of a normal job but gave up far more because of this book. My wife, Jean, is a gem. Her intelligence, honesty, thoughtfulness, and dead-on knack for the essential have been a cornerstone of my life and work for fifteen years. Thanks to her, I hope this book has not just content, but spirit. Our children, Kirsti, Silva, and Justin, are potent lessons in the value, challenge, and joy of life. Getting more time again to grow and play with them was special motivation for me to bring this project to conclusion. The household had one frequently asked question that couldn't be answered until the very end: "When will the book be done?" Well, the answer to that is finally, happily, at hand.

Jonni Kanerva
Mountain View, California
June, 1997

CHAPTER 1

Classes, Interfaces, and Packages

Objects, Classes, and Methods (Q1.1–Q1.10)

Subclassing, Overloading, and Overriding (Q1.11–Q1.19)

Interfaces and Abstract Classes (Q1.20–Q1.28)

Packages and Access Modifiers (Q1.29–Q1.34)

OBJECTS, CLASSES, AND METHODS

Q1.1

What is an object?

An object is a software unit that combines a structured set of data with a set of operations for inspecting and manipulating that data.

Object-oriented programming reverses the function–data relationship familiar from non–object-oriented languages, such as C. Programs in C (similarly Pascal, or Basic) are often based on direct data manipulation: they define data structures and provide functions that inspect or change that data from anywhere else in the program. Intimate knowledge of data structures can be spread throughout the program, and changing a structure in one part can have drastic consequences for many other parts of the program.

Object-oriented programming provides standard tools and techniques for reducing dependencies between different parts of a program. An object starts with a structured set of data, but also includes a set of operations for inspecting and manipulating that data. In an object, all operations that require intimate knowledge of the data structure are directly associated with the structure, rather than being spread throughout the program.

A *class* (Q1.2) defines a type of object. It defines the data an object can hold and the *methods* (Q1.3) for operating on that data. Each object belongs to some class and is called an *instance* of that class (Q1.7).

Grouping operations together with their data permits you to request operations from the object rather than directly manipulating the object's data. This seemingly small step has the great benefit of decoupling the requester of an operation from the performer. The requester (some part of the program) need know only what actions to request; the performer (the object) is responsible for the detailed knowledge of how to fulfill the requests. Parts of a program now depend on each other, not through data structures, but through functionality they promise to provide (sometimes called the "contract" of each participating class).

The Java^TM programming language is object-oriented, which means that classes, instances, and methods constitute the core of your program's design.

See also: Q1.2, Q1.3, Q1.7

Q1.2

What is a class?

A class is a blueprint for objects: it defines a type of object according to the data the object can hold and the operations the object can perform.

Classes are the fundamental units of design in object-oriented programming. A class is a pattern that defines a kind of object (Q1.1). It specifies a data structure for the object together with a set of operations for acting on the object's data. A class is usually also a factory that creates objects. You can use a class to create one or more objects (instances of the class) when the program is run (Q1.7). Each instance carries its own data, such that you can change one instance and leave others unaffected. Classes specify capabilities for objects, and objects do the actual work.

The Java String class, for example, defines an object type for character strings. A String instance holds a sequence of Unicode characters and provides a large number of methods (Q1.3) for getting information about that string. Although there is just one String class, there can be any number of String instances (objects) in a Java program.

A class declaration in Java looks much like a struct declaration in C. It contains at the very least the class keyword, the class's name, an opening brace, and a closing brace. Class declarations also have many optional parts, such as access modifiers (Q1.32), a superclass specification (Q1.12), interface specifications (Q1.20), and various parts in the body of the class. The following simple example defines a class with one piece of data (called a *field*) and one method for acting on that data:

```
class SimpleClass {
    int count;  // field
    void incrementCount() {
        ++count;
    }
}
```

Understanding the difference between a class and an instance is one of the fundamental steps in learning object-oriented programming. Table 1.1 shows a few analogies for this difference:

Table 1.1: Class versus Instance

Class	Instance
cookie recipe and cutter	cookie
housing tract blueprint	specific house
rubber stamp	stamped image
photographic negative	printed picture

Note: From here on, this book follows *The Java Language Specification* (JLS; p. 38) in using the term *object* to refer to class instances *and* arrays (Q2.19). This broader use of the term takes a little getting used to but is clear and consistent. Where only class instances are under discussion, they will be referred to as *class instances* or simply *instances*.

See also: Q1.1, Q1.3, Q1.7, Q1.12, Q1.20, Q1.32, Q2.19, JLS p. 38

Q1.3

What is a method?

A method is the basic unit of functionality in an object-oriented language—a body of executable code that belongs to a class and that can be applied to (*invoked on*) a specific object or the class itself.

Methods are the object-oriented counterpart to functions or subroutines. Like a function, a method consists of:

- a name

- a (possibly empty) list of input names, called parameters, and their types

- an (optional) output type, called the return type (the void keyword declares that a method has no return type)

- a body of executable code

The following code fragment declares a method whose output (of type double) is the average of its two input values (also of type double):

```java
double average(double a, double b) {
    return (a + b) / 2.0;
}
```

Because methods belong to classes (Q1.2), you can define a method only in the body of a class definition. Note that the code fragment, however, follows the convention of this book in not showing the enclosing class definition unless relevant.

You usually use a method to inspect or manipulate the data stored in an object. For example, the Java String class provides a length method for determining the length of a String instance. The length method has no parameters and its return value is an int indicating the length of the String instance you invoke it on; for instance:

```java
String aString = "Bicycle Shop Quarterly News";
int howLong = aString.length();
```

Methods are not simply activated—they are *invoked* on a specific object (or on a class; see Q1.6). Consider the following code, which creates two Abstract Window Toolkit (AWT) Button instances and then sets the label for each one:

```
/* in Java: */
Button button1 = new Button();
Button button2 = new Button();
button1.setText("Push Me First");
button2.setText("Push Me Second");
```

Invoking `setText` on `button1` amounts to asking the `Button` class to look up its definition for `setText` and then execute that code with respect to the data in `button1`. Invoking `setText` on `button2` results in the same method lookup, but the resulting code is applied to `button2` rather than `button1`. In a non–object-oriented language, such as C, you might use an equivalent `setButtonText` function that includes the button explicitly as an argument:

```
/* in C: */
struct Button *button1 = makeButton();
struct Button *button2 = makeButton();
setButtonText(button1, "Push Me First");
setButtonText(button2, "Push Me Second");
```

(For further discussion of the relationship between a `struct` in C and an object in Java, see Q2.10.)

Because each class is responsible for its own methods, different classes can use the same name, parameters, and return type, yet still define different methods. For example, the AWT `Label` class also defines a `setText` method that takes a `String` parameter:

```
/* using Label's setText method rather than Button's: */
Label aLabel = new Label();
aLabel.setText("Read me -- I'm a label.");
```

In this example, the `Label` class provides its own definition for `setText`, and this definition could be entirely different from what the `Button` class provides.

The ability of different methods to look alike from the caller's perspective is a crucial part of object-oriented programming: it separates the request for action from the details of how that request is fulfilled. Your code can invoke a method on an object without having to know the exact class of the object—only that it has a method with the same name, parameter list, and return type (Q1.14). What actual code gets executed is selected by the class of the target object, not by the invoker.

See also: Q1.2, Q1.4, Q1.6, Q1.14, Q2.10

Q1.4

What is the signature of a method?

The signature of a method is the combination of the method's name and the method's input types (that is, number of parameters and their types).

The signature of a method provides precisely enough information to identify a method uniquely within a given class. Put another way, each method signature functions as a distinct lookup key when the class maps from method invocations to executable method bodies.

For example, the following are signatures for several methods in the Java AWT `Rectangle` class (in the JDK 1.1):

a. `isEmpty()`

b. `intersection(Rectangle)`

c. `setLocation(int, int)`

d. `contains(int, int)`

e. `contains(Point)`

(Note that method signatures as represented here are not valid Java code; they represent only the information in the signature itself.) The method signatures in a, b, and c differ from each other in every way—name, number of parameters, and types of parameters; items c and d differ only in name; and items d and e match in name but differ in number and types of parameters.

It is important to remember that a method's output information—its return value or declared exceptions—does not contribute to the method's signature. The compiler uses this information, though, to check the validity of method overriding (Q1.14, Q2.24).

See also: Q1.13, Q1.14, Q2.24

Q1.5

What is the difference between an instance variable and a class variable?

An instance variable represents a separate data item for each instance of a class, whereas a class variable represents a single data item shared by the class and all its instances.

An instance variable represents data for which each instance has its own copy. An instance variable corresponds roughly to a field of a structure (`struct`) in C or C++. If your program contains twenty `Button` instances, for example, each instance has its own `label` instance variable holding the label string for that button.

A class variable, in contrast, belongs to the class as a whole. All instances of the class have access to the same single copy. A class variable can therefore function as a shared resource and an indirect means of communication among the instances of the class. Class variables are declared with the `static` keyword.

The following code fragment declares a class with two instance variables and one class variable:

```
class Example {
    int i1;  // no static keyword, therefore instance variable
    String s;
    static int i2;  // static keyword, therefore class variable
}
```

See also: Q1.6

Q1.6

What is the difference between an instance method and a class method?

An instance method has a `this` instance reference, whereas a class method does not.

An instance method always works hand in hand with a class instance. An instance method must be invoked on a specific class instance, and it has special access to the data in that instance. For example:

```
String s1 = "abcde";   // one String instance
String s2 = "fgh";     // another String instance
int i1 = s1.length();  // i1 = 5
int i2 = s2.length();  // i2 = 3
```

The `length` method returns the number of characters in its target object (`s1` or `s2` in this example), just as if that target were an argument to a `length` function (cf. `strlen(aString)` in C). When defining an instance method, you can use the `this` keyword to refer to the target instance.

Class methods have no target instance and thus no implicit `this` reference. Class methods can always be used, even if you have no instance of the class on hand. Class methods, like class variables, are declared with the `static` keyword.

For example, the `currentThread` method in class `Thread` is a class method. You invoke it on the `Thread` class itself, and it determines the currently executing thread and returns a reference to it.

```
Thread activeThread = Thread.currentThread();
```

As alternates to the names instance variable, instance method, class variable, and class method, some Java programmers prefer to use terms such as member, field, static field, method, and static method. Table 1.2 summarizes how the various terms are related.

Table 1.2: Names for Elements in a Class

member	field	instance variable (or nonstatic field)
		class variable (or static field)
	method	instance method (or nonstatic method)
		class method (or static method)

Note: The term *field* is useful for distinguishing variables defined in a class, as opposed to local variables, which are defined inside a method.

VariableExample.html

See also: Q1.2, Q1.3, Q1.5

Q1.7

How do I create an instance of a class?

The usual way to create a class instance is to invoke a constructor for the class.

In Java, all objects (class instances and arrays) are created with space allocated from system-managed memory, but you never access that heap directly. The Java language and Virtual Machine manage it for you via the `new` keyword, the `newInstance` method in class `Class`, and automatic garbage collection (Q3.5).

The standard way to create a class instance is with the new keyword followed by the name of the class and arguments for one of the class's constructors. For example:

```
Button myButton = new Button("Press Me");
```

This line of code declares a variable named myButton, creates a new Button instance labeled Press Me, and sets the myButton variable to refer to that button. Common coding style in Java is to declare a class-type variable and initialize it to point to a newly created instance all in the same line of code.

For comparison, if you simply declare an instance variable of type Button, as in:

```
Button myButton;
```

then all you've created is a variable named myButton initialized with a null reference (by default initialization; see Q1.10). Or if you declare a local variable (that is, a method-internal variable) as above, the compiler will require you to set it to some value before you can use it.

You can also create or obtain class instances by invoking methods. Some methods always return a new instance, such as the newInstance method in class Class (Q2.15, Q3.7) and the valueOf method in class Integer (Q10.4). Other methods, such as InetAddress's getByName method (Q10.16), may return an instance, but without any guarantee that the instance is distinct from others it returned earlier.

See also: Q1.10, Q2.15, Q3.5, Q3.7, Q10.4, Q10.16

Q1.8

What is an abstract method?

An abstract method is a method that defines all aspects of itself except what code it executes.

An abstract method declares the method's name, parameter types, return type, and exceptions, but does not provide an implementation for the method. You declare an abstract method with the abstract keyword and with a semicolon in place of the method body. For example:

```
public abstract void drawFigure();  // abstract method declaration
```

Abstract methods let you design a class with some or all pieces left for subclasses to fill in. A class containing abstract methods is also called abstract, and must also be declared with the abstract keyword (Q1.9). By including an abstract method in a class, you require that anyone who implements a fully functional (*concrete*) subclass (Q1.11) will have to include an implementation for that method.

For example, the Number class in the java.lang package consists entirely of abstract methods. The full JDK (1.0.2 and 1.1) class definition is:

```
/* in Number.java (JDK 1.0.2 and 1.1): */
public abstract class Number {
    public abstract int intValue();
    public abstract long longValue();
    public abstract float floatValue();
    public abstract double doubleValue();
}
```

The java.lang package also contains several concrete subclasses of Number: Integer, Long, Float, Double, and (starting with the JDK 1.1) Byte and Short. Each of these subclasses defines implementations for the four abstract methods just listed.

As another example, the InputStream class in the java.io package provides the base for a large family of subclasses that handle specific types of byte-oriented input streams. The JDK 1.0.2 class definition implements all its methods except one. (In the JDK 1.1, InputStream's available method is also defined as abstract.) The core no-parameter read method, responsible for reading one byte of input, is left abstract so that subclasses must define it:

```
public abstract int read() throws IOException;
```

The other read methods in InputStream are defined to eventually result in calls to read(). In this way, when you implement read() in a subclass, the rest of the class is already integrated around your new method definition.

See also: Q1.9, Q1.11

Q1.9

What is an abstract class?

An abstract class is a class designed with implementation gaps for subclasses to fill in.

An abstract class is deliberately incomplete. It defines a skeleton that various subclasses (Q1.11) can flesh out with customized implementation details. The different *concrete* (nonabstract) subclasses provide a family of variants.

An abstract class must be explicitly declared with the abstract keyword. Note that declaring a class as abstract suffices to make it abstract—it need not even have any abstract methods. By declaring it abstract, you signal that it is functionally incomplete, and you ensure that no one can create instances of that class.

The AWT Component class (Q5.1), for example, is the abstract superclass for all AWT user-interface elements. Although it provides default implementations for all its methods, it is nevertheless declared abstract. Component is not meant to be instantiated directly. Instead, it provides a common infrastructure within which more specific subclasses, such as Button and TextField, can be defined and instantiated.

See also: Q1.8, Q1.11, Q5.1

Q1.10

What is an object reference?

An object reference is essentially an object pointer with strong restrictions for integrity and safety.

As a Java programmer, you can access objects (class instances and arrays) only by means of object references. Behind the scenes, an object reference provides two kinds of information to the run-time system:

- a pointer to the object's instance information—its data
- a pointer to the object's class information—its run-time type and its table of methods

Although pointers exist inside the Java run-time system, you cannot manipulate them directly. The Java language does not expose a numerical notion of references or pointers: you cannot do pointer arithmetic, nor can you fabricate pointers from numeric data.

The operations you can perform on an object reference all treat the reference as an opaque entity. Table 1.3, adapted from *The Java Language Specification* (p. 39), summarizes the possible operations on an object reference:

Table 1.3: Possible Operations on an Object Reference

assign the reference to a variable
invoke a method on the reference
extract a field from the reference
cast the reference to another type
test the reference's run-time type using the `instanceof` operator
concatenate the reference with a `String` instance
test the reference for equality with another reference using `==` and `!=`
provide the reference as a value in the conditional operator `?:`

The integrity of object references in Java is a cornerstone of security (protection from malice) and safety (protection from mistakes).

As an example, consider the following code fragment:

```
String s1;
String s2;
s1 = "a string";
s2 = s1;
```

The first two lines declare two `String` variables; at this stage, `s1` and `s2` are simply uninitialized local variables. The third line sets `s1` to refer to the `String` instance represented by the string literal `"a string"` (Q2.8). The fourth line sets `s2` to refer to the same object as `s1`. There is still just one `String` instance, but now two separate references to it.

When you declare a variable of a class, interface, or array type, the value of that variable is always an object reference or the `null` reference. The following chart compares similar definitions in Java and C++:

Java	C++
`Button b;`	`Button *b;`
`String s;`	`String *s;`

See also: Q2.8, JLS p. 39

SUBCLASSING, OVERLOADING, AND OVERRIDING

Q1.11

What is a subclass?

A subclass is a class defined as an extension or modification of another class.

Except for the Object class in the java.lang package, every class in the Java language is a subclass of some other class (called its *immediate superclass*, or *superclass* for short). A subclass behaves like its superclass, except where it specifies extensions or modifications.

A subclass can extend its superclass by defining additional instance variables and methods for the subclass instances, or by defining additional class variables and class methods for the subclass. A subclass can also modify the behavior of its superclass by replacing some of the superclass's method definitions with its own. In both cases, the Java language uses the extends keyword to declare subclass relationships. In the JDK (1.0.2 and 1.1), for example, the FileInputStream class in the java.io package is defined as a subclass of InputStream:

```
/* in FileInputStream.java (JDK 1.0.2 and 1.1): */
public class FileInputStream extends InputStream {
    // ... fields and method definitions
}
```

If a class definition omits the extends clause, the class is defined as an immediate subclass of the root Object class.

The subclass relation is transitive: if class Z is a subclass of class Y, and class Y is a subclass of class X, then class Z is a subclass of class X:

Z subclass of Y, Y subclass of X $\implies$ Z subclass of X

By means of transitivity, Object is the ultimate superclass; all other classes are direct or indirect subclasses of Object.

Subclasses are fundamental to object-oriented programming. They enable substitutability (also called *polymorphism*), the property by which a subclass instance can be used anywhere that one of its superclasses is expected:

Substitutability (Polymorphism)	
Using a subclass instance where a superclass type is expected	as the object on which a method is invoked
	as the argument to a method or constructor
	as the value assigned to a variable

As a final note, the immediate superclass–subclass relationship in the Java language is one-to-many. A subclass has only one immediate superclass (*single inheritance;* see Q1.25), but a superclass can have any number of subclasses.

See also: Q1.12, Q1.25

Q1.12

What is inheritance?

Inheritance is the way a subclass uses method definitions and variables from a superclass just as if they belonged to the subclass itself.

In general, any instance method or instance variable not defined in a subclass is *inherited* from its superclass. (There are systematic exceptions to this rule; see Q1.32.) A subclass can use the inherited methods and variables just as if it had defined them itself. Inheritance is a powerful mechanism for reusing code: you can start from existing (and, hopefully, reliable) classes and write code to provide just the extra functionality you require.

Inheritance provides a chain in which a class inherits not only from its immediate superclass, but also from any superclass upwards to the Object class. All Java classes ultimately inherit from Object.

For example, the Button class in the java.awt package is defined as a subclass of the powerful, generic Component class (Q5.1). The Java language uses the extends keyword to declare this subclass relationship:

```
/* in Button.java, JDK 1.0.2: */
public class Button extends Component {
    // ... class definition code
}
```

The class definition for Button in the JDK 1.0.2 is surprisingly small. The key extensions from Component to Button are one instance variable and two methods:

- `label`: a `String` instance—the button's text label

- `getLabel()`: returns the button's text label

- `setLabel(String)`: sets the button's text label

Nevertheless, a `Button` instance possesses full `Component` functionality: you can send events to a Button instance, you can draw it on screen, you can resize and reposition it, you can enable or disable it, and so on. All of this functionality is inherited from the `Component` class, and is accessed using methods defined in the `Component` class.

See also: Q1.5, Q1.6, Q5.1

Q1.13

What is an overloaded method?

An overloaded method, strictly speaking, is more than one method: it is two or more separate methods (defined or inherited) in the same class that share the same name.

Methods belong to classes, and methods within a class are distinguished according to their signatures: the combination of method name, number of parameters, and types of parameters (Q1.4). Accordingly, you can use the same name for different methods only if the methods contain different parameter lists.

Method overloading allows you to group conceptually similar methods under the same name, and to use simpler names in general. Your method names can reflect the behavior of the methods without having to worry about how many or what types of parameters the methods take.

The `Math` class in the `java.lang` package illustrates method overloading based on parameter types. It defines four different methods with the name `max`:

- `max(int, int)`, returns an `int`

- `max(long, long)`, returns a `long`

- `max(float, float)`, returns a `float`

- `max(double, double)`, returns a `double`

Without method overloading, each `max` method would need to have its own distinct name, such as `maxInt`, `maxLong`, `maxFloat`, and `maxDouble`. Using the same method name is simpler and conveys the unity of purpose among these four methods.

As a second example, the `String` class has two methods named `substring`. One uses two parameters to specify both a starting point and an ending point from which to extract the substring; the other uses one parameter to specify just the starting point:

- `substring(int, int)`, returns a `String` instance
- `substring(int)`, returns a `String` instance

Again, using the same name for both methods highlights their common functionality; the difference in parameter lists makes enough of a distinction.

Note: Java, unlike C++, allows inherited methods to coexist with overloaded methods. In a subclass, you can define a method with the same name as a method inherited from a superclass, and the superclass method will be accessible provided the two method signatures are distinct. (If the signatures are the same, you've overridden rather than overloaded the method; see Q1.14.)

See also: Q1.2, Q1.3, Q1.4, Q1.12, Q1.14

Q1.14

What does it mean to override a method?

Instead of inheriting a method from its superclass, a subclass can override the method by providing its own definition for it.

Overriding complements inheritance (Q1.12): it lets you choose which behaviors of a superclass to accept as is (inherit) and which to replace with code that you need specifically for your subclass (override). Overriding also lets you provide implementations for methods that the superclass declares as abstract.

Overriding requires a precise replacement of the superclass's method: the subclass's method must have the same name, parameter list, and return type as the superclass's method. Its declared exceptions must also be compatible with those of the superclass. In the JDK 1.0.2, for example, the `Applet` class inherits `Component`'s `update` method (Q5.1, Q8.5), which completely clears the background before redrawing (via `paint`):

```
/* in Component.java (JDK 1.0.2): */
public void update(Graphics g) {
    g.setColor(getBackground());
    g.fillRect(0, 0, width, height);
    g.setColor(getForeground());
    paint(g);
}
```

You can define an `Applet` subclass and change this behavior by overriding `update` in that subclass, for instance, to avoid clearing the background first:

```
/* overriding update in an Applet subclass: */
public void update(Graphics g) {
    paint(g);
}
```

A key point is that, from the subclass's perspective, overriding a method completely replaces the superclass's method. Whenever you invoke the method on an instance of the subclass, you execute the subclass's code for the method rather than the superclass's. To include the superclass's implementation as part of your subclass's method, you use the `super` keyword (Q1.17).

OverrideMethodExample.html

See also: Q1.4, Q1.12, Q1.16, Q1.17, Q2.26, Q5.1, Q8.5

Q1.15

What is the difference between overloading and overriding?

Overloading occurs when two or more methods use the same name (but different parameter lists), such that both methods are available side by side in the same class; overriding occurs when a subclass method and a superclass method use the same name (and matching parameter lists), such that the subclass method blocks out the superclass method.

Overloading (Q1.13) and overriding (Q1.14) are often confused with each other, because the words are similar and because they both involve a single method name referring to potentially several different method implementations.

There are clear differences, however, when you compare the two point by point, as done in Table 1.4.

Table 1.4: Overloading versus Overriding

Overloading	Overriding
relationship between methods available in the same class	relationship between a superclass method and a subclass method
does not block inheritance from the superclass	blocks inheritance from the superclass
separate methods share (overload) the same name	subclass method replaces (overrides) the superclass method
different method signatures	same method signature
may have different return types	must have matching return types
may have different declared exceptions	must have compatible declared exceptions

For example, both the `Object` class and the `String` class (an immediate subclass of `Object`) in the `java.lang` package define an `equals` method:

- in `Object`: `public boolean equals(Object obj) { /* ... */ }`
- in `String`: `public boolean equals(Object obj) { /* ... */ }`

This is a case of overriding, since `String` is a subclass of `Object`, and `String`'s `equals` method has the same name, parameter types, and return type as `Object`'s `equals` method.

Now suppose that a `String2` class defined `equals` to take a `String2` parameter instead of an `Object` parameter:

- in `Object`: `public boolean equals(Object obj)`
- hypothetical `String2`: `public boolean equals(String2 str)`

This would be a case of overloading. The `String2` class would have two alternate `equals` methods: one defined in `String2` and one inherited from `Object`. Even though the two methods have the same name and return type, they differ in what parameter they take.

See also: Q1.13, Q1.14, Q1.16

Q1.16

Can I override the `equals` *method or* `clone` *method from class* `Object` *to take a parameter or return a value of the type that I specify?*

No; you can override a method from a superclass only if your subclass's method has the same signature and return type.

Overriding a method requires a close match between the superclass method and the subclass method:

- the subclass method and superclass method must have the same signature

- the subclass method and superclass method must have the same return type

- the subclass method's level of access must be equal to or greater than that of the superclass method

Note that the `native` and `abstract` keywords do not have to match between the subclass and superclass methods.

To override `Object`'s `equals` method, you must define precisely the same return type and parameter type as defined by the `Object` class. (You are free, though, to vary the parameter name—`obj` in the following example—since parameter names are not carried over into class files.) For example:

```
/* overriding equals in a subclass of Object: */
public boolean equals(Object obj)  { /* ... */ }
```

Similarly, you can override `Object`'s `clone` method only to return `Object`:

```
/* overriding clone in a subclass of Object: */
public Object clone()  { /* ... */ }
```

Attempting to return any class other than `Object` yields a compile-time error:

```
/* failed attempt to override clone: */
public MySubclass clone()  { /* ... */ }
```

The Vector class in the java.util package, for example, overrides Object's clone method and therefore returns Object rather than Vector. To assign the cloned Vector instance to another Vector variable, you must cast the returned value from Object to Vector (Q2.9):

```
Vector vector1 = new Vector();
Vector vector2 = (Vector)vector1.clone();
```

Note: Method overloading is an option if you really want to provide a more specific parameter type than Object, but it is not an option for return types. Whether you are overriding or overloading, the return types must match *exactly*— a compile-time error occurs if they don't.

See also: Q1.4, Q1.13, Q1.14, Q1.15, Q2.9

Q1.17

What is the super keyword used for?

The super keyword gives a class explicit access to the constructors, methods, and variables of its superclass.

The super keyword works hand in hand with inheritance (Q1.12) to connect a class to its superclasses. Inheritance gives a class *implicit* access to its super-classes. When you invoke an instance method, for example, you automatically get an inherited superclass method implementation if the instance's class doesn't define the method for itself. Implicit access is blocked, though, by method over-riding (Q1.14), or by defining instance or class variables with the same names as the superclass versions (called *hiding*). This is where super comes in. The super keyword gives a class *explicit* access to its immediate superclass's parts, even if that access is otherwise blocked. The two common uses of super are to access the superclass's constructor and to access the superclass's version of an overridden method.

The super keyword is essential to the workings of constructors. Unlike methods, constructors are not inherited; the super keyword thus provides the only means to access a constructor in a superclass. Within a constructor, using super(...) triggers a call to the superclass constructor with a matching parameter list. (The compiler issues an error if the superclass contains no such constructor.) This is how each instance of a class performs a chain of initializations. An instance initializes itself as an Object instance and then steps down from each superclass to an immediate subclass until it finally initializes those parts that are specific to the subclass at the end of the chain.

For example, the following `Frame` subclass defines two constructors to match the two constructors provided by the `Frame` class:

```
class ExampleFrame extends Frame {
    public ExampleFrame() {
        super();
    }
    public ExampleFrame(String title) {
        super(title);
    }
    // ... field and method definitions
}
```

Even though the constructors in this example do nothing more than invoke the superclass constructors, you need to include them because constructors are not inherited. (If your constructor invokes the superclass constructor, this invocation must occur as the first statement in your constructor definition.)

The chain of initialization is so important that the Java system automatically includes a call to the superclass constructor if you don't provide one yourself. The automatic superclass constructor is always a no-parameter constructor. For example, the JDK 1.0.2 `Button` class contains the following constructor code:

```
/* in Button.java (JDK 1.0.2): */
public Button(String label) {
    this.label = label;
}
```

Because of the automatic inclusion of the superclass constructor, the above code is equivalent to:

```
/* Equivalent Button constructor: */
public Button(String label) {
    super();
    this.label = label;
}
```

The automatic default constructor has no parameters, but you can use whatever parameter list you need by invoking the superclass constructor explicitly.

The second common use of `super` is within a method definition, to access the superclass version of the same method. This makes sense in a method definition that is overriding the method from its superclass. In this context, `super` allows you to define an overriding method that builds around its superclass method rather than replacing it outright. The AWT `Button` class again provides a simple example:

```
/* in Button.java (JDK 1.0.2) */
protected String paramString() {
    return super.paramString() + ",label=" + label;
}
```

Because `Button` is a subclass of `Component`, this `paramString` method will invoke `Component`'s version of `paramString`, which returns a `String` instance describing parameters relevant to all components, and will then append the button's label to that string. Invoking `paramString` on a button thus returns a `String` instance that includes the button's size and on-screen position (information all components have) together with the button's label (information specific to the `Button` subclass).

Finally, you can use `super` to access a variable in a superclass that is hidden by a variable in the subclass with the same name. The following code fragment illustrates how, for a variable named foo:

```
class X {
    int foo = 1;  // declares instance variable foo
}

class SubX {
    int foo = 2;  // declares own version of foo, which hides the
                  // superclass version
    int getSuperFoo()  {
        return super.foo;  // returns 1, not 2
    }
}
```

SuperExample.html

See also: Q1.11, Q1.12

Q1.18

Does the Java language provide virtual methods, like C++?

Yes; but Java methods are virtual by default, whereas C++ methods are not.

"Virtual methods" are an essential ingredient for taking advantage of inheritance and polymorphism. Because of inheritance and polymorphism, an object reference need not match exactly the class of the object it refers to: the object can belong to a subclass of the reference's type. For example, the aThread reference below is of type Thread, but the object it refers to is of type MyThread, a subclass of Thread:

```
class MyThread extends Thread { /* ... overrides start() ... */ }
class Example {
    // ...
    Thread aThread = new MyThread();    • dynamic by default
    myThread.start();
    // ...
}
```

When you invoke a method on a reference, such as the anObject.start() expression above, the virtual machine must know which class to use for looking up the method definition; there are two basic choices:

- *static binding*—use compile-time type of object reference

- *dynamic binding*—use run-time type of referred-to object

In the preceding Thread example, dynamic binding will pick up the overridden start method in the MyThread subclass, whereas static binding would find only the Thread version. Programmers familiar with C++ will recognize this distinction as the difference between nonvirtual and virtual methods.

In the Java language and Virtual Machine, dynamic binding is the default, and there is no virtual keyword. The distinction between dynamic and static binding is generally expressed in terms of whether a method can be overridden:

Method overridable?	Java	C++
yes	[default]	use virtual keyword
no	use final keyword	[default]

Note: Besides final methods, two further situations in Java use static rather than dynamic binding. Class methods and method invocations involving the super keyword cannot involve method overriding; hence, they do not require dynamic binding.

See also: Q1.10, Q1.12, Q1.14, Q1.19, Q1.26

Q1.19

What is a final class?

A final class is a class that is declared with `final` keyword so that it can never be subclassed.

Using the `final` keyword in the Java language has the general meaning that you define an entity once and cannot change it or derive from it later. More specifically:

- a `final` class cannot be subclassed
- a `final` method cannot be overridden
- a `final` variable cannot change from its initialized value

Classes are usually declared `final` for either performance or security reasons. On the performance side, the compiler can optimize `final` classes to avoid dynamic method lookup because their method implementations are never overridden. Methods in a `final` class can work at the speed of straight function calls, or even as inline code, which may be several times faster than a typical method invocation on current virtual machine implementations. The `String` class, for instance, is declared `final` in large part because of the performance optimizations that can be achieved. Note, however, that the performance advantage of final classes (or final methods for that matter) is likely to fade in the next year or two as Java Virtual Machine implementations apply increasingly sophisticated techniques to handle method invocation. Relying heavily on `final` in your current designs may confine you unnecessarily in the future.

On the security side, making a class `final` is like putting a lock on the class — it prevents other programmers from subclassing a secure class to invoke insecure methods.

Note: Making an entire class final is a fairly extreme measure and should be done only in exceptional cases. You most often can achieve the security and performance effects you desire by making selected methods in a class final, while leaving the class available for subclassing.

See also: Q1.18

INTERFACES AND ABSTRACT CLASSES

Q1.20

What is an interface?

In the Java language, an interface is like a stripped-down class: it specifies a set of methods that an instance must handle, but it omits inheritance relations and method implementations.

Object-oriented programming is sometimes modeled as communication between objects—one object talks to, or sends a message to, another object by invoking a method on it. In this view, an interface in the Java language specifies the bare minimum one object needs to know in order to talk to another object: a set of abstract methods (Q1.8), that is, methods minus any implementation information. Put another way, an interface specifies how you can talk to an object, but says nothing about what kind of object will handle your messages. It is the job of one or more class instances to provide the substance behind an interface's promise (Q1.21).

Interfaces are a close cousin to classes (Q1.2), and their declarations resemble class declarations. For example, the Runnable interface in the java.lang package (JDK 1.0.2 and 1.1) is declared as follows:

```
/* in Runnable.java (JDK 1.0.2 and 1.1): */
public interface Runnable {
    public abstract void run();
}
```

An interface can also contain static final variables, called class constants; see *The Java Language Specification*, pp. 186–188, for details.

Interfaces provide the minimal level of dependence between interacting objects. An interface focuses purely on the role an object plays—what services it can provide—without making any restrictions on the class of the object (Q1.24).

See also: Q1.2, Q1.21, Q1.24, JLS pp. 186–188

Q1.21

How does a class implement an interface?

A class implements an interface by declaring that it implements the interface and by providing implementations for all methods contained in the interface.

Despite not having any implementation, an interface embodies both form and intent. When you define an interface, you specify the set of methods in the interface; you should also specify the intended meaning of each method. Correspondingly, implementing an interface requires that a class match the interface in both form and intent:

- the class provides implementations for all the methods in the interface

- the class declares explicitly that it implements the interface

Because both steps are required, implementing an interface is guaranteed to be a deliberate choice by the class's author. Simply having the same methods as an interface is not sufficient.

For example, `Applet` subclasses commonly implement the `Runnable` interface in order to run themselves in a separate thread (Q9.16). The `Runnable` interface in the `java.lang` package declares just a single `run` method taking no parameters (Q1.20). A `Runnable` `Applet` subclass must therefore declare that it implements the `Runnable` interface and must define a `run` method:

```
public class MyApplet extends java.applet.Applet
                       implements Runnable
{
    // ...
    public void run() {
        // ... code to run the applet in a separate thread
    }
}
```

Note: If a class implements an interface, all its subclasses automatically implement the interface, too. Also, you can declare that an abstract class (Q1.9) implements an interface yet omit some of the method declarations. This amounts to a promise (checked by the compiler) that any concrete subclasses of that abstract class will fully declare and implement the methods in the interface.

See also: Q1.9, Q1.20, Q1.22, Q9.16

Q1.22

Can I instantiate an interface?

You can't; you must instantiate a class that implements the interface.

Interfaces specify a vocabulary of methods by which objects can communicate. Instead of instantiating an interface, you instantiate a class (Q1.7) that implements the interface (Q1.21). You can then use that object anywhere the interface type is required.

InstantiateInterfaceExample.html

See also: Q1.7, Q1.20, Q1.21

Q1.23

Why does a method in an interface appear to be public even though I didn't declare it to be public?

The Java language defines all methods and variables in an interface to be public, regardless of whether you use the `public` keyword or not.

The Java language requires that all methods and variables in an interface be public. The compiler thus allows you to omit the `public` keyword (Q1.32). Similarly, all methods in an interface are abstract (Q1.8), and you do not need to include the `abstract` keyword in any interface declarations.

The compiler will accept `public` and `abstract` modifiers on interface methods for compatibility with older code, but you are encouraged as a matter of style to omit them (*The Java Language Specification*, p. 187).

See also: Q1.8, Q1.20, Q1.32, JLS p. 187

Q1.24

How is an abstract class different from an interface?

Although the Java language makes a clear distinction between abstract classes and interfaces, in practice the difference is often a matter of degree and intent.

Abstract classes (Q1.9) fill in the wide range between concrete classes and interfaces. Table 1.5 lists several distinctions that are relevant to typical uses.

Table 1.5: Concrete Class versus Abstract Class versus Interface

Concrete Class	Abstract Class	Interface
specifies the full set of methods for an object	specifies the full set of methods for an object	specifies a subset of methods for an object
implements all of its methods	implements none, some, or all of its methods	implements none of its methods
can have instances	can't have instances	can't have instances
can have subclasses	must have subclasses; useless without them	can't have subclasses; must have classes that implement it; useless without them

If the differences in Table 1.5 leave you uncertain about whether to use an abstract class or an interface, one further factor may be decisive. A class can have only one immediate superclass, but it can implement any number of interfaces (Q1.25). An abstract class, even one with all abstract methods, ties its subclasses to a particular inheritance hierarchy. An interface, in contrast, leaves an object free to implement other interfaces as needed by the object's class.

Beyond the details, it is important to understand how classes and interfaces differ in spirit. Classes generally specify the full identity of an object: who/what it is (its parentage), what roles it can perform (its vocabulary of methods), and how it specifically performs those roles (its implemented behavior). Interfaces specify neither parentage nor behavior for an object—they focus exclusively on the role(s) an object can play.

Consider, for example, the Observer interface and Observable class in the java.util package. An Observer object is one that expects to be notified when an object it is watching (an Observable object) changes state. An Observable object is one that knows how to register, unregister, and notify a collection of Observer objects.

The Observer interface (JDK 1.0.2 and 1.1) defines a single method:

```
/* in Observer.java (JDK 1.0.2 and 1.1): */
public interface Observer {
    void update(Observable o, Object arg);
}
```

Because `Observer` is an interface, you can define whatever class you like to implement the interface. For instance, you could define a `Button` subclass to serve as an `Observer`:

```
public class ObserverButton extends Button
                            implements java.util.Observer {
    public static void update(Observable o, Object arg) {
        // ... respond to notification
    }
}
```

This independence of interfaces from any class hierarchy is a *huge* benefit.

In contrast, `Observable` is defined as a class, which restricts all `Observable` objects to belong to the `Observable` class or to a subclass of `Observable`. Unlike `ObserverButton` above, you simply *cannot* define an `ObservableButton` as a subclass of `Button`. Java allows only single class inheritance, which forces you to choose between one or the other inheritance hierarchy (Q1.25).

See also: Q1.9, Q1.20, Q1.25

Q1.25

Does the Java language allow multiple inheritance?

Yes and no.

A class in Java can implement any number of interfaces (*multiple interface inheritance*) but can extend exactly one immediate superclass, from which it inherits implementations (*single class inheritance*).

Similarly, an interface can have any number of superinterfaces, which are declared with the extends keyword. For example:

```
// ... interfaces Readable, Writable declared elsewhere
public interface StreamInputOuput extends Readable, Writable {
    // ... additional methods not in Readable or Writable
}
```

Finally, does an interface have any superclasses? Yes, all interfaces are treated as having one superclass: the `Object` class. This amounts to a claim that whatever class implements the interface will be a subclass of `Object`; the Java language guarantees this to be true (Q1.11).

See also: Q1.2, Q1.11, Q1.12, Q1.20

Q1.26

What is the instanceof *keyword, and what does it do?*

The instanceof **keyword is a two-argument operator that tests whether the run-time type of its first argument is assignment compatible with its second argument.**

An expression using instanceof, such as X instanceof Y, tests whether the object referred to by X could be assigned to a variable of type Y. If Y is a class, this test checks whether X's object belongs to class Y or to a subclass of Y. If Y is an interface, the test checks if X's object's class implements that interface.

The instanceof operator performs tests at both compile time and run time. For example, testing whether a String instance in a String variable can be an instance of Integer fails at compile time:

```
String aString = "abadcafe";
if (aString instanceof Integer)  { /* ... */ }
```

The error message from the JDK (1.0.2 and 1.1) compiler is unequivocal:

```
Impossible for java.lang.String to be instance of
java.lang.Integer.
```

Failure at compile time signals gross errors, such as checking two class types, neither of which is a subclass of the other.

The primary use of instanceof, however, is to check at run time the actual object type (run-time type) of its left-hand argument, regardless of the static type of the reference. For example, the AWT Component class includes a getParent method that returns an object reference of type Container. The actual (run-time) type of the parent object, though, could be Panel, Applet, Frame—any of a number of subclasses of Container. You can then use the instanceof operator to test which specific subclass you have:

```
/* code in your Component subclass: */
// ... myButton has been created and built into a user interface
Container cont = myButton.getParent();
if (cont instanceof Frame) { /* ... code to handle Frame ... */ }
```

InstanceofExample.html

Q1.27

Why do I get the error message `Can't access protected method` `clone...` *when I try to clone an object?*

The `clone` **method in class** `Object` **signals an error if you invoke it on an object whose class does not explicitly support cloning.**

The `clone` method in class `Object` creates a new object that is essentially a bit-for-bit copy of the source object. This is a simple but risky behavior for classes in general, so classes are not allowed to inherit it by default. (Remember that any nonprivate method in class `Object` is potentially inherited by all other Java classes.) `Object`'s `clone` method thus has two built-in safety measures:

- `clone` is `protected`, which restricts access from outside the `java.lang` package

- `clone` checks that the target object's class implements the `Cloneable` interface

The upshot of these restrictions is that you can invoke `clone` on an object only if that object's class has been designed explicitly to allow cloning. See Q1.28 for a discussion of how to design a class for cloning.

Cloning an object from a class set up for cloning, however, is straightforward. You invoke `clone` on an instance of that class, as in the following hypothetical example:

```
DollarBill genuine = new DollarBill();
DollarBill counterfeit = (DollarBill) genuine.clone();
```

The `clone` method returns an object reference of type `Object`, which you must cast to the appropriate class.

See also: Q1.28, Q1.33

Q1.28

How do I design a class so that it supports cloning?

Declare that the class implements the `Cloneable` **interface and override** `Object`**'s** `clone` **method with a version suited to your class.**

Designing a class that supports cloning involves two parts: a promise of cloneability and a clone method to back it up. First, you mark your class as fit for cloning by declaring that it implements the Cloneable interface. For example:

```
public class DollarBill implements Cloneable { /* ... */ }
```

The Cloneable interface contains *no* methods; it is purely a flag.

Second, you define a clone method that correctly copies the parts within each instance of your class. Some parts of a class may require *shallow copying;* others may require *deep copying*. Shallow copying merely copies the value of a data element bit for bit—this is what the default clone method in class Object does. Shallow copying is appropriate when a data element directly represents a value, such as an int, float, or boolean, rather than a reference to a value. Shallow copying may occasionally be used for reference values as well, the result being two references sharing the same referred-to object. Deep copying is often required for reference-type data elements. Deep copying creates both a new reference and a new object for the reference to refer to. The following code fragment sketches a DollarBill class that performs both shallow and deep copying in its clone method:

```
public class DollarBill implements Cloneable {
    int value = 1;   // value of the bill (1, 5, 10, 20, ...)
    String name;   // personalized name given to individual bill

    // ... constructors and various methods

    /**
     * Clones a DollarBill by copying its value and making a deep
     * copy of its String name.
     */
    public Object clone() {
        DollarBill copy = null;
        try {
            copy = (DollarBill) super.clone();   // shallow copy
            copy.name = new String(this.name);   // deep copying
        } catch (CloneNotSupportedException e) {
            e.printStackTrace();
        }
        return (Object) copy;
    }
}
```

CloneExample.html

See also: Q1.27, Q1.32, Q1.33

PACKAGES AND ACCESS MODIFIERS

Q1.29

What are packages, and what are they used for?

A package is a collection of classes and interfaces that provides a high-level layer of access protection and name space management.

Although the class (Q1.2) is arguably the central unit of design in Java programs, Java language *packages* provide a vital additional level of support for program modularity. A package groups together a set of classes and interfaces (Q1.20) that needs to work as a coherent whole. The java.io package, for instance, contains classes and interfaces for managing various kinds of input and output.

Packages define boundary lines to govern how classes and interfaces may interact with one another. Access control modifiers (Q1.32) use package boundaries to:

- facilitate a high degree of interaction and interdependency within a package

- reduce access and interaction across package boundaries

For instance, the default access to methods and variables, if you don't specify an access modifier, is that a method or variable defined in one class cannot be used by classes belonging to a different package.

Packages also reduce the potential for name clashes, because class names and interface names are ultimately reckoned relative to the package to which they belong (Q1.30). Thus, you could define your own Button class, distinct from the Button class in the java.awt package, provided that you place it in a package other than java.awt. In general, you should not deliberately reuse well-known class names like this; the name space protection provided by packages is more of a safety measure against accidental clashes.

Every class and interface belongs to some package. For each compilation unit (typically a source file), you can declare what package its classes and interfaces belong to with a package declaration at the beginning. For example:

```
package myPackage;  // if present, must come first in the file
public interface Xyz { /*  ... */ }
class Uvw { /*  ... */ }
```

Any number of source files (compilation units) can be declared to belong to the same package. If you omit the `package` declaration, the classes and interfaces in that file will be assigned to a system-provided unnamed package. Although the package is nameless, the same rules for package-internal versus package-external access privileges still apply.

See also: Q1.2, Q1.20, Q1.30, Q1.32, JLS p. 119

Q1.30

I've seen both `java.applet.Applet` *and* `Applet` *used to refer to the* `Applet` *class—what's the difference?*

The shorter name is definitely easier to use, but it requires that you provide an `import` declaration to specify which package the class belongs to.

The name `java.applet.Applet` is the *fully qualified name* of the `Applet` class in the `java.applet` package. Fully qualified class or interface names come in the form:

```
packageName.simpleClassName
packageName.simpleInterfaceName
```

The package name itself can be a compound name with its own internal periods, such as `java.applet` and `java.awt.image`.

You can always refer to a class or interface by its fully qualified name, but it is more common and more convenient to use just the *simple name* of the class or interface. To let the compiler know which package a simple name belongs to, you provide an `import` declaration at the head of your source file (or, strictly speaking, after the package declaration, if there is one). For example:

```
import java.applet.Applet;
```

After this, the compiler will know to treat each occurrence of the simple name `Applet` the same as if it were the fully qualified name `java.applet.Applet`. Import declarations let the compiler do the extra name work for you. Using an import declaration for a class (or interface) is often called *importing the class* (or interface).

An alternate form of import declaration lets you import as many classes as needed from a package. A *type import on demand* uses an asterisk (*) in place of a specific class or interface name. For example:

```
import java.awt.*;
```

This form of import declaration makes *all* the classes and interfaces in the specified package available as simple names.

Although package names are hierarchical, import declarations are not. In the example above, the `import` declaration imports only classes and interfaces from the `java.awt` package. It does not import from subpackages in `java.awt`—you must include separate import declarations for each subpackage you want to import; for example:

```
import java.awt.*;        // the main AWT package
import java.awt.image.*;  // the image subpackage
import java.awt.event.*;  // the event subpackage; in JDK 1.1
```

Remember: Importing classes and interfaces affects only the names by which your code refers to classes. It does not send additional code to the compiler, like C's `include`, or perform other behind-the-scenes manipulations.

See also: Q1.29, Q1.31, JLS pp. 120ff

Q1.31

Why can I get some simple class names "for free," without using an `import` *declaration?*

Java language programs automatically imports all classes in the `java.lang` **package.**

The `java.lang` package contains classes and interfaces that provide crucial support to the Java language and Virtual Machine, including `Class`, `Exception`, `Object`, `Runnable`, `String`, `System`, and `Thread`. To ensure that these classes and interfaces are always easily available, and to prevent programs from inadvertently calling on nonstandard versions, the `java.lang` package is always automatically imported. The compiler treats each source file as if its first `import` statement were

```
import java.lang.*;  // implicit in every Java source file
```

The automatic importing of java.lang class and interface names is one of three sources of simple class names in a source file:

- automatic importing from java.lang package
- explicit import declarations
- classes and interfaces in unnamed package

See also: Q1.29, Q1.30, JLS p. 119

Q1.32

Is there a default access modifier for classes and interfaces? For class members (methods, constructors, and fields)?

There is no default access modifier; the absence of a modifier, though, signals package-level access, which is access only from classes in the same package.

You can assign two different levels of access to classes and interfaces: public and package (also called *package private*). Public access is marked with the public keyword, and package access has no keyword, as shown in Table 1.6:

Table 1.6: Access Levels for Classes and Interfaces

public keyword	accessible to all classes
no keyword	accessible only to classes in same package

(The Java language has a package keyword, but it is used in a different context, for package declarations; see Q1.29.)

Table 1.7 lists the four possible levels of access for class and interface members (methods, constructors, and fields); again, package access has no keyword.

Table 1.7: Access Levels for Class and Interface Members

public keyword	accessible to all classes
no keyword	accessible only to classes in same package
protected keyword	accessible to classes in same package, and in limited circumstances to subclasses in other packages (Q1.33)
private keyword	not accessible to any other classes

Good program design seeks to isolate parts of a program from unnecessary, unintended, or otherwise unwanted outside influences. Access modifiers provide an explicit and checkable means for the language to control such contact.

See also: Q1.27, Q1.29, Q1.33

Q1.33

What does protected *access mean?*

A method, constructor, or field with protected **access is accessible to all classes in the same package, and to** *subclasses* **in other packages provided that the class granting the access is the same as or a subclass of the class making the access.**

The protected level of access augments the default package-level access with limited access for subclasses outside the package of the class defining the protected element (call these package-external subclasses). The basic idea is that access from a subclass outside the protected element's package is reckoned relative to the object or class through which the access is occurring—access is allowed only if the target class is the same as or a subclass of the package-external class attempting the access.

For example, consider the access facts for the following scenario:

package P	contains class X and class SubX (a subclass of X)
	class X defines protected method M
package Q	contains class Y (a subclass of X) and class SubY (a subclass of Y)

First, code in class X or SubX can always invoke M:

Method invocation	Access allowed?
code in class X or SubX invokes M on instance of class X or SubX	Yes; access is from inside the protected element's package
code in class X or SubX invokes M on instance of class Y or SubY	Yes; access is from inside the protected element's package

In contrast, when code in class Y or SubY attempts to invoke M, whether or not access is allowed depends crucially on the target instance:

Method invocation	Access allowed?
code in class Y invokes M on instance of class X or SubX	No; package-external access allowed from class Y only if target instance belongs to class Y or a subclass of Y.
code in class Y invokes M on instance of class Y or SubY	Yes; package-external access allowed from class Y because target instance belongs to class Y or a subclass of Y.
code in class SubY invokes M on instance of class Y	No; package-external access allowed from class SubY only if target instance belongs to class SubY or a subclass of SubY.

Admittedly, the details of protected access are tricky—for a full specification and further examples, see *The Java Language Specification* (p. 100).

See also: Q1.29, Q1.32, JLS p. 100

Q1.34

What is the accessibility of a public method or field inside a nonpublic class or interface?

A public method or field inside a nonpublic class is accessible only inside its package, unless some other public access point—a public interface or public superclass—can be used.

The accessibility of members (methods and fields) within a class or interface is limited by the class or interface through which they are accessed. A nonpublic class receives the default package access so that even public methods or fields inside that class are generally not visible outside the class's package.

In two circumstances, though, a public class member can have full public access even though the class that defines it has only package access. First, a public interface can expose methods from a package-private class that implements the interface. When an instance of the class is accessed through the interface (that is, through a reference of the interface type), the methods implementing the interface are visible outside their package.

A public superclass with public methods can also expose methods from a package-private subclass. When an instance of the subclass is accessed through a reference of the superclass type, any public method of the superclass is accessible to all classes. By dynamic binding (Q1.18), however, the actual method body invoked will be the one belonging to the package-private subclass.

See also: Q1.18, Q1.29, Q1.32

CHAPTER 2

Java Language

Constants and Expressions (Q2.1–Q2.10)

Variables and Methods (Q2.11–Q2.18)

Arrays (Q2.19–Q2.21)

Exceptions (Q2.22–Q2.26)

CONSTANTS AND EXPRESSIONS

Q2.1

What is the difference between Integer *and* int *in Java—why do I get the following error:* Can't convert java.lang.Integer to int*?*

Integer **is a class defined in the** java.lang **package, whereas** int **is a primitive data type defined in the Java language itself; Java does not automatically convert from one to the other.**

The Java language makes a fundamental distinction between two kinds of data: reference types and primitive types. A reference type holds a reference to a value rather than the value itself (Q1.10, Q2.11). Reference types comprise all the object-related types of the Java language:

Reference types in Java: class types, interface types, array types

Reference types provide an open-ended type system. You can define new types by defining new classes, new interfaces, or arrays containing components from those classes or interfaces.

Primitive types hold raw values without any object-oriented support. The primitive types in Java are shown in Table 2.1.

Table 2.1: Primitive Types in Java

`boolean`: binary value, either `true` or `false`
`byte`, `short`, `int`, `long`: 8-, 16-, 32-, and 64-bit signed integer values
`char`: Unicode characters as unsigned 16-bit integer values
`float`, `double`: 32- and 64-bit IEEE 754 floating point numbers

Although the Java language is strongly object-oriented, it includes the primitive types because of their speed, simplicity, and compactness.

In this light, consider again the difference between `Integer` and `int`. At a basic level, elements of `Integer` and `int` both represent a 32-bit signed integer value. Which of these you use depends on what you want to do, as described in Table 2.2.

Table 2.2: Using a Class versus Using a Primitive Type

Use `Integer` (or other numeric class)	Use `int` (or other primitive data type)
as an argument for a method that requires an `Object`	for calculations
for storage in general-purpose `Object` containers	for storage in large arrays

For example, to store an integer value as part of a `Vector` (a class in package `java.util`), you need to wrap the value in an `Integer` instance:

```
Vector v = new Vector();
v.addElement(new Integer(5));
```

In contrast, if you want to keep a counter variable that you increment repeatedly, by all means use an `int`:

```
int count;
// ...
++count;
```

Finally, the `Integer` class lets you translate back and forth between `Integer` and `int` representations of the same value:

```
int i = 5;
Integer myInteger = new Integer(i);
int j = myInteger.intValue();
```

Note: The extra effort required to convert between `int` and `Integer` can be a nuisance, but is consistent with Java's emphasis on type safety.

See also: Q2.11

Q2.2

How do I treat all 8 bits of a `byte` as an unsigned quantity?

When the unusual need arises, perform a logical-and of your `byte` value and the hexadecimal value `0xFF`—this counteracts the automatic sign extension that occurs when a `byte` value undergoes promotion to an `int`.

The Java language strictly defines the sizes and arithmetic properties of its primitive numeric data types. The integral types `byte`, `short`, `int`, and `long` are all represented in 2's-complement form with sizes of 8, 16, 32, and 64 bits, respectively.

In several circumstances, the Java language promotes a `byte` value to an `int`:

- *assignment conversion:* when you assign a byte value to a variable of type `int` (*The Java Language Specification*, p. 61)

- *method invocation conversion:* when you provide a byte value as an argument to a method that expects an `int` (JLS, p. 66)

- *casting conversion:* when you explicitly cast a byte value to `int` (JLS, p. 67)

- *numeric promotion:* when you use a byte operand in an arithmetic expression (JLS, p. 72)

If you assume, as the Java language does, that a byte represents an 8-bit signed value, these promotions occur without surprising side effects.

Promoting `byte` to `int` (or `short` to `int`, for that matter) occurs by sign extension: the highest bit of the smaller type is copied to all new bits in the larger type. For example, the following display shows the value –4 represented as a `byte`, and then sign-extended to an `int`:

–4 as an 8-bit signed byte	11111100
sign-extend to 32 bits	11111111 11111111 11111111 11111100
interpret value as `int`	–4

Suppose, however, that you want to treat the same eight bits as an unsigned value, in which case that value would be 252. As soon as you sign-extend the `byte` to an `int` (for any of the reasons above), you're back to the value –4:

252, in 8 unsigned bits	11111100
sign-extend to 32 bits	11111111 11111111 11111111 11111100
interpret value as `int`	–4

Assuming that you really have a good reason for using the `byte` as an unsigned value, the fix is to counteract the automatic sign extension by setting the extra bits to zero. Perform the logical-and (&) of your `byte` value with the hexadecimal constant `0xFF`:

252, in 8 unsigned bits	11111100
sign-extend to 32 bits	11111111 11111111 11111111 11111100
`0xFF` in 32 bits	00000000 00000000 00000000 11111111
logical-and (&)	00000000 00000000 00000000 11111100
interpret value as `int`	252

Note: The Java language provides an unsigned right shift operator, `>>>`, as another means of averting automatic sign extension. For example, the expression (`value >>> 4`) shifts `value`'s bits 4 places to the right and fills in the vacated high-order bits with 0s (rather than 1s). Thus, an alternate, and more complex, way to extract an 8-bit unsigned value is ((value << 24) >>> 24).

UnsignedByteExample.html

See also: Q2.1, JLS pp. 61–75

Q2.3

How do I work around Java's lack of true enums?

Use class constants—they provide symbolic names for integer-like constants.

Two of Java's cousin languages, C and C++, contain a notion of enumeration or enumerated type, called enum for short. An enum is a user-defined type that can take symbolic, identifier-like, constant values. Consider, for example, the following two statements, in either C or C++:

```
/* in C or C++ */
enum season {winter, spring, summer, fall};
season now = fall;
```

The first statement defines an enum with the name season, and the second declares a variable of type season and assigns an appropriate enum value to it.

The closest match to enum in the Java language is an integer class constant—a final static variable of type int. A class constant has the following properties:

- It is declared with the keywords final and static.
- It must be initialized with a value as part of its declaration.
- It can be used only for its value; it cannot be assigned to.

The corresponding season example in Java, therefore, would be:

```
/* in Java: */
public final static int WINTER = 0;
public final static int SPRING = 1;
public final static int SUMMER = 2;
public final static int FALL = 3;
int now = FALL;
```

It is conventional to use all capital letters for Java class constant names.

See also: Q2.1

Q2.4

Why is goto *a reserved keyword in Java—shouldn't it be outlawed?*

The word goto **is reserved in the Java language precisely so that it can be outlawed.**

The Java language sets aside 47 words as keywords—words reserved by the language itself and therefore not available as names for variables or methods. Here is the list from *The Java Language Specification* (p. 18):

```
abstract, boolean, break, byte, case, catch, char, class, const,
continue, default, do, double, else, extends, final, finally,
float, for, goto, if, implements, import, instanceof, int,
interface, long, native, new, package, private, protected,
public, return, short, static, super, switch, synchronized,
this, throw, throws, transient, try, void, volatile, while
```

Two of these are not currently used by the Java language: goto and const. They are deliberately set aside so that a Java-compatible compiler can produce more specific error message if it finds one of these forbidden keywords in a source file. This is intended to help former C or C++ programmers who are migrating code to Java.

The Java language retains limited goto powers in the form of labeled statements reachable from break and continue statements. These are especially useful for exiting from multiple layers of loops, as sketched in the following example:

```
topLoop:     // label for the following while statement
while (checkCondition()) {
    for (int i = 0; i < max; ++i) {
        for (int j = 0; j < i; ++j) {
            // ...
            if (foundAnswer()) {
                break topLoop;   // exits the top-level while loop
            }
        }
    }
}
```

KeywordExample.html

See also: JLS p. 18, JLS pp. 283–286

Q2.5

What are some guidelines for using uppercase and lowercase letters in my identifiers?

Use lowercase letters in general, but capitalize the first letter of class and interface names, as well as the first letter of any non-initial word.

Case sensitivity is part of Java's deliberate design choice to maintain compatibility with C programming habits where reasonable. Case distinctions take part in some naming conventions employed by the Java system and standard classes. *The Java Language Specification* recommends (but does not require) that such conventions be used in all Java programs. For example:

- "Names of packages intended only for local use should have a first identifier that begins with a lowercase letter." (p. 107)

- "Names of class types should be descriptive nouns or noun phrases, not overly long, in mixed case with the first letter of each word capitalized." (p. 108)

- "Method names should be verbs or verb phrases, in mixed case, with the first letter lowercase and the first letter of any subsequent words capitalized." (p. 108)

- "Names of fields that are not final should be in mixed case with a lowercase first letter and the first letters of subsequent words capitalized." (p. 109)

Table 2.3 presents some examples from the JDK 1.1:

Table 2.3: Examples of Capitalization in Identifiers

Kind of identifier	Names in the JDK 1.1
class	`Button, BufferedReader`
interface	`Runnable, DataInput`
method	`start(), getAbsolutePath()`
variable	`int offset, String anotherString`

See also: JLS pp. 106–111

Q2.6

Is there any limit to the length of an identifier?

Yes; 65,535 characters is the maximum possible identifier length, because identifier names must be representable in Java class files.

The Java language in principle does not limit the length of identifiers. According to *The Java Language Specification* (p. 6), "An identifier is an unlimited-length sequence of Unicode letters and digits, the first of which must be a letter." However, Java source code is compiled into Java class files, and the specification for class files does, in effect, place an upper bound on the size of identifiers. This limit is well beyond the practical needs of human codes, but it is interesting to understand where it comes from.

Java class files must store symbolic names for all fields, methods, classes, and interfaces referenced in a class definition. (In contrast, class files represent method parameters and local variables not by name but by index.) In a class file, the maximum space a single name can take is 65,535 bytes. If the name contains only ASCII characters, then the class file can fit 65,535 Unicode characters into those 65,535 bytes. Unicode characters beyond the ASCII range (that is, values above 127), however, require two or even three bytes of storage apiece, because they are encoded in the UTF-8 format (see *The Java Virtual Machine Specification*, p. 100, for details). Names containing such characters have a correspondingly lesser maximum length. You could precisely calculate this maximum, depending on the characters in the string, but you should never need to even approach it.

See also: JVMS p. 100

Q2.7

Why doesn't Java have user-defined operator overloading?

The Java language forgoes the expressive power of user-defined operator overloading for the sake of simplicity and readability.

The Java language aims to be powerful and practical, yet simple and readable. It was the experience of the Java language designers that operator overloading too often makes programs hard to read. The code itself no longer tells you which parts have standard meanings and which parts are defined by the author. (This highly contentious issue has received copious discussion on various Java-related mailing lists and newsgroups.)

The Java language allows only one very limited case of operator overloading. The + operator doubles as an arithmetic addition operator (when both its operands are numeric) and as a string concatenation operator (when at least one operand is a String instance). The following three statements, for example, contrast the uses of the + operator:

```
String string1 = "box " + (5 + 3);   // Result:  "box 8"
String string2 = ("box " + 5) + 3;   // Result:  "box 53"
String string3 = "box " + 5 + 3;     // Result:  "box 53"
```

The first line involves both the string concatenation operator and the arithmetic addition operator; the second line involves two applications of the string concatenation operator; and the third line shows that it is a good idea to provide explicit parentheses whenever mixing the two uses of the + operator.

For the same goals of simplicity and clarity, the Java language also omits typedefs and preprocessor macros. Thus, a piece of Java code, even out of context, makes sense. You know which parts are defined by the language itself and which parts are defined by the author.

See also: Q11.1

Q2.8

Why do I have to put an f after a floating point constant?

The f (or F) suffix directs the compiler to create a float value from a sequence of characters representing a floating point number (a *float literal*)—otherwise the compiler would by default create either a double value or an int value.

A literal is a string of characters in a source file that the compiler translates directly to a value of a specific type. The Java language recognizes literals for integral numbers, floating point numbers, strings, Unicode characters, boolean values, and null. Table 2.4 shows examples of literals in the Java language, with the types as indicated.

Table 2.4: Examples of Java Literals

Literal	Type
34	`int`
0xFF	`int`
3.14159	`double`
1.25e11	`double` (the value is 1.25×10^{11})
'9'	`char`
'\uFF01'	`char`
true	`boolean`
false	`boolean`
"Cancel"	`String` (the quotes are part of the literal)
"null"	`String`
null	special `null` literal

Numerical literals have the option of containing a suffix as well, which directly specifies the type that the compiler should use when creating the value from the literal, as shown in Table 2.5.

Table 2.5: Suffixes on Numerical Literals

Suffix on literal	Type	Examples
`d` or `D`	`double`	34d, 0xffD
`f` or `F`	`float`	34F, 3.14159f
`l` or `L`	`long`	34l, 0xffL

By default, an integer-like literal (with no decimal point or exponent) creates a value of type `int`, and a floating point literal creates a value of type `double`. If you need a nondefault type for the value, use the appropriate suffix on the literal. There are two common cases that require this.

First, to specify a long literal outside the range of an int, you cannot count on automatic promotion; you must use the l or L suffix:

```
long valueOne = 1234567890123;   /* WRONG */
long valueTwo = 1234567890123L;  /* RIGHT */
```

In the first line, the integer literal is silently be treated as an int, with the resulting value of 1,912,276,171 (the int value of the lower 32 bits of the literal).

Second, to specify a float literal as an initial value for a float variable or as an argument to a method, again you cannot count on automatic type conversion; you must use the f or F suffix:

```
float floatVal1 = 3.14159;   /* WRONG--compiler will complain */
float floatVal2 = 3.14159f;  /* RIGHT */
```

In this case, the compiler issues an error message for the first line because the types are incompatible: it cannot assign a value of type double to a variable of type float without an explicit cast (Q2.9). With an explicit cast, the compiler is again satisfied:

```
float floatVal3 = (float) 3.14159;  /* OKAY */
```

See also: Q2.9

Q2.9

How and when can I cast from one class to another?

You can't change the class of an object, but you can change the class by which a reference accesses an object.

A Java object has a fully specified, unchangeable class at run time. (Invoking getClass on an object returns a Class instance describing the object's class; see Q2.15.) Although objects and their classes cannot be cast, object references (Q1.10, Q2.11) can.

To cast a reference to a specified class or interface, place the class or interface name in parentheses preceding the reference. For example:

```
String aString = "abadcafe";
Object anObject = (Object) aString;   // OKAY
anObject = aString;                   // OKAY
```

Java allows you to cast an object reference both from subclass (Q1.11) to superclass and from superclass to subclass. An upward cast—subclass to super-class—is checked at compile time.

A downward cast (superclass to subclass) works only if the cast passes a run-time type check: the run-time type of the object must be same as (or a subclass of) the type it is being cast to. Any downward cast failing the run-time check will throw a ClassCastException. For example:

```
String aString = "abadcafe";
Object anObject = (Object) aString;          // OKAY - compile time
String testString = (String) anObject;       // OKAY - run time

Integer anInteger = new Integer(1);
anObject = (Object) anInteger;               // OKAY - compile time
Integer testInteger = (Integer) anObject;    // OKAY - run time

testString = (String) anObject;              // ClassCastException
```

Note: The cast operator can also apply to interfaces and to Java's primitive numerical types, such as int and double (Q2.8).

See also: Q1.10, Q1.26, Q2.8, Q2.11, Q2.15

Q2.10

Can I use C-like data structures in Java?

If you really want just a structured data container with no methods, then create a class containing nothing but public instance variables.

A class (Q1.2) in the Java language provides a structured data container together with executable code (methods; see Q1.3) for inspecting and manipulating that data. A structure (struct) in C provides merely the structured data container. If you really want to, you can strip down a Java class to look and behave much like a structure in C. For example:

```
/* a structured data container in Java: */
class Point {
    public int x;
    public int y;
}

/* a structured data container in C: */
struct point {
    int x;
    int y;
} ;
```

However, once you have your data nicely packaged like this, it almost always makes sense to add some functionality to manipulate the data held in such a container. In object-oriented programming, this means defining one or more methods in the class.

See also: Q1.1, Q1.2, Q1.3

VARIABLES AND METHODS

Q2.11

Are Java objects pointers?

No; Java objects are objects (typed containers for data plus associated methods), but the Java language lets you access objects only via references.

The Java runtime is filled with objects—created by the system and by your program. An object is a programming entity that holds data and is associated with a class; the class defines both the data and services that its objects support.

Although objects are the heart of your Java program, you never get direct access to them. The Java language lets you handle only object references—values that refer to objects but completely lack arithmetic (pointer-like) properties (Q1.10). Whenever a variable, method argument, or method return value appears to work with an object, it is in fact working indirectly through an object reference.

See also: Q1.1, Q1.2, Q1.10, Q2.1, Q2.12, Q2.13

Q2.12

In a method invocation, does Java pass arguments by reference or by value?

Java method invocations pass arguments by value.

Java method invocations pass *all* arguments by value—primitive data types and reference data types alike (Q2.1). This means that the value of each argument is copied to a corresponding method-internal variable before the method's code is executed. The method's code can act only on this internal copy of the data.

Consider the following minimal class, which defines and invokes a `zeroIt` method:

```
class Example {
    static void zeroIt(int intVal) {
        intVal = 0;
    }

    public static void main(String[] args) {
        int myInt = 5;
        zeroIt(myInt);
        System.out.println("Does myInt equal 0 or 5?  " + myInt);
    }
}
```

Running this class shows that the `int` argument is unchanged:

```
> java Example
Does myInt equal 0 or 5?  5
```

Because `zeroIt`'s `int` argument is passed by value, `zeroIt` zeroes only its internal copy of the `int` value; it doesn't affect the original `int` value stored in `myInt`.

What about objects, then? The key here is that the Java language provides only reference-type (pointer-like) variables for objects (Q1.10, Q2.11). The values of such variables are not objects, but references to objects. When you invoke a method with object-like arguments, the object references are passed by value; in other words, the reference itself is copied to a corresponding method-internal variable. The result is that two different references now refer to the same object.

Copying references still allows you to affect the referred-to object from inside the method, as long as the internal reference copy keeps referring to the original object. Consider a slightly different class, `ZeroItExample2`, that works on `StringBuffer` instances (modifiable character strings; Q11.1):

```
class Example2 {
    static void zeroIt(StringBuffer buf) {
        buf.setLength(0);
        buf.append("0");
    }

    public static void main(String[] args) {
        StringBuffer myStringBuffer = new StringBuffer("abc");
        zeroIt(myStringBuffer);
        System.out.println("Does myStringBuffer equal abc or 0?  "
                            + myStringBuffer);
    }
}
```

The answer this time is:

```
> java Example2
Does myStringBuffer equal abc or 0?  0
```

Here, the zeroIt method does affect data outside the method, but only because it could reach it indirectly, via the reference copied in.

As a final exercise, try replacing zeroIt in Example2 with the following tryToZeroIt method:

```
static void tryToZeroIt(StringBuffer buf) {
    buf = new StringBuffer("0");
}
```

Why does this version *not* affect the value of myStringBuffer? (Hint: Consider which operations in zeroIt and tryToZeroIt affect references and which affect referred-to objects.)

See also: Q1.10, Q2.1, Q2.11, Q11.1

Q2.13

If the Java language lacks pointers, how do I implement classic pointer structures like linked lists?

Use object references in place of pointers.

Object references in Java are like object pointers minus the arithmetic. The Java language lets you point to (refer to) objects; it just doesn't let you change numbers into references, references into numbers, or otherwise treat references in any numerical way (Q1.10, Q2.11). This property makes it straightforward to implement classic pointer-dependent data structures such as lists and trees. The following example shows a minimal linked-list implementation of a stack:

```java
/** A bare-bones stack class that holds objects of any class. */
public class SimpleStack {
    LinkedObject stackTop = null;
    public void push(Object obj) {
        if (obj != null) {
            stackTop = new LinkedObject(obj, stackTop);
        }
    }

    public Object pop() {
        if (stackTop != null) {
            Object oldTop = stackTop.value;
            stackTop = stackTop.nextObject;
            return oldTop;
        }
        return null;
    }
}

/** A bare-bones class for linking objects of any class. */
class LinkedObject {
    Object value;
    LinkedObject nextObject;
    LinkedObject(Object obj, LinkedObject next) {
        value = obj;
        nextObject = next;
    }
}
```

Even better, you often don't need to reinvent the wheel; you can use a class that's already been designed to provide the behavior you need. A Stack class already exists in the java.util package, for example. The java.util package also provides a Vector class, which represents a growable array for Object instances that you can use in place of a linked list, at least for some applications. The above code, for instance, could be rewritten as:

```java
import java.util.Vector;
public class VectorStack {
    Vector stackElements;
    public void push(Object obj) {
        if (obj != null) {
            stackElements.addElement(obj);
        }
    }
}
```

```
    public Object pop() {
        if (stackElements.isEmpty()) {
            return null;
        }
        Object oldTop = stackElements.lastElement();
        stackElements.removeElementAt(stackElements.size() - 1);
        return oldTop;
    }
}
```

LinkedListExample.html

See also: Q1.10, Q2.11, Q2.12

Q2.14

What does the following error message mean: `Can't make a static reference to nonstatic variable?`

The compiler is complaining that you are trying to reference the implicit instance variable `this` **from within a class method.**

The Java language lets you define three kinds of variables: class variables, instance variables, and local variables (Q1.5). Class variables are defined on a per-class basis, and all instances of a class can access them. Instance variables are defined on a one-per-object basis, and you can access them only in connection with some specific instance of a class. Local variables are defined inside individual methods and can be accessed only from inside that same method.

The "`Can't make a static reference ...`" error message most commonly arises in a class's `main(String[])` method, which the Java language requires to be a class method (declared with the `static` keyword; see Q1.6). The following code exemplifies the error:

```
/* The compiler will complain about this: */
class StaticError {
    String myString = "hello";
    public static void main(String[] args) {
        System.out.println(myString);
    }
}
```

The `myString` variable is an instance variable; you cannot access it unless you have created one or more instances of the class. There are therefore two minimal ways to fix the example: either change the variable to be a class variable, or create an instance of the class in order to access the instance variable.

The first fix simply requires that you use the static keyword when defining the variable:

```
/* This works. */
class NoStaticError {
    static String myString = "hello";
    public static void main(String[] args) {
        System.out.println(myString);
    }
}
```

The second fix requires creation of an instance of the class:

```
/* This also works. */
class NoStaticError2 {
    String myString = "hello";
    public static void main(String[] args) {
        NoStaticError2 obj = new NoStaticError2();
        System.out.println(obj.myString);
    }
}
```

See also: Q1.5, Q1.6

Q2.15

In a class method, how can I get the name of the class, or create a new instance of the class?

You can't, in general; these operations require that you obtain an instance of class Class representing the current class, which in turn requires that you either (a) already know the name of the class, or (b) already have an instance of the class.

The Java platform includes a special class, the Class class, that lets your program inspect Java data types at run time. Each instance of class Class represents a different class or interface type that has been loaded into the current Java Virtual Machine.

You can query a Class instance for many kinds of information about the class. In the JDK 1.0.2, you can query the class's name, class loader, superclass, and interfaces; you can also create a new instance of the class with the newInstance method. The JDK 1.1 opens much more to inspection, including the class's fields, methods (Q2.16), and constructors.

One way to obtain a Class instance is to ask for it by name, using the forName method (Q3.7). The following code, for example, fetches three distinct Class instances from the virtual machine:

```
Class c1 = null;
Class c2 = null;
Class c3 = null;

try {
    c1 = Class.forName("java.lang.Thread");
    c2 = Class.forName("java.lang.String");
    c3 = Class.forName("java.lang.Integer");
} catch (ClassNotFoundException e) {
    e.printStackTrace();
}
```

Note that the forName method requires that you provide the fully qualified name of the class, that is, the class's simple name preceded by the name of the package containing the class (Q1.30).

In the JDK 1.1, if you know the class's name at compile time, you can get the Class instance more directly, by means of a *class literal*:

```
/* using JDK 1.1: */
Class c1 = Thread.class;
Class c2 = String.class;
Class c3 = Integer.class;
```

Alternatively, if you have an object and want to get at its corresponding Class instance, you can invoke the getClass method on the object. For example:

```
Class c4 = "a string".getClass();
```

Finally, what about accessing the Class instance for the class of the currently executing method? If the method is an instance method, there is a simple, general way to get the Class object—use the ever-present this field, which refers to the object the method was invoked on:

```
/* works inside an instance method: */
Class thisClass = this.getClass();
```

Even simpler, you can take advantage of the fact that this can be left implicit:

```
Class thisClass = getClass();   // same as this.getClass()
```

Class methods, however, have no notion of a current instance (no `this`), so you must manually provide an instance (or the class's name) before you can fetch the `Class` instance. This requirement, unfortunately, often forces the cart before the horse.

ClassClassExample.html

See also: Q1.30, Q2.16, Q3.7

Q2.16

Can I write a method that delivers dynamically (at run time) all public methods of an object?

Don't write this yourself; use the `getMethods` **method in class** `Class`**, available in the JDK 1.1.**

The JDK 1.1 enhances the ability of class `Class` to inspect Java classes at run time, by means of classes in the `java.lang.reflect` package:

- `Method`: instances of this class let you inspect and manipulate a specific method of a class.

- `Field`: instances of this class let you inspect and manipulate a specific field of a class.

- `Constructor`: instances of this class let you inspect and manipulate a specific constructor of a class.

Following are several of the new (1.1) methods in class `Class`:

- `getMethods()`: returns an array of `Method` objects corresponding to the public methods of this class.

- `getFields()`: returns an array of `Field` objects corresponding to the public fields (variables) of this class.

- `getConstructors()`: returns an array of `Constructor` objects corresponding to the public constructors of this class.

Thus, inspecting methods, fields, or constructors at run time requires that you obtain the `Class` instance for the class you're interested in, then invoke the appropriate accessor methods. The following example method takes an object argument and prints out all the accessible methods, fields, and constructors in the class of that object:

```
public static void printClassInfo(Object obj) {
    Class c = obj.getClass();
    Method[] methods = c.getMethods();
    Field[] fields = c.getFields();
    Constructor[] constructors = c.getConstructors();

    System.out.println("\nMethods:");
    for (int i = 0; i < methods.length; ++i) {
        System.out.println("    " + methods[i]);
    }
    System.out.println("\nFields:");
    for (int i = 0; i < fields.length; ++i) {
        System.out.println("    " + fields[i]);
    }
    System.out.println("\nConstructors:");
    for (int i = 0; i < constructors.length; ++i) {
        System.out.println("    " + constructors[i]);
    }
}
```

Note: The getMethods method returns *all* public methods belonging to a class—the methods declared by the class together with the methods inherited from superclasses.

GetMethod11Example.html

See also: Q2.17, Q2.18

Q2.17

Can I invoke methods dynamically, from names (String instances) that are determined at run time?

Yes; the reflection API in the JDK 1.1 lets you invoke methods by means of run-time strings representing method names, but use of this facility is *not* recommended as a general design strategy.

Starting in the JDK 1.1, the Class class and the new java.lang.reflect package expand your ability to inspect and manipulate classes and methods at run time. The preceding FAQ (Q2.16) illustrates how to inspect class information at run time using Class's getMethods, getFields, and getConstructors methods.

The reflection API also lets you pull out individual elements from a class or class instance and act on them. You can:

- invoke a method by means of a Method instance fetched at run time (using Method's invoke method)

- change the value of a field by means of a Field instance fetched at run time (using one of Field's set... methods)

- create a new class instance by means of a Constructor object fetched at run time (using Constructor's newInstance method)

These capabilities are essential for component integration frameworks, such as JavaBeans™, and for application builder tools.

Let's focus now on methods. Invoking a method dynamically requires two basic steps:

1. Obtain a Method instance using Class's getMethod method.

2. Invoke the invoke method on that Method instance.

(The English description is almost comical here because of the multiple levels of reference to object-oriented constructs.) As an example of step 1, the following code obtains a Method instance representing the substring(int, int) method in class String:

```
/* Get Method instance representing String.substring(int, int). */
Class theClass = String.class;
Class[] parameters = {int.class, int.class};
Method theMethod  = null;
try {
    theMethod = theClass.getMethod("substring", parameters);
} catch (NoSuchMethodException e) {
    // ... handle exception
}
```

A significant restriction in using getMethod is that getMethod requires a Class object to represent each method parameter. If the parameter is already of a class or interface type, this step is straightforward. However, if the method parameter has a primitive data type, such as int or double, you need to provide an instance of class Class specially designed to represent that primitive type. Table 2.6 lists the Class objects and corresponding class literals (introduced in the JDK 1.1) that you can use to represent the primitive types.

Table 2.6: `Class` **Instances and Class Literals**
for the Primitive Types

Primitive type	Class instance	Class literal
double	Double.TYPE	double.class
float	Float.TYPE	float.class
long	Long.TYPE	long.class
int	Integer.TYPE	int.class
short	Short.TYPE	short.class
byte	Byte.TYPE	byte.class
char	Character.TYPE	char.class
boolean	Boolean.TYPE	boolean.class
void	Void.TYPE	void.class

Note that `void`, strictly speaking, is not a type, but it still needs a `Class` instance representing it for use with the `java.lang.reflect` classes.

Once you obtain the `Method` instance, you can invoke the `invoke` method on it. Just as `getMethod` requires an array of `Class` instances to represent the parameter types, `Method`'s `invoke` method requires an array of `Object` instances to represent the actual arguments to the method when you invoke it. If a method argument is a primitive data type, you must use one of the wrapper classes in the `java.lang` package, such as `Integer` or `Double`, to place the argument value inside an appropriate class instance:

```
/* Execute "123".substring(1, 2). */
Object[] arguments = {new Integer(1), new Integer(2)};
String s1 = null;
try {
    s1 = (String) method.invoke("123", arguments);
} catch (InvocationTargetException e) {
    // ... handle exception
} catch (IllegalArgumentException e) {
    // ... handle exception
}
```

These examples also illustrate the kinds of exceptions (Q2.22, Q2.23) that the methods can throw: `getMethods` can throw `NoSuchMethodException`, and `invoke` can throw `InvocationTargetException` and `IllegalArgumentException`.

Invoking methods dynamically from string names is an important piece of flexibility in the Java system. However, this capability circumvents Java's many built-in mechanisms for compile-time name checking and type checking—it should be used sparingly and with caution.

InvokeMethodDynamically11Example.html

See also: Q2.1, Q2.16, Q2.22, Q2.23

Q2.18

How can I accomplish the equivalent of function pointers in Java, for instance, for use in an array?

To treat executable code as an assignable, run-time swappable unit, you need to package it in a (small) class; the inner class facility added to the Java language starting with the JDK 1.1 simplifies this work.

In the Java language, the smallest unit of code that you can treat in an object-like fashion is the class. ("The quanta of behavior are classes," is James Gosling's terser version of this idea.)

To encapsulate code so that you can assign it to variables, pass it from object to object, and so on, you need to create one or more classes to contain the code. You can use either an interface or a simple superclass as the type for the code objects you want to manipulate. The following sample code shows one simple way to accomplish this, within the JDK 1.0.2 Java language:

```
interface DoIt {
    public void doIt();
}

class PrintMonth implements DoIt {
    public void doIt() {
        String[] monthNames = {"January", "February", "March",
                               "April", "May", "June",
                               "July", "August", "September",
                               "October", "November", "December"
                              };
        int monthIndex = new java.util.Date().getMonth();
        System.out.println(monthNames[monthIndex]);
    }
}
```

```
class PrintDay implements DoIt {
    public void doIt() {
        String[] dayNames = {"Sunday", "Monday", "Tuesday",
                             "Wednesday", "Thursday",
                             "Friday", "Saturday"};
        int dayIndex = new java.util.Date().getDay();
        System.out.println(dayNames[dayIndex]);
    }
}

class Demonstration_1_0_2 {
    public static void main(String[] args) {
        DoIt[] thingsToDo = {new PrintMonth(), new PrintDay()};
        for (int i = 0; i < thingsToDo.length; ++i) {
            thingsToDo[i].doIt();
        }
    }
}
```

The JDK 1.1 release augments the Java language with the notion of *inner classes:* classes and interfaces that can be declared as members of another class. Inner classes, especially anonymous inner classes, make it significantly easier to define small classes (Q7.2).

MethodTable11Example.html

See also: Q7.2

ARRAYS

Q2.19

Can I allocate an array dynamically?

Yes and no; you can create an array with a size determined at run time, but you cannot change the size of an array once you've created it.

Arrays in Java are full-fledged, object citizens of the language. Like other Java objects, they are created dynamically at run time, and their storage space is allocated from the virtual machine's system storage. Because arrays are created at run time, you don't have to prespecify an array's size at compile time.

There are two ways to create an array: with an array initializer when declaring an array-type variable, or with an array creation expression. An array initializer specifies the complete set of values to be stored in an array. For example, the following declaration and initializer create an array holding 5 int values:

```
int[] myInts = {5, 4, 3, 2, 1};  // int myInts[]... also allowed
```

A plain array creation expression, using the new keyword, creates an array filled with default values for the element type in the array. You specify the size of the array with any expression that evaluates to an int. The following code, for instance, creates an array of sine values; the array's size is specified by the method's argument:

```
public static float[] sineArray(int size) {
    float[] sineVals = new float[size];
    for (int i = 0; i < sineVals.length; ++i) {
        sineVals[i] = (float) Math.sin( (i * 2 * Math.PI) / size);
    }
    return sineVals;
}
```

Starting with the JDK 1.1, you can also include an array initializer directly in an array creation expression. For example:

```
/* using JDK 1.1: */
// int[] myInts declared elsewhere
myInts = new int[] {5, 4, 3, 2, 1};
```

Once a Java array is created, its size is fixed for the lifetime of the array. If you need more dynamism—an array-like object that can grow as needed when you use it—consider using the Vector class in the java.util package.

See also: Q2.20, JLS p. 193

Q2.20

How do I initialize an array of objects?

Write a loop that initializes the base elements of your array one by one.

In the Java language, what looks like an array of objects is really an array of object references—basically, pointers to objects (Q2.11). The objects themselves are stored separately in space managed by the Java Virtual Machine. When you create an object-type array, you are in fact creating an array of object references. Unless you explicitly initialize the array, moreover, each object reference receives the default initial value of `null`. In other words, creating an object array in Java automatically gives you an array filled with null object references.

After creating an array, you need to set each object reference to refer to some bona fide object. The usual technique for this is to allocate and initialize objects in a loop through the array, as illustrated:

```java
String[] sArray = new String[10];
for (int i = 0; i < sArray.length; ++i) {
    sArray[i] = "string at index " + i;
}
```

The behavior of arrays containing objects follows from the fact that Java array components are in fact nameless variables (*The Java Language Specification*, p. 193). These nameless variables are related to their array in much the same way that (named) instance variables are related to the class instance containing them. Table 2.7 compares arrays and class instances as two different kinds of object; you might find this alternate view of Java arrays a surprising yet useful one.

Table 2.7: Class versus Array as Two Kinds of Object

Class instance (`obj`)	Array instance (`arr`)
stores per-object data in named instance variables	stores per-object data in nameless (but numbered) variables
can have variables of different types in one object	all variables in object have same type
accesses variables by name: `obj.fieldName`	accesses variables by index: `arr[index]`
reference-type variables hold object references	[same as class instance]
instance variables have default initialization	[same as class instance]

InitialializeObjectArrayExample.html

See also: Q2.11

Q2.21

If arrays are objects, why can't I use a length *method to determine an array's size?*

Such a method would be reasonable, but it doesn't exist; the Java language designers decided to expose array length like a public final instance variable rather than a method.

In Java, arrays are objects. They are created dynamically from central, system-managed memory like other objects; they all have Object as a superclass; and you can invoke any Object method on them. Given this, it would have been possible to define a length instance method on arrays to return the length of the array, much like the length method in class String.

However, the Java language designers chose to represent length simply as an instance variable of the array. The length variable is always accessible but never changeable; its value is fixed at the time the array is created.

EXCEPTIONS

Q2.22

What is an exception?

An exception is a condition (typically an error condition) that transfers program execution from a thrower (at the source of the condition) to a catcher (handler for the condition); information about the condition is passed as an Exception or Error object.

An exception provides a communication channel between one portion of code that detects and signals an (error) condition, and another portion of code that responds to the condition. Exceptions in some ways resemble method invocations, as highlighted in Table 2.8. In both cases, information and control of execution pass from one portion of code to another. And in both cases, the initiator of the exchange typically doesn't know, and doesn't need to know, precisely what code will respond (Q1.1, Q1.18).

Table 2.8: Throwing an Exception versus Invoking a Method

Instigator/Requester	Communication mechanism	Responder/ Performer
`throw` statement	`Exception` object	executes catch clause
method invocation expression	dynamic method lookup; arguments and return value	executes method body

It is important to remember, however, that exceptions should be used only for *exceptional* control flow needs. Exceptions typically signal unexpected error conditions, such as:

- `IllegalArgumentException`: a method argument violates some requirement

- `NullPointerException`: a method is invoked on a `null` reference

- `ArrayIndexOutOfBoundsException`: an array index is too small or too large

The Java language represents exceptions as objects, all of which belong to the `Throwable` class or one of its subclasses. Because exceptions belong to classes, you can readily define your own exception types by subclassing an existing exception class.

There are four main ways to interact with Java's exception system, listed below in a common order that programmers learning Java encounter them:

- catching exceptions thrown by other people's code

- writing your own code to throw exceptions

- declaring exceptions that a method can throw

- defining your own `Exception` classes

What follows is a bare-bones how-to introduction for each of these facets.

To catch an exception, you specify a body of code to watch, a type of exception to watch for, and a body of code to execute if an appropriate exception type is thrown within the watched body of code. For example:

```
int anIntValue;
String str = solicitStringFromUser();
try {
    anIntValue = Integer.parseInt(str);
} catch (NumberFormatException e) {
    reportError("string could not be parsed as an integer.")
}
```

To throw an exception, use the `throw` statement and provide a newly created `Exception` instance, which can include a message providing information about this particular exception:

```
int speed;  // an instance variable
public void setSpeed(int value) throws IllegalSpeedException {
    if (value < 0) {
        throw new IllegalSpeedException(
                "speed cannot be negative");
    }
    speed = value;  // executed only for valid speed values.
}
```

The above code also illustrates how to declare an exception: you provide a `throws` declaration following the method's parameter list. Note that both methods and constructors can throw and declare exceptions.

Finally, to define a new `Exception` class, subclass `Exception` or one of its subclasses, and provide appropriate constructors. The `IllegalSpeedException` used in the previous example is not a predefined Java class; you could define it yourself:

```
class IllegalSpeedException extends Exception {
    public IllegalSpeedException() { super(); }
    public IllegalSpeedException(String s) { super(s); }
}
```

ExceptionExample.html

See also: Q2.23

Q2.23

Why does the compiler complain about `InterruptedException` *when I try to use* `Thread`'s `sleep` *method?*

The compiler is complaining, as it is required to do, that your code invokes a method that might throw a *checked exception*, but your code is not prepared to handle that exception; to stop the compiler from complaining, your method must either declare or catch the `InterruptedException` that `Thread`'s `sleep` method can throw.

InterruptedException belongs to the set of *checked exceptions*—a subset of exceptions that a Java compiler is required to track through any source code it handles (Q2.22). One of the compiler's restrictions is that a method declare all the checked exceptions that it might throw. A method can throw an exception either by an explicit throw statement or by invoking another method that throws the exception.

Thread's sleep method declares that it can throw an InterruptedException; therefore, the compiler will examine any method that invokes sleep to check whether the exception is being dealt with. You have two options when writing a method that invokes sleep:

- declare that your method can throw InterruptedException
- catch the exception inside your run code

To declare the exception, add a throws clause to your method definition:

```
public void myMethod() throws InterruptedException { /* ... */ }
```

This is a simple fix, but it also means that you are leaving it up to some other method to catch and deal with the exception.

It is often better to catch an exception right at the point it is generated, where you usually have more information about what triggered the exception. To catch the exception, surround your call to sleep in a try-catch block:

```
try {
    Thread.sleep(sleepTime);
} catch (InterruptedException e) {
    // ... handle the exception here (good)
    // or leave this blank to ignore the exception (risky)
    // but still satisfy the compiler
}
```

See also: Q2.22, Q2.24

Q2.24

Why do methods have to declare the exceptions they can throw?

The simple answer is that the Java language requires it; the more meaningful answer is that the language requires exception declarations because they enhance the usability and robustness of code as part of an API.

The Java language requires that a method declare any *checked exceptions* that the method might throw. Whether an exception is checked or not depends on the exception's class. As shown in Table 2.9, the base `Throwable` class splits into two main subclass branches, `Error` and `Exception`. All `Exception` subclasses are checked exceptions except for `RuntimeException` and its subclasses (Q2.25).

Table 2.9: Checked Exceptions versus Unchecked Exceptions

Class hierarchy under `Throwable`			Checked?
`Throwable`	`Error` and its subclasses		no
	`Exception`	`RuntimeException` and its subclasses	no
		all other `Exception` subclasses	yes

The intent of checked exceptions is that you declare exceptions as a meaningful part of your class's programming interface. Together with a method's return value, exceptions define the output behavior of the method. Any code that invokes a method must be prepared to handle either of these:

- the method's return value, if the method completes normally

- any of the method's checked exceptions, if the method terminates abnormally

Checked exceptions thus complement the return value as indicators of a method's exit status.

For example, the `InputStream` class in the `java.io` package includes a `read` method that is declared as follows:

```
public byte read() throws IOException;
```

This means that any method invoking this `read` method must be prepared to handle two kinds of outcome from the method: a `byte` return value if the read succeeds, or an `IOException` if the read fails. The invoking method itself must therefore either catch the exception or declare that it, too, throws `IOException` (Q2.23).

The requirement that checked exceptions be declared or caught is not just good programming practice—it is a rule enforced by the Java compiler. More specifically, the compiler enforces the following condition:

> If method X invokes method Y, and method Y can throw a checked exception, then either method X must catch the exception, or method X must declare the exception (or a superclass of the exception).

The real power of this check is that the compiler performs it transitively, following the often-complex chain of possible method invocations (method X invokes method Y, which in turn might invoke method Z, and so on).

This moderate degree of automated error checking provides surprisingly strong help in writing robust, error-tolerant code. One example comes from the development of Java and HotJava themselves. When exception declarations and exception checking were added to the language, this immediately turned up a number of cases in which the HotJava developers hadn't noticed they needed to catch certain important types of exceptions. Instead of being caught further down the road as tricky run-time bugs, these mistakes were now being flagged as compile-time errors. The developers thus were able to find and fix the problems much more efficiently. The extra effort of declaring checked exceptions was repaid many times. Such experiences advise against circumventing these built-in checks without strong reason (and even then, think twice).

See also: Q2.22, Q2.23, Q2.25

Q2.25

What's the difference between a runtime exception and a plain exception—why don't runtime exceptions have to be declared?

The Java language specifies that all runtime exceptions are exempted from the standard method declarations and compiler checks; such exceptions belong more to the system as a whole than to the method that happens to be executing when the exception is thrown.

The Java language lets you signal conditions (usually error conditions) by *throwing* an object at one point in your code, such that an enclosing block can *catch* the object and infer from it the trigger condition. The object you throw must belong to the Throwable class or one of its subclasses. The class hierarchy under Throwable further classifies the nature of the unusual condition. Throwable subdivides into two subclasses, which *The Java Application Programming Interface (Vol. 1)* demarcates nicely:

- `Error`: "indicates serious problems that a reasonable application should not try to catch." (p. 175)

- `Exception`: "indicates conditions that a reasonable application might want to catch." (p. 162)

Errors are never declared—they are entirely unexpected and practically always fatal. When an `Error` instance is thrown and not caught, it works its way up the method invocation stack until the Java Virtual Machine detects it, prints out a diagnostic error message (usually including a useful stack trace), and then kills that thread. (Uncaught `Exception` instances have this same behavior.)

Exceptions come in two basic varieties—those that can be ascribed to the execution of a single method and those that belong more to the system as a whole:

- `Exception` (in general): meaningful, specific, recoverable condition that can be expected to arise occasionally in the execution of this method (for instance, a `NumberFormatException` thrown when trying to parse a `String` instance as an integer value).

- `RuntimeException`: a condition that can arise in principle anytime, largely independent of which particular method happens to be executing (for instance, an `ArrayIndexOutOfBoundsException`).

Exceptions in general must be declared by methods (and by constructors) and are checked by the compiler (Q2.24). Runtime exceptions are exempted from this because the Java designers judged that having to declare them would be too much work, would involve too many methods, and would not pay back the extra effort sufficiently in terms of increased program robustness.

The difference between runtime exceptions and other exceptions is not always clear-cut—it requires human judgment as to the relative merits of including the exception as a method-specific condition versus a can-happen-anytime general condition. Nevertheless, making the distinction reflects Java's pragmatic streak:

- It presents a balance between theoretical purity and practical needs.

- It helps developers write convenient yet robust code.

Recommendation: Use general (declared) exceptions wherever possible. In the experience of many Java developers, the benefits of automatic compile-time checking more than offset the extra effort of declaring or catching exceptions.

See also: Q2.22, Q2.23, Q2.24, Q2.26

Q2.26

Given a method that doesn't declare any exceptions, can I override that method in a subclass to throw an exception?

No; subclasses must honor the API contract established by their superclasses, and this includes the types of checked exceptions that a method can throw.

An API (application programming interface) establishes a contract of intent, not just of form or interpretation. To borrow terminology from linguistics and philosophy, an API contract involves both extension and intension: the boundaries of the current state of the world (extension) as well as the intended boundaries for other possible states of the world (intension: possible future implementations). In object-oriented programming, a common source of "possible future implementations" is subclassing from an existing class in an API.

A method defines a contract for any subclass method that would override it; it constrains possible implementations that a subclass could provide. In Java, the bare minimum contract for a method's inputs and outputs is the following:

- A method's parameter list is fixed; an overriding method in a subclass must declare precisely the same number and types of arguments.

- A method's return type is fixed; an overriding method in a subclass must declare precisely the same return type.

- The set of checked exceptions a method can throw (the method's declared exception classes and all their subclasses) establishes an upper bound. An overriding method in a subclass cannot throw any checked exceptions outside of that; it can, however, throw fewer exception types, or even none at all.

Note that the contract on exceptions concerns only checked exceptions; errors and runtime exceptions (that is, `Error`, `RuntimeException`, and their subclasses; see Q2.25) are always permitted.

If a method, such as `Object`'s `toString` method, is declared as throwing no checked exceptions, any overriding method you define must live within those bounds. You cannot define your own subclass of `Exception` and have your `toString` method throw that. In such a case, if you really need some exception to be thrown, you can resort to a subclass of `RuntimeException`, which is not checked or constrained by the compiler.

See also: Q2.24, Q2.25

CHAPTER 3

Virtual Machine

Virtual Machine (Q3.1–Q3.9)

VIRTUAL MACHINE

Q3.1

When, and by whom, is the main *method of a class invoked?*

Normally, you don't invoke main **yourself; the Java Virtual Machine invokes it for you if it uses your class as its starting point of execution.**

A Java Virtual Machine always starts execution from the main method of some class. Even a large Java application, such as the HotJava™ browser, starts execution in one class's main method. The main method must be declared as public and static, it must have no return value, and it must declare a String array as its sole parameter:

```
public static void main(String[] args) {
    // ...
}
```

You can include such a main method in any class you define. The Java compiler does not complain about classes containing unused main methods.

How you as a user start a Java Virtual Machine can vary in different implementations. In some implementations, such as the JDK (1.0.2 and 1.1) on Solaris and Win32, you start the virtual machine with a command line that specifies a class and an optional list of strings for your program to start with. For example, suppose that your Java Virtual Machine is stored in a command named java, and you have written and compiled the following CountWords class:

```
public class CountWords {
    public static void main(String[] args) {
        System.out.println(args.length);
    }
}
```

If you now issue the command:

```
java CountWords argyle baldric corral delirium
```

the Java Virtual Machine starts up by seeking and loading your CountWords class, checking that it has an appropriate main method, and invoking that main method with an array of four strings ("argyle", "baldric", "corral", and "delirium") as its sole argument. In this example case, the main method merely prints out the number of strings in the argument String array.

Most classes are never meant to provide the starting point for an application, but it is often useful to include a main method in them anyway. You can use main as a convenient way to test your class repeatedly as you develop it. When you later integrate your class into an application containing other classes, these extra main methods are automatically ignored, except for the single class you use as your application's starting point.

MainExample.html, SimpleTimer.html

See also: Q1.2, Q1.3

Q3.2

What are bytecodes?

Java bytecodes are a language of machine instructions understood by the Java Virtual Machine and usually generated (compiled) from Java language source code.

Java bytecodes encode instructions for the Java Virtual Machine. These instructions specify both operations and operands, always in the following format:

- opcode (1 byte): specifies what operation to perform

- operands (0–n bytes): specify data for the operation

The 1-byte opcode is simply a number that the Java Virtual Machine interprets as a specific instruction. For instance, opcode value 104 (0x68 in hexadecimal representation) is the instruction to multiply two int values — it instructs the virtual machine to take the top two values off the Java operand stack, multiply them, and push the product back on the stack. In addition to its numerical value, each opcode has a conventional short name, called its *mnemonic*. The mnemonic for opcode 104 is imul.

Following each opcode come any operands the opcode may require. The Java Virtual Machine uses the opcode to determine just how many following bytes are operands for that opcode. In some cases, such as the imul instruction, the opcode's single byte represents the entire instruction — no operands are needed. In other cases, the opcode may require one or more operands. For example, the fload instruction (opcode value 23, or 0x17 in hexadecimal) loads a float value from a local variable, and it uses an index operand to specify which local variable to load from. If the local variable of interest is at index 5, the complete instruction would have the following two bytes:

```
23 5    [fload from local variable at index 5]
```

There are different approaches for learning more about Java Virtual Machine instructions. If you want the comprehensive, detailed picture, read *The Java Virtual Machine Specification* (Tim Lindholm and Frank Yellin, 1996, Addison Wesley). It covers each virtual machine instruction — its name (mnemonic), what it does, what operands it takes, how it interacts with the operand stack, and more. It's not light reading, but it's a wonderful resource when you need it.

You can also learn by experimentation, using javap, as described in Q3.3.

See also: Q3.3

Q3.3

What is javap?

The javap **program is a class file disassembler that comes with the JDK (1.0.2 and 1.1).**

The JDK (1.0.2 and 1.1) provides a Java class file disassembler, the javap program, which can translate from binary opcodes and operands to a human-readable format with opcode mnemonics, decimal numbers, and so on. javap is a simple, useful tool for exploring compiled class files and for learning about the Java Virtual Machine instruction set.

The rest of this answer uses `javap` to explore the bytecodes generated from the following Java source file:

```
public class BytecodeExample {
    public float multiply(byte a, short b, int c, float d) {
        return a * b * c * d;
    }
}
```

After you compile this source file to a class file, run the `javap` program on the resulting class (use the `-c` option to see the virtual machine instructions):

```
javap -c ByteCodeExample
```

(Note that you provide *just* the class name, not the full name of the file containing the class.) The output from this command on the JDK 1.1 includes the virtual machine instructions for the `multiply` method:

```
Method float multiply(byte,short,int,float)
    0 iload_1
    1 iload_2
    2 imul
    3 iload_3
    4 imul
    5 i2f
    6 fload 4
    8 fmul
    9 freturn
```

Following are the same instructions, explained one by one; in each case the stack referred to is the Java operand stack.

`iload_1`	load `int` value of first method argument onto stack
`iload_2`	load `int` value of second method argument onto stack
`imul`	take two `int` values from top of stack, multiply them, place product (`int` value) on stack
`iload_3`	load `int` value of third method argument onto stack
`imul`	take two `int` values from top of stack, multiply them, place product (`int` value) on stack
`i2f`	convert `int` value on top of stack to `float` value

`fload 4`	load `float` value of fourth method argument onto stack
`fmul`	take two `float` values from top of stack, multiply them, place product (`float` value) on stack
`freturn`	take `float` value from top of stack, return it as value from this method

To appreciate the convenience provided by the `javap` program, consider the same 10 bytes of the `multiply` method in plain numerical (decimal) form:

    27 28 104 29 104 134 23 4 106 174

See also: Q3.2

Q3.4

What does it mean to say that Java is interpreted?

Several implementations of the Java Virtual Machine, including the JDK (1.0.2 and 1.1), interpret compiled Java code (virtual machine instructions) — for each instruction, the virtual machine carries out the specified behavior before reading the next instruction.

Java technology uses both compilation and interpretation. Compilation is the process of translating content (such as code) from one language to another, and storing the results of that translation for later use. Many well-known programming languages, such as C, Pascal, and Fortran, are usually compiled straight from source code to native machine code. In contrast, the Java programming language is compiled into Java class files, which contain architecture-independent instructions for the Java Virtual Machine (see Q3.2 and *The Java Virtual Machine Specification*, Ch. 4).

Interpretation also involves translating code from one language to another, except you directly execute the translation instead of storing it. Languages (or language families) such as Lisp and Basic are typically interpreted straight from source code to execution. In many Java implementations, interpretation picks up where compilation left off. Java Virtual Machine instructions, which were compiled from source code, are interpreted by the virtual machine — converted on the fly into native machine code, which is then executed rather than stored.

Interpreting virtual machine instructions is common on existing implementations of the Java Virtual Machine (such as the JDK 1.0.2 and 1.1), but is not required by either *The Java Language Specification* or *The Java Virtual Machine Specification*. A virtual machine implementation may also use just-in-time (JIT) compilation: translating virtual machine instructions into native machine code at run time on the local platform, and then executing from that stored machine code. (It is even possible to have hardware that directly implements the Java Virtual Machine instruction set; such machines would then run compiled Java code natively.)

Interpreted code is generally more flexible and adaptive than compiled code, but you usually pay a considerable price in execution speed because of the extra translation work performed as the program executes. This point is especially clear when you consider code with loops. The example below shows Java source code for a simple loop to sum integers from 1 to 1000:

```java
int sum = 0;
for (int i = 1; i <= 1000; ++i) {
    sum += i;
}
```

After compilation into virtual machine instructions (and displayed by `javap -c`), the loop looks like:

```
 0 iconst_0
 1 istore_1
 2 iconst_1
 3 istore_2
 4 goto 14
 7 iload_1
 8 iload_2
 9 iadd
10 istore_1
11 iinc 2 1
14 iload_2
15 sipush 1000
18 if_icmple 7
21 return
```

Using just-in-time compilation, the above virtual machine instructions can be translated once into native machine code, and then the machine code is used directly each time through the loop. Using interpretation, on the other hand, means that the machine code for executing the loop is not stored for reuse — the virtual machine instructions are read and translated into machine code *each time* through the loop.

See also: Q3.2, Q3.3, JVMS Ch. 4

Q3.5

What kind of garbage collection does the Java Virtual Machine use?

The Java Virtual Machine specification does not require any particular algorithm; the virtual machine implementation in the JDK 1.0.2 and 1.1 uses a partially conservative mark-and-sweep garbage collector, but other implementations may use other techniques.

The Java Virtual Machine is required to provided automatic storage management for objects (class instances and arrays). In the JDK (1.0.2 and 1.1), for instance, storage space for all objects is allocated from a central Java heap, and a running Java program uses pointers into the heap area, called object references (Q1.10, Q2.11), to access its objects. When the program no longer holds a reference to an object, that object's space on the heap can be reclaimed, or *garbage collected*. Automatic garbage collection means that the run-time system, not the programmer, is responsible for tracking memory use and deciding when to free memory that is no longer needed. This strongly boosts programmer productivity and code robustness.

A Java Virtual Machine implementation must include some form of garbage collection, but the implementation can choose what kind. The JDK (1.0.2 and 1.1) implements garbage collection with a partially conservative mark-and-sweep algorithm.

A round of mark-and-sweep garbage collection starts by identifying any element in a running program (that is, any element on one of the the program's active thread execution stacks) that might refer to an object. For pure Java code, there is no question about precisely which elements are object references, but Java programs can also include non-Java `native` methods, which might have their own object pointers. The garbage collector is *conservative* in that it errs on the side of safety: if an element even looks like it might point to an object in the central heap, that element gets treated as an object reference. The garbage collector traces all potential references to corresponding objects on the heap, and from any references held by those objects to yet further objects, and so on. It *marks* all objects encountered in this transitive process; these objects are considered the program's set of live objects that must be maintained. Finally, the garbage collector scans (*sweeps*) the heap for all unmarked objects and reassigns their space back to the pool of free memory available for new allocation. Note that this method correctly picks up dead reference cycles (e.g., X refers to Y, which refers to Z, which refers to X, but the program no longer refers to any of the three), which escape detection by some other algorithms, such as simple reference counting.

See also: Q1.10, Q2.11

Q3.6

Is finalization broken—why does my `finalize` *method never seem to get invoked?*

Your object's `finalize` method will get invoked, but the Java system makes no guarantees about when; it requires only that an object be finalized before it is garbage collected.

Objects use system resources, and a well-behaved object should free its resources for reuse once the object is no longer needed. One system resource, storage space for objects, is managed automatically by the Java Virtual Machine: the virtual machine detects when an object is no longer usable and eventually reclaims the object's space for use by new objects (Q3.5). If your object uses any other system resource, such as a graphics context, an open file, or a network connection, it is up to you to explicitly manage that resource. Java's system of finalization provides a simple notification service with which you can define how your objects free up their resources.

The core of Java's finalization system is the `finalize` method:

```
protected void finalize() throws Throwable { ... }
```

The `Object` class defines an empty version of this method, which you override in a subclass when you need to specify finalization actions for that class. The following code fragment illustrates a class that provides a method to explicitly clean up system resources, but also defines `finalize` as a backup measure:

```
class MyClass {
    AudioDevice device = AudioDevice.acquire();
    void cleanUp() {
        // ...
        if (device != null) {
            device.release();
            device = null;
        }
    }

    protected void finalize() throws Throwable {
        if (device != null)
            device.release();
        }
        super.finalize();
    }
    // ...
}
```

The most common confusion about finalization is *when* it occurs. There is much leeway — a virtual machine is required only to obey the following sequence:

1. Your program removes its last reference to an object.

2. The virtual machine invokes `finalize` on that object.

3. The virtual machine garbage collects the object.

What this means in practice, such as on the JDK 1.0.2 and 1.1 virtual machines, is that finalization waits for garbage collection, and then runs immediately prior to the actual reclamation of space. You can wait indefinitely for finalization to occur, because garbage collection usually waits until either the system runs low on memory or there is sufficient slack time in the application. If you need to, you can initiate finalization and garbage collection explicitly by invoking `System.runFinalization()` or `System.gc()`, but these methods provide no guarantees either. Finalization or garbage collection (depending on which method you invoke) will occur, but there is no guarantee that some specific object of yours is ready to be finished off.

Because the timing of finalization is implementation dependent, and even circumstance dependent, you can't rely on finalization for consistent, timely behavior. Wherever possible, you should free critical system resources explicitly in your code and rely on finalization as more of a backup measure. The AWT code for the Graphics class (in JDK 1.0.2 and 1.1), for instance, disposes of each system graphics context explicitly as soon as it can; for safety, the class also invokes `dispose` from its `finalize` method:

```
/* in Graphics.java (JDK 1.0.2 and 1.1): */
public void finalize() {
    dispose();
}
```

See also: Q8.20

Q3.7

I'm having trouble invoking methods on the objects returned from `Class`'s `forName` *method — how should I use* `Class.forName`?

Invoke `newInstance` on the `Class` object returned by `forName` and then cast the resulting instance to a type that the compiler can access; only then can your program invoke a method on the instance of the newly loaded class.

The forName method in class Class is a hidden gem in the Java system. This method lets your code create a new class type from a dynamic name—that is, a name given to your program as a string at run time. What's particularly powerful about using forName is that neither you nor the compiler needs to know the exact details of the new class, only what superclass it extends or interfaces it implements. The forName method is what enables a Java-capable browser, for instance, to load arbitrary applets, even though the browser can't know in advance what Applet subclasses it will be called on to create.

The forName method takes a String argument as the name of a class, and attempts to create a binary representation for a class with that name. (This process is called *class loading*.) If it succeeds, it returns an instance of class Class that represents the newly created class type. The following code illustrates:

```
Class newClass = null;  // initialize local variable, in case
                        // forName throws exception
String packageName = "myPackage";
String className = "myClass";
try {
    newClass = Class.forName(packageName + "." + className);
} catch (ClassNotFoundException e) { /* ... */ }
```

The Class instance returned by forName only represents the new class type; it is not an instance of that class. To obtain an instance of the new class, invoke newInstance on the Class object, which returns an object reference of type Object. (Note that newInstance requires that the target class have an accessible no-parameter constructor.) To access more than plain Object functionality, you need to cast the object reference to a more specific type—but what type?

Although the forName method can create a new class type at run time, the way your code uses that class is still checked by the compiler, before your program has a chance to run. This restricts your code to using the new class and its instances only in terms of a superclass or interfaces that the compiler can check. For example, suppose that myPackage.myClass in the previous code fragment implements the Runnable interface, which contains the single method run. You can then cast (Q2.9) the new instance to Runnable, after which the compiler will allow you to invoke run on it:

```
Object foo = null;
try {
    foo = (Runnable) newClass.newInstance();
    foo.run();  // invoke method on new instance
} catch (IllegalAccessException e) { // ...
} catch (InstantiationException e) { // ...
}
```

Thus, the newly loaded class may have all kinds of wonderful functionality, but the compiler doesn't know this at compile time; the compiler lets your code access only those methods (and fields) belonging to an interface or superclass that it can check.

ForNameExample.html

See also: Q2.9

Q3.8

Why do I get verifier errors when loading a class file produced by javac?

Chances are the class was compiled with optimization, which can cause the class file to fail verification; this is an unfortunate flaw in existing implementations.

The Java Virtual Machine performs three general processes when it first attempts to execute code belonging to a class:

1. *loading:* given the class name, determine the binary form for the class
2. *linking:* convert the class's binary form so that it can be merged into the currently executing virtual machine
3. *initialization:* execute the static initializers for the class and the class variable initializers

All three processes are managed by a class loader (an instance of a ClassLoader subclass). A Java program can have more than one class loader, to define different policies for finding classes and constraining their behavior.

The process of linking usually starts with verification — checking that the class's binary representation is well formed and the virtual machine instructions in it obey the constraints of the Java language and Virtual Machine. Verification adds both security and robustness — it protects a virtual machine from malicious executable code, and it weeds out class files that may have been accidentally corrupted in transmission. An error detected during verification is thrown as an instance of the VerifyError class.

The javac compiler is meant to generate only valid executable code, and should always do so when run in normal mode. However, when you compile with optimization (javac -0 in the JDK 1.0.2 and 1.1), you run the risk of obtaining code that a verifier will not understand and will therefore reject.

Java implementations have the leeway of omitting verification for trusted, local class files, and the JDK (1.0.2 and 1.1) takes advantage of this. The Applet-Viewer application, for instance, uses different class loaders for local classes versus classes loaded over the network. Its network class loader verifies each class as it comes in, but its local class loader omits the verification phase in order to save time. If you have a class file that loads successfully from the local file system, but fails when loaded over the network, you are quite likely seeing the difference between two class loaders, only one of which is using verification.

You can test your own class files for well-formedness by using the javap tool in the JDK (1.0.2 and 1.1). When given the -verify option, javap simply runs the class you specify through its verifier and reports success or failure:

```
% javap -verify packageFoo.ClassE
Class packageFoo.ClassE succeeds
```

See also: Q3.3

Q3.9

How fast are Java programs compared to equivalent C or C++ programs?

The relative speed depends on the type of program and on whether the virtual machine implementation uses interpretation or just-in-time compilation — GUI-intensive programs may have little noticeable difference, but computation-intensive programs run about 10–20 times slower in interpreted Java Virtual Machine instructions than in compiled native code.

The execution speed of a Java program depends on how you run it. Most of the initial Java Virtual Machine implementations run interpretively — they translate Java Virtual Machine instructions to native machine code each time immediately prior to executing the code (Q3.4). Common estimates are that an interpretive virtual machine implementation runs around 10–20 times slower than comparable code compiled directly to the native platform.

This slowdown represents the worst-case behavior for computation-bound programs, where intensive, uninterrupted computation comprises most or all of the program. GUI-dominated programs, on the other hand, typically spend most of their time waiting for user input; in such programs, the perceived difference in performance is often minor.

If raw execution speed is the bottleneck, you might consider using a virtual machine implementation that includes a just-in-time (JIT) compiler, which are becoming more and more common. A JIT compiler translates Java Virtual Machine instructions into native machine code at run time on the local platform. Once the virtual machine implementation has this translation, it can run the native code at speeds comparable to other compiled languages.

See also: Q3.4, Q11.12

CHAPTER 4

Applets

Applets versus Applications (Q4.1–Q4.3)

Installing Applets (Q4.4–Q4.10)

Applet User Interface (Q4.11–Q4.15)

Applet Program Structure (Q4.16–Q4.19)

Applet Communication (Q4.20–Q4.22)

Miscellaneous (Q4.23–Q4.24)

APPLETS VERSUS APPLICATIONS

Q4.1

What is an applet?

An applet is a Java™-compatible program that you can embed in a web page.

An applet itself is fairly simple; it is usually composed of several pieces:

- code: the Java class files that represent the executable code of the applet

- other resources: data needed by the applet, including images and sounds

These pieces, however, only begin to tell the story. The real action happens when you bring in the applet's supporting cast:

- the applet context

- the APPLET tag

- http servers and the Internet

To execute applets, you need an applet context—a larger program, typically a Java-enabled web browser, that automatically finds and loads the applet code across the network and then runs the applet code locally. The applet context must know how to interpret an APPLET tag—an HTML (HyperText Markup Language) tag that points to the applet's executable code and provides information on how to run the applet (Q4.7). In addition, the applet context defines a security policy to prevent arbitrary applets from harming the host system.

Finally, to deliver applets across the Internet, you need a standard http server that can deliver the applet code and resources across the network when requested (Q4.24).

An applet is much more than just a fancy way to spice up a web page. It is real application code, running on the user's machine, complete with a graphical user interface. Correspondingly, an applet can:

- draw interactively on screen, rather than merely presenting static images

- respond directly to the user's keyboard and mouse events

- perform calculations on the user's machine

In other words, an applet transforms a rectangular area of a web page into a fully interactive computational engine powered by the Java Virtual Machine.

See also: Q4.7, Q4.24, JavaSoft's Security FAQ web page
> (http://java.sun.com/sfaq/)

Q4.2

How do applets differ from applications?

Applications are stand-alone, full-featured programs, whereas applets are embeddable, almost full-featured programs.

Java applets and Java applications have much in common (Q4.3), but there are clear differences as well. Table 4.1 summarizes some of the key ones.

Table 4.1: Java Applications versus Applets

Java application	Java applet
must be installed on local machine	needs no explicit installation on local machine
must be run explicitly within a Java-compatible virtual machine	loads and runs itself automatically in a Java-enabled browser
can run with or without a graphical user interface	must run within a graphical user interface (using the Abstract Window Toolkit)
starts execution with its `main` method	starts execution with its `init` method
once started, manages its own flow of execution	has its flow of execution determined partly by its browser context (Q4.16)
has no inherent security restrictions (apart from safety features in the Java language itself)	has significant security controls to prevent malicious or poorly written applets from harming the user's system

Note: Differences arising from applet security are extensive and are detailed separately in the JavaSoft Security FAQ web page: `http://java.sun.com/sfaq/`.

See also: Q4.3, Q4.16, JavaSoft's Security FAQ
(`http://java.sun.com/sfaq/`)

Q4.3

Can I write Java code that works both as an applet and as a stand-alone application?

Yes, but with limitations.

Applets and applications share the standard Java class libraries, including the user-interface tools in the Abstract Window Toolkit (AWT). These classes let you present a user interface, handle events, manage input and output (subject to security restrictions), and generally define objects and their interactions.

To work as a combined applet/application, your `Applet` subclass must include a `main` method; `main` is the required starting point for all applications (Q3.1):

```
public static void main(String[] args) { ... }
```

Your `main` method must create an applet instance and place it within a frame (the AWT class for a top-level window with borders). This method also needs to call the applet's `init`, `start`, `stop`, and `destroy` methods at appropriate times to simulate how a browser would have invoked those methods; a code skeleton (written for JDK 1.1) illustrating these method calls follows:

```
/* using JDK 1.1: */
import java.awt.*;
import java.awt.event.*;
import java.applet.Applet;
public class AppletAndApplicationExample extends Applet {

    public void init() { /* ... (Q4.16, Q4.17) ... */ }

    public void start() { /* ... (Q4.16, Q4.18) ... */ }

    public void stop() { /* ... (Q4.16, Q4.18) ... */ }

    public void destroy() { /* ... (Q4.16) ... */  }

    public static void main(String[] args) {
        /* Set up the frame that holds the applet. */
        Frame appletFrame = new Frame("My Applet");
        Applet theApplet = new AppletAndApplicationExample();
        appletFrame.pack();  // create peer frame (hack)
        appletFrame.add(theApplet, "Center");  // applet fills
                                               // frame
        appletFrame.setLocation(40, 40);
        appletFrame.addWindowListener(new AppQuitter());

        /* Now start invoking applet methods. */
        theApplet.init();
        appletFrame.pack();  // resize frame to fit initialized
                             // applet
        appletFrame.show();  // bring frame and initialized
                             // applet on screen
        theApplet.start();
        theApplet.stop();
        theApplet.destroy();
    }

    /** An inner class for quitting the application. */
    static class AppQuitter extends WindowAdapter {
        public void windowClosing(WindowEvent e) {
            e.getWindow().dispose();
            System.exit(0);
        }
    }
}
```

Combined applets/applications are interesting and useful (in testing your code, for example), but there are considerable limitations on what functionality is common to both sides. Because of applet security restrictions, applications can do much more than applets. On the other hand, applets running in Java-enabled browsers have some capabilities that are not available to applications in the JDK (1.0.2 or 1.1). Table 4.2 notes some of these differences.

Table 4.2: Some Differing Application and Applet Capabilities

Applications only	reading from and writing to the local file system
	making socket connections to arbitrary hosts on the net
	loading native code (e.g., functions written in C)
Applets only	loading and playing audio (Q11.8)
	communicating with applets on a web page (Q4.20)

For further details on applet security restrictions, consult the JavaSoft Security FAQ at `http://java.sun.com/sfaq/`.

AppletAndApplicationExample.html

See also: Q3.1, Q4.16, Q4.17, Q4.18, Q4.20, Q11.8, JavaSoft's Security FAQ
(`http://java.sun.com/sfaq/`)

INSTALLING APPLETS

Q4.4

How do I put an applet into a web page?

Use the APPLET tag; its attributes let you specify the applet's code, its resources, and its positioning on the web page.

When a Java-enabled browser visits your page and encounters an APPLET tag, it uses information in the tag to start fetching the applet's executable code, and to reserve a space on the page for displaying the applet. These steps correspond to the three required attributes noted in Table 4.3.

Table 4.3: APPLET Tag Attributes

Required	`code`, `width`, `height`
Optional	`codebase`, `alt`, `name`, `align`, `vspace`, `hspace`

For example, the following APPLET tag

```
<applet code="DreamWeaver.class" width=250 height=150>
</applet>
```

specifies that the applet's code (more specifically, its main class file) resides in a file named `DreamWeaver.class`. By default, the browser looks for the applet class file in the same place that it fetched the web page from. This tag also specifies that the applet should initially occupy a space on the page 250 pixels wide by 150 pixels high.

Of the six optional APPLET tag attributes, `codebase` is the most important. It works together with the `code` attribute to give a complete specification of where to find the main applet class file: `code` specifies the name of the file, and `codebase` specifies the URL for the directory containing the file. You need to use `codebase` anytime your main applet class is not in the same directory as the HTML page containing the APPLET tag. As for the other optional attributes, their meanings are explained in Q4.7.

Finally, to allow custom parameter information to be passed from the HTML page to an applet, Java-enabled browsers recognize any PARAM tag between the opening `<applet>` and closing `</applet>` as providing applet-specific parameter information. The `Animator` applet, for example, makes rich use of custom parameters to let you control animations and sound sequences without modifying the applet's code. The APPLET tag on the web page at `http://java.sun.com/applets/applets/Animator/example3.html` includes the following lines:

```
<applet code="Animator.class" width=460 height=160>
<param name=imagesource value="images/Beans">
<param name=endimage value="10">
<param name=backgroundcolor value="0x00FF00">
<param name=soundsource value="audio">
<param name=soundtrack value="spacemusic.au">
</applet>
```

See also: Q4.7

Q4.5

Can I put more than one applet in a web page?

Yes; include a separate APPLET tag for each applet you wish to put on your web page.

Each APPLET tag represents a unique applet copy running in the space you give it. Thus, you can you can put different applets on the same page, or multiple copies of the same applet. You can also specify a name in each APPLET tag so that the different applets on the page can locate and communicate with each other (Q4.20).

See also: Q4.20

Q4.6

How do I use the APPLET tag if I want to show users of non–Java-enabled browsers what they're missing?

Include the desired substitute HTML material between the opening `<applet>` **and closing** `</applet>` **(and after any PARAM tags belonging to the applet).**

The APPLET tag has both a beginning `<applet>` and an end `</applet>`, so that additional HTML material can be placed between the two. A Java-enabled browser ignores everything between `<applet>` and `</applet>`, except for PARAM tags. As a result, you see the applet, but none of the in-between HTML material. A non-Java browser does just the opposite: it ignores the begin and end APPLET tags as well as any PARAM tags between them. Instead, it shows just the in-between HTML material. You can use this space to provide a written description of what the viewer is missing, or a static image of what your applet looks like.

The following example APPLET tag is adapted from the README page in the JDK 1.0.2 release:

```
<applet codebase="http://java.sun.com/applets/applets/NervousText"
    code="NervousText.class" width=400 height=75 align=center >
<param name="text" value="This is the Applet Viewer.">
<hr>  If you were using a Java-enabled browser, you would see an
 active applet in place of the following static image:
<img ....>  <hr>
</applet>
```

See also: Q4.4, Q4.7

Q4.7

What is the complete syntax for using the APPLET tag?

The README file in the JDK 1.0.2 release contains a description of the APPLET tag; below is the APPLET tag syntax information from that file:

```
Here's the complete syntax for the APPLET tag:
'<'  'APPLET'
    ['CODEBASE' '=' codebaseURL]
    'CODE' '=' appletFile
    ['ALT' '=' alternateText]
    ['NAME' '=' appletInstanceName]
    'WIDTH' '=' pixels 'HEIGHT' '=' pixels
    ['ALIGN' '=' alignment]
    ['VSPACE' '=' pixels] ['HSPACE' '=' pixels]
'>'
['<' 'PARAM' 'NAME' '=' appletAttribute1 'VALUE' '=' value '>']
['<' 'PARAM' 'NAME' '=' appletAttribute2 'VALUE' '=' value '>']
. . .
[alternateHTML]
'</APPLET>'

'CODEBASE' '=' codebaseURL
    This optional attribute specifies the base URL of the applet --
    the directory that contains the applet's code.  If this attribute
    is not specified, then the document's URL is used.

'CODE' '=' appletFile
    This required attribute gives the name of the file that contains
    the applet's compiled Applet subclass.  This file is relative to
    the base URL of the applet.  It cannot be absolute.

'ALT' '=' alternateText
    This optional attribute specifies any text that should be
    displayed if the browser understands the APPLET tag but can't
    run Java applets.

'NAME' '=' appletInstanceName
    This optional attribute specifies a name for the applet instance,
    which makes it possible for applets on the same page to find (and
    communicate with) each other.

'WIDTH' '=' pixels 'HEIGHT' '=' pixels
    These required attributes give the initial width and height (in
    pixels) of the applet display area, not counting any windows or
    dialogs that the applet brings up.

'ALIGN' '=' alignment
    This optional attribute specifies the alignment of the applet.
    The possible values of this attribute are the same as those for
    the IMG tag: left, right, top, texttop, middle, absmiddle,
    baseline, bottom, absbottom.
```

```
'VSPACE' '=' pixels 'HSPACE' '=' pixels
```
These optional attributes specify the number of pixels above and below the applet (VSPACE) and on each side of the applet (HSPACE). They're treated the same way as the IMG tag's VSPACE and HSPACE attributes.

```
'<' 'PARAM' 'NAME' '=' appletAttribute1 'VALUE' '=' value '>' . . .
```
This tag is the only way to specify an applet-specific attribute. Applets access their attributes with the getParameter() method.

The JDK 1.1 introduces two new attributes for the APPLET tag: ARCHIVES and OBJECT. These attributes are described as follows on the APPLET tag page at `http://java.sun.com/products/JDK/1.1/docs/guide/misc/applet.html`:

```
ARCHIVES = archivesList
```
This OPTIONAL attribute describes one or more archives containing classes and other resources that will be "preloaded". The classes are loaded using an instance of an AppletClassLoader with the given CODEBASE.
NB: in JDK1.1, multiple APPLET tags with the same CODEBASE share the same instance of a ClassLoader. This is used by some client code to implement inter-applet communication. In JDK1.2, we *may* provide a cleaner mechanism for inter-applet communication and we *may* give each APPLET instance its won [sic] ClassLoader instance (thus gaining security).

```
OBJECT = serializedApplet
```
This attribute gives the name of the file that contains a serialized representation of an Applet. The Applet will be deserialized. The init() method will *not* be invoked; but its start() method will. Attributes valid when the original object was serialized are *not* restored. Any attributes passed to this APPLET instance will be available to the Applet; we advocate very strong restraint in using this feature. An applet should be stopped before it is serialized.
One of CODE or OBJECT must be present.

See also: the applet DTD page (`http://java.sun.com/applets/applet.html`) **and the applet TAG page** (`http://java.sun.com/products/JDK/1.1/docs/guide/misc/applet.html`)

Q4.8

What are the different pieces that can make up an applet, and how do I install them?

An applet can be composed of class files, data files, and media files; installation is mainly a question of putting these resources in places where your applet's code knows to look for them.

Every applet must have a main applet class file — you create this by compiling your applet source file, which must define a subclass of `java.applet.Applet`. This class file is what the code attribute in the APPLET tag points to.

Any nontrivial applet, however, uses additional resources, such as additional class files, image files, sound files, and so on. Usually these resources are grouped together in the same directory as the main applet class file, or in obviously named subdirectories, such as `images` or `sounds`. Installing an applet, then, requires:

- including an appropriate APPLET tag in your web page

- placing your applet's resources in appropriate locations so that a Java-enabled browser can find them

As an illustration, consider a hypothetical `Calculator` applet that uses `Parser` and `Computation` classes to parse the input and perform the calculations, and that provides the option of playing a different short sound for each key pressed. Your web page and applet can be divided into the following pieces:

- the web page with the Calculator APPLET tag: `index.html`

- the main applet class file: `Calculator.class`

- additional class files: `Parser.class`, `Computation.class`

- sound files: `snd1.au`, `snd2.au`, `snd3.au`, `...`

These pieces can be arranged within a main directory named `Calculator` in the following manner (shown in Windows 95/NT-style pathnames):

- in `c:\home\me\public_html\Calculator`:

      index.html
      Calculator.class
      Parser.class
      Computation.class

- in `c:\home\me\public_html\Calculator\sounds`:

      snd1.au
      snd2.au
      snd3.au
      ...

In this example, because the web page with the APPLET tag is in the same directory as the class files for the applet, the APPLET tag needs only the code attribute and not codebase:

```
<applet code="Calculator.class" width=250 height=250>
</applet>
```

See also: Q4.9, Q4.10

Q4.9

Where can I put my applet's class files, and how do I indicate their location using the APPLET tag?

Your applet's class files need to be either in the same directory as the applet's web page or in a directory pointed to by the APPLET tag's codebase attribute.

Each APPLET tag defines a base URL for the applet, which should be a directory, and all class loading for the applet is done relative to this URL. The base URL can be either the directory from which the document containing the APPLET tag was retrieved (the "document base"), or it can be a separate location specified by the optional codebase attribute. The codebase attribute can specify either the relative URL (for a subdirectory of the document base) or an absolute URL (for a completely independent location of class files). Following are three hypothetical examples showing different arrangements of class files.

Example 1 — an APPLET tag in a web page at http://www.somewhere.com/webPages/dreaming.html:

```
<applet code="DreamWeaver.class" width=250 height=150>
</applet>
```

For this example, the applet's main class file, DreamWeaver.class, must be located in the same directory as the HTML page, that is, in the webPages directory:

```
HTML page:    ....../webPages/dreaming.html
document base:  ....../webPages
class file:    ....../webPages/DreamWeaver.class
```

Example 2 — an APPLET tag in a web page at http://www.somewhere.com/webPages/daydreaming.html:

```
<applet code="Reverie.class" width=250 height=150
        codebase="classes">
</applet>
```

For this example, the applet's main class file, `Reverie.class`, should be located in the `classes` subdirectory of the document base:

```
HTML page:    ....../webPages/daydreaming.html
document base:  ....../webPages
class file:   ....../webPages/classes/Reverie.class
```

Example 3—an APPLET tag in a web page at `http://www.somewhere.com/webPages/nervousDreaming.html`:

```
<applet code="NervousText.class" width=400 height=75 align=center
    codebase="http://java.sun.com/applets/applets/NervousText">
<param name="text" value="To sleep, perchance to dream.">
</applet>
```

In this example, the applet's main class file is totally separate from the document base:

```
HTML page:    ....../webPages/nervousDreaming.html
document base:  ....../webPages
class file:   http://java.sun.com/applets/applets/NervousText/NervousText.class
```

Note: If your applet's classes have their own package structure, then your classes may also occur in subdirectories of the code base, in accordance with the common directory-package correspondence in Java: packages and subpackages containing classes correspond to directories and subdirectories containing class files.

See also: Q4.8, Q4.10

Q4.10

Can I put my reusable custom classes in a special place so that many different applets can use them?

Applets and their associated classes must stick closely together—you are quite limited in how you can place your reusable custom classes to allow access by more than one applet.

As specified in Q4.9, the classes needed by your applet must all be in the base URL directory, or in a subdirectory of that base if your classes have their own package structure. The simplest approach is to put your web pages (HTML files) and all your class files — main applet class files and reusable custom classes alike — in a single large directory. This approach allows you to use just the `code` attribute in your APPLET tag, rather than using both `code` and `codebase`.

Alternatively, you can put all your class files together in a directory, but place your web pages wherever else you like. This approach requires that you use the `codebase` attribute in your APPLET tags to specify the directory that holds your class files.

What you specifically can't do is put your main applet class file in one place (such as the document base directory) and put your custom class files in a separate place. The Java-enabled browser would not then know where to search for them.

See also: Q4.8, Q4.9

APPLET USER INTERFACE

Q4.11

How do I determine the width and height of my applet?

Use the `getSize` **method (or** `size` **in the JDK 1.0.2), which the** `Applet` **class inherits from the** `Component` **class (Q5.1) in the** `java.awt` **package.**

The `getSize` method (in JDK 1.1) returns the size of the applet as a `Dimension` object, from which you can extract separate `width` and `height` fields:

```
/* Using JDK 1.1: */
Dimension dim = getSize();
int appletWidth = dim.width;
int appletHeight = dim.height;
```

In the JDK 1.0.2, use the method name `size` in place of `getSize`.

See also: Q5.1

Q4.12

How do I set the background color within the applet area?

Use the `setBackground` **method, which the** `Applet` **class inherits from** `Component`.

`Component`'s `setBackground` method specifies the background color for an AWT component. For applets, this sets the color with which the entire applet area is covered before anything else is drawn on top (lines, images, or even other components, such as buttons and text fields).

Unless you're changing background colors repeatedly, you should set the background color in your applet's `init` method:

```
public void init() {
    // ...
    setBackground(Color.green);
    // ...
}
```

You can also set a background image for the applet, on top of which you place any user-interface components the applet may require (Q8.9).

AppletSizeExample.html

See also: Q4.13, Q5.1, Q8.9

Q4.13

How can I create a transparent background for my applet?

You can't create transparent backgrounds for applets in the JDK (1.0.2 and 1.1), but you can fake it in some cases.

Applets inherit from the `Component` class. In the JDK 1.0.2, `Component` instances are always opaque. (The JDK 1.1 provides the basic infrastructure for lightweight components that can have transparency, but instances of the `Applet` class still come with an opaque background.) Even if an applet doesn't draw itself in any interesting way, it still fills its rectangular space with a solid background color. The only way to achieve the effect of transparent background is by a chameleon trick: attempt to make your applet's background indistinguishable from the underlying HTML page background. Yes, this is a *hack* rather than a solution, but you might find it useful.

If the HTML background is a solid color, your work is fairly easy. You can write your applet such that it takes background color as one of its parameters. Then set that parameter in the APPLET tag to match to color of the HTML page you are putting the applet in.

If the HTML page background is a GIF image or pattern, you're basically out of luck. You can still write your applet to take the relevant information as a parameter (in this case, the name of the GIF file that is providing the background image), but your applet's location on the page may cause noticeable discontinuities in the background image. Some patterns are easier to blend in with than others.

MatchBackgroundExample.html

See also: Q8.7

Q4.14

Can I put menus and a menu bar on my applet?

No; you can't put a menu bar (or menus) directly on the applet itself.

The JDK (1.0.2 and 1.1) restricts menu bars to occur only on frames (instances of the Frame class or a Frame subclass). Frames represent independent top-level windows with a border. The Applet class inherits from Panel rather than Frame, though.

To provide a menu bar for your applet, the current workaround is to create a new Frame instance from your applet and put a menu bar on that. For example:

```java
import java.awt.*;

public class AppletMenuExample extends java.applet.Applet {
    static final String FILE = "File;
    static final String FILE_NEW = "New...";
    static final String FILE_OPEN = "Open...";
    // ...
    AppletMenuFrame myFrame;
    MenuBar myMenuBar;
    Menu fileMenu;
```

```
public void init() {
    myFrame = new AppletMenuFrame(this,
                             "Applet frame with a menu");

    myMenuBar = new MenuBar();
    fileMenu = new Menu(FILE);
    myFrame.setMenuBar(myMenuBar);
    myMenuBar.add(fileMenu);
    fileMenu.add(FILE_NEW);
    fileMenu.add(FILE_OPEN);
    // ...
    myFrame.pack();
    myFrame.show();
    }
}
```

AppletMenuExample.html

See also: Q6.8, Q7.8

Q4.15

I know that cursors can be changed from within frames, but how do I change the cursor in my applet?

In the JDK 1.0.2 you must find the Frame **instance that contains the applet and change its cursor, but the JDK 1.1 allows you to set the cursor for instances of any** Component **subclass, including** Applet.

The JDK 1.0.2 lets you control one cursor per Frame instance. (The Frame class represents top-level, bordered windows.) Since applets aren't a kind of Frame, you can't set the cursor for an applet directly. You can, however, trace up the containment hierarchy until you finally find a Frame instance:

```
/* using JDK 1.0.2: */
Frame myFrame;
Container parent = getParent();
while (parent != null &&  !(parent instanceof Frame)) {
    parent = parent.getParent();
}
myFrame = (Frame)parent;
if (myFrame != null) {
    myFrame.setCursor(Frame.CROSSHAIR_CURSOR);
}
```

The JDK 1.1 fixes this shortcoming by letting you set the cursor on individual components. You can set your applet's cursor by invoking Component's setCursor method on the applet itself. For example:

```
/* using JDK 1.1: */
public void init() {
    setCursor(new Cursor(Cursor.HAND_CURSOR));
    // ...
}
```

An additional benefit of the cursor-per-component service in the JDK 1.1 is that the AWT automatically switches the cursor as needed to match the component pointed to by the mouse. In contrast, the JDK 1.0.2 forces you to manage the cursor switching by yourself, which is doable but tedious.

ChangeCursorExample.html, ChangeCursor11Example.html

See also: Q5.14

APPLET PROGRAM STRUCTURE

Q4.16

Several applet methods seem special, in that I need to define them even if my own code doesn't invoke them — what are the methods, and when (and by whom) are they invoked?

The applet context (for instance, a Java-enabled browser), invokes init, start, stop, **and** destroy **to control the applet's life cycle; and the Abstract Window Toolkit (AWT) invokes** update **and** paint **for on-screen rendering as well as a whole family of event-handling methods.**

It is easy to think of an applet as a separate entity, but applets execute within a larger context provided by a Java-enabled browser and the AWT. This context impinges on the applet significantly, in the form of method invocations signaling stages in the applet's life and events that the applet can respond to.

The creation, initialization, running, stopping, and destruction of an applet are all managed by the browser that loads the applet. Four methods control the applet's life cycle, as shown in Table 4.4.

Table 4.4: Methods that Control an Applet's Life Cycle

Method	When invoked
init	after the applet is loaded (this invocation is guaranteed to precede invocation of start)
start	after init
	each time the applet's page is revisited
stop	each time the applet's page is exited
	one final time before invocation of destroy
destroy	just before the applet is garbage collected (this invocation is guaranteed to follow all invocations of stop)

Keeping the applet's on-screen appearance up to date is controlled in part by the AWT, with two methods (Q8.1, Q8.5), shown in Table 4.5.

Table 4.5: Methods that Control an Applet's On-Screen Appearance

Method	When invoked
update	in response to repaint; should invoke paint in turn
paint	when the applet needs to be redrawn: • when first brought on screen • when re-exposed after being covered or miniaturized • when scrolled
	when needed by update

Finally, the applet receives its events from the AWT, in the form of calls to a range of event-handler methods. See Chapters 6 and 7 for details on the general AWT framework(s) for delivering and handling events.

See also: Q4.17, Q4.18, Q8.1, Q8.5

Q4.17

Should applets have constructors?

No; use the `init` **method to initialize your applet.**

A Java-enabled web browser creates an instance of your applet class as part of loading the applet over the network. The browser essentially uses a default constructor on your behalf and then invokes your applet's `init` method. Any constructor you provide will simply be ignored.

Your applet should therefore define its own version of the `init` method. An applet's `init` method typically performs initialization tasks such as reading APPLET tag parameter values, initializing instance variables, and building the applet's interface.

See also: Q4.16, Q4.18

Q4.18

How can my applet tell when a user leaves or returns to the web page containing my applet?

The browser invokes your applet's `stop` **method each time the user leaves the page (either by visiting another page or by iconifying the browser) and invokes your applet's** `start` **method each time the user returns.**

It is important for browser performance that you restrain your applet's activity while the user is visiting other web pages. Your applet should either be completely idle or consume a bare minimum of resources when it's not on center stage. The `start` and `stop` methods give you the necessary control points; you override them to define the behavior you need at those critical times. Common uses for the `stop` method are:

- to stop animations
- to pause other computation-intensive activity

Typical corresponding uses for the `start` method are to restart animations and resume the activities stopped by `stop`.

InitStartStopExample.html

See also: Q4.16, Q4.17, Q9.2, Q9.3

Q4.19

How do I read number information from my applet's parameters, given that Applet's getParameter *method returns a* String?

Use the parseInt **method in the** Integer **class, the** Float(String) **constructor in class** Float, **or the** Double(String) **constructor in class** Double.

The getParameter method in the Applet class is an all-purpose tool for requesting a named parameter and getting back its value as a string. It leaves to you the task of converting the string into an appropriate value.

The java.lang package (in the JDK 1.1) provides classes corresponding to each of the floating point and integral types: Double, Float, Long, Integer, Short, and Byte. (The JDK 1.0.2 lacks the Short and Byte classes.) Each of these classes provides a means of converting from a String instance to an appropriate numerical value and vice versa (Q10.4).

Extracting integer values is the simpler case. All four integral classes provide a parseX method for extracting a numerical value from a string representation: parseLong in class Long, parseInt in class Integer, parseShort in class Short, and parseByte in class Byte. Consider the parseInt method in the Integer class, for example. If the method can successfully interpret the string as an integer value, it returns that value as an int; otherwise, it throws a NumberFormatException. The following code fragment shows a typical pattern for using parseInt:

```
/* code in an Applet subclass: */
int anIntValue = 10;  // some default value
String param = getParameter("myInt");

if (param != null) {
    try {
        anIntValue = Integer.parseInt(param);
    } catch (NumberFormatException e) {
        // ... recover from malformed parameter value
    }
}
```

The floating point classes of the JDK (1.0.2 and 1.1) lack an analogous parseFloat or parseDouble method, so you have to do a little more work. You can construct a floating point object from the string and then ask it for its value as a primitive floating point type:

```
float aFloatValue = 1.0f;   // some default value
double aDoubleValue = 2.0;  // some default value
String param = getParameter("myFloat");
if (param != null) {
    try {
        aFloatValue = new Float(param).floatValue();
    } catch (NumberFormatException e) {
        // ... recover from malformed parameter value
    }
}

param = getParameter("myDouble");
if (param != null) {
    try {
        aDoubleValue = new Double(param).doubleValue();
    } catch (NumberFormatException e) { /* ... */ }
}
```

NumericalParametersExample.html

See also: Q10.4

APPLET COMMUNICATION

Q4.20

How can I arrange for different applets on a web page to communicate with each other?

Name your applets inside the APPLET tag and invoke `AppletContext`**'s** `getApplet` **method in your applet code to obtain references to the other applets on the page.**

The `AppletContext` interface in the `java.applet` package gives an applet limited access to the applet's context of execution: the browser that the applet is running in, the web page the applet is on, and other applets on the same page. You can attain a limited form of inter-applet communication by naming your applets and using the `AppletContext` class to find other applets by their names.

First, you name an applet by setting the name attribute in the APPLET tag. For example, the following APPLET tags place two named applets, Kim and Sandy, on a web page:

```
<applet code="ChatApplet.class"
        name="Kim"
        width=400 height=120>
</applet>
<applet code="QuietApplet.class"
        name="Sandy"
        width=400 height=120>
</applet>
```

Second, your applet code must query the AppletContext object to obtain references to the other applets it wants to communicate with. If you want the Sandy applet, for instance, to invoke methods on the Kim applet (such as a beQuiet method), your QuietApplet code would include lines like the following:

```
/* in QuietApplet.java: */
AppletContext context = getAppletContext();
ChatApplet kimApplet = (ChatApplet) context.getApplet("Kim");
kimApplet.beQuiet();
```

AppletContext's getApplet method returns a reference with the type of Applet. As just shown, you need to cast that reference to the relevant Applet subclass.

Unlike the code fragment, general-purpose applets should not hardwire specific names for other applets. Instead, they should be written to obtain the names from parameter values passed in through the APPLET tag.

Note: Communication between applets is part of the standard Java Applet API and is supported by the JDK 1.0.2 and 1.1, but some Java-enabled browsers do not yet support it.

InterappletExample.html

See also: Q4.7

Q4.21

How do I select a URL from my applet and send the browser to that page?

Ask the applet for its applet context and invoke showDocument **on that context object.**

When an applet runs in a Java-enabled browser, it has limited access to the browser by means of the `AppletContext` interface. `AppletContext` provides two methods for requesting the browser to display new documents:

```
showDocument(URL url)
showDocument(URL url, String target)
```

The one-parameter version of `showDocument` replaces the current web page with the one specified by the URL argument. For example:

```
URL targetURL;
String urlString = ...
AppletContext context = getAppletContext();
try {
    targetURL = new URL(urlString);
} catch (MalformedURLException e) {
    // ... recover from malformed URL
}
context.showDocument(targetURL);
```

The two-parameter version of `showDocument` lets you control where the new web page will appear, in terms of HTML "frames." HTML frames (not related to the AWT `Frame` class) subdivide a single browser window into subregions, each of which can display a web page. (Note that numerous web users regard HTML frames as a confusing and counterproductive addition to the hypertext model.) The `String` `target` parameter in `showDocument` specifies which HTML frame will display the new page (or whether to use a new, separate window altogether), as listed in Table 4.6.

Table 4.6: Controlling HTML Frames with `showDocument`

target parameter	Where to show new page
`"_self"`	the current HTML frame
`"_parent"`	the parent of the current HTML frame
`"_top"`	the topmost HTML frame
`"_blank"`	a new, unnamed top-level window
name	a new top-level window with the specified *name*

See also: Q10.14

Q4.22

Can applets on different pages communicate with each other?

No, not directly.

In the JDK (1.0.2 and 1.1), applets can communicate directly with each other only if they are on the same web page (Q4.20). Otherwise, applets must arrange a meeting place at which to exchange information, either on the local file system (that is, the file system of the machine that is running the applet) or at a remote server.

Communicating via the local file system can work in principle but is currently not a general solution. Different Java-enabled browsers vary in how, or even if, they allow applets to read and write files.

Alternatively, your applets could communicate back to a common server, but applet security strongly restricts your options here, too. Applets loaded over the net are allowed to make network connections only to the host that served the applet's class file. You could create a server program on the host machine that tracks several applets and assists communication between them.

Upcoming developments, such as signed applets and finer-grained security configurations, should considerably enhance the ability of applets to cooperate over the network.

See also: Q4.20

MISCELLANEOUS

Q4.23

Can I load an applet dynamically into a Java application, and if so, how does the applet get the parameter information it would normally get from the APPLET tag?

Applets can be loaded into Java applications like other user-interface elements, but you must use care to provide them with the connections and support they normally expect to receive from a web browser.

Applets are a subclass of `Panel`, which in turn is a subclass of `Component` — the base class for all Abstract Window Toolkit (AWT) user-interface elements (Q5.1). In terms of building an interface (Q5.2), you can add an applet to a panel or window/frame just the same as you would a button:

```
Applet myApplet = ...
Panel p = new Panel();
p.add(myApplet);
p.add(new Button("Press me."));
```

Applets generally require much more care, though, in how they are hooked up to the rest of the application. For an application to provide a general framework for linking in applets, it must provide objects that implement the `AppletContext` and `AppletStub` interfaces. (Note that one class can implement both interfaces.) For example, in the JDK (1.0.2 and 1.1), an applet call to `getParameter` gets relayed to an `AppletStub` object:

```
/* in Applet.java (JDK 1.0.2 and 1.1): */
public String getParameter(String name) {
    return stub.getParameter(name);
}
```

At the very minimum, you can provide an `AppletStub` object that returns `null` strings to any request for a parameter. A well-written applet should then provide its own default values.

See also: Q5.1, Q5.2

Q4.24

Do I need any special server software or setup to deliver applets?

No; applets can be delivered by standard http servers, just like other nontext data files.

On the server side, applets exist as Java class files, image files, and any other data files needed by the applet. An http server can deliver these files the same as any others — it needs no special knowledge of Java technology. All the special behavior occurs on the client side, when a Java-enabled browser dynamically loads the class files and builds a running Java applet from them.

Occasionally, you may encounter an http server that corrupts class files by serving them as text files — MIME type `http/text` — which is intended for files that use only the lower 7 out of the 8 bits in a byte. Java-compatible class files, however, are binary files; they use all 8 bits in a byte, so they must be sent in a binary mode—MIME type `application/octet-stream`. A symptom of this kind of corruption is a class format error, such as the following error message from Netscape Navigator:

```
# Applet exception: error: java.lang.ClassFormatError
java.lang.ClassFormatError
        at netscape.applet.AppletClassLoader.loadClass.....
```

If you encounter an http server that you suspect is corrupting its class files in this way, you can advise the server administrators to fix the problem: the relevant server configuration file should be changed to serve `.class` files as MIME type `application/octet-stream`.

See also: Q4.1

CHAPTER 5

Abstract Window Toolkit

Components, Containers, and Peers (Q5.1–Q5.10)

Windows, Frames, and Dialogs (Q5.11–Q5.16)

Miscellaneous (Q5.17–Q5.21)

COMPONENTS, CONTAINERS, AND PEERS

Q5.1

What are the Component *and* Container *classes?*

Component **and** Container **are the two fundamental classes in the Abstract Window Toolkit (AWT);** Component **instances** (*components*) **represent individual user-interface elements, and** Container **instances** (*containers*) **represent groups of components.**

Component is the abstract base class for all AWT user-interface elements except menu components. A component can be presented on screen, relocated, resized, or hidden; it can be drawn or printed; and it can receive, handle, and deliver events. Components can also be grouped and formatted in containers.

Container is an abstract subclass of Component with the added property of containing a group of components. Containers can also contain other containers, which can contain other containers, and so on to arbitrary depth. The term *containment hierarchy* refers to this nested arrangement of containers and components (sometimes also called a window hierarchy). Another useful bit of terminology is to refer to a container as the *parent* of each component that it contains.

It is important when learning to use components and containers not to confuse the containment hierarchy with the inheritance hierarchy. The following diagram illustrates the contrast:

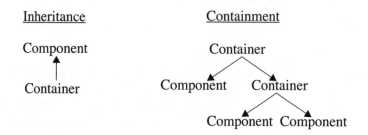

Besides handling the normal component tasks, a container also manages the components it contains. A container can add components, remove components, and (with the help of a layout manager; see Q5.2) control the layout of its components.

The Component and Container classes constitute the backbone of the Java™ Abstract Window Toolkit—you'll want to get to know these classes and their methods well.

ButtonCanvasExample.html

See also: Q5.2

Q5.2

How do I control the positioning of my interface components?

Assign an appropriate layout manager to each container in your interface, or let the AWT assign default layout managers for you; the layout manager automatically calculates layout positions for the container's components.

In the AWT, a container tracks the components (Q5.1) that belong to it, but calls on a LayoutManager object to control their layout. LayoutManager is an interface (Q1.20). The objects serving as layout managers come from classes that implement the LayoutManager interface (Q1.21). (Starting with the JDK 1.1, the LayoutManager2 interface extends LayoutManager to provide better support for constraint-based layout managers.) By setting the layout manager for a container, you are telling the container what strategy to use when laying out its components.

A layout manager is responsible for calculating the sizes and locations of the components in a container. Different layout managers use different strategies for this. A BorderLayout, for example, allocates five distinct regions ("North", "South", "West", "East", and "Center") within a rectangle and allows one component in each region. A GridLayout handles any number of components by arranging them as a grid of equal-sized cells. The number of rows and columns in the grid can be set when the GridLayout instance is created. A FlowLayout arranges its components much like the flow of words in a paragraph: all in a single row if space permits, otherwise wrapped around to one or more additional rows.

You can choose a layout manager for each container. If you don't, the AWT assigns a default layout manager depending on the class of your container. Window and Window subclasses (such as Frame and Dialog) use a BorderLayout by default; Panel and Panel subclasses (including Applet) use a FlowLayout by default.

Typical steps for laying out components are:

- creating your components and containers

- setting the layout manager for each container (or use the default)

- adding components to the appropriate containers

You can also define your own layout manager by implementing the Layout-Manager or LayoutManager2 interface. This is a nontrivial undertaking, though, and requires a strong, detailed understanding of existing layout managers. A rule of thumb is that you should feel you understand 98 percent of the code in the existing JDK 1.1 layout managers (excluding, perhaps, GridBagLayout) before writing your own.

See also: Q5.1, Q5.3, Q5.4, Q5.5

Q5.3

What are inset values, and how do I set them?

Inset values specify how much of a container's space is reserved for a border, inside of which the container's components are arranged; you set these values by overriding getInsets **(or** insets **in JDK 1.0.2) in your own** Container **subclasses.**

Each container, for example a `Frame` instance, `Panel` instance, or `Applet` instance, provides a rectangular space in which to position the container's components. In the default case, the components in a container can occupy the full space of the container. Inset values, represented as an instance of the `Insets` class, allow you to specify an amount of space at one or more margins—a boundary inside which all components must be placed. For example, a top inset of 10 means that a component's top edge can be placed no higher than 10 units (the space covered by 10 pixels) from the top of the container.

Inset values are useful for containers that have border material surrounding their content area. The `Frame` class, for instance, provides top-level windows that have a title bar. The space for the title bar is figured into the `Insets` instance, so that any components placed in the `Frame` instance will neither overlap nor lie underneath the title bar. Layout managers in general take into account a container's inset values when calculating where to place components.

You can specify inset values only for a `Container` subclass that you define (Q5.8). This is because containers have no `setInsets` method; instead, your subclass must override the `getInsets` method (or `insets` in JDK 1.0.2) to return the inset values you desire. For example:

```
/* using JDK 1.1: */
public class myApplet extends java.applet.Applet {
    // ...
    public Insets getInsets() {
        return new Insets(10, 6, 15, 3);
    }
}
```

This code defines an `Applet` subclass with the following inset values: top 10, left 6, bottom 15, and right 3.

Note: You shouldn't override the inset values for `Frame` and `Dialog` objects. These values are set by the native toolkit to ensure that native border material, such as the title bar, does not cover any content you place in the frame or dialog.

See also: Q5.1, Q5.2, Q5.8, Q5.12

Q5.4

Can I exert complete control over the size and placement of components in my interface?

Yes, you can—but please don't.

The AWT is designed to let layout managers handle layout details so that resizing is handled automatically, and layouts behave consistently across platforms. This is a central objective of Java technology: writing applications once and running them anywhere.

You can, however, handle all your layout work manually by not using any layout manager for your container. To do so, set the container's layout manager to null. For example:

```
myPanel.setLayout(null);
```

It is then up to you to choose sizes and locations for all the components, right down to the last pixel in your container.

Note: hand-done layouts are *strongly* discouraged. What works on one specific hardware-software platform can fail gracelessly on another. Differences in native toolkits, font dimensions, and local language preference can change a finely hand-tuned layout on one platform into a mishmash of misalignments and overlaps on another.

Q5.5

What do the invalidate *and* validate *methods do?*

The invalidate **and** validate **methods control when a container lays out its components.**

Component layouts in the AWT are dynamic. A change in one container, such as resizing a text field or adding a button, can spread up the containment hierarchy and trigger layout adjustments in many other containers. For efficiency, the AWT splits the process into two independently controllable parts:

1. marking the containers whose layouts are no longer valid

2. redoing the layout of containers marked as invalid

The invalidate method handles the first step. It marks containers as needing a new layout but doesn't perform that layout itself. If a text field is resized, for instance, the AWT will invoke invalidate on the text field and on the text field's parent. When needed, the AWT propagates invalidate calls up through the containment hierarchy.

All the real action happens in validate. Invoking validate on a container checks whether that container is marked as invalid, that is, in need of a new layout.

If the container is invalid, `validate` invokes the `dolayout` method on it (or `Layout` in the JDK 1.0.2), and then repeats this process on any components in the container. The relayout process triggered by `validate` is thus recursive, and can descend arbitrarily far down a containment hierarchy.

If you plan to override `validate` or `layout` in your own `Container` subclasses, be careful of the following two implementation details. First, although the effects of `validate` descend the containment hierarchy, you cannot count on the `validate` method itself being invoked on every container along the way. Second, `validate` code, including calls to `dolayout` (or `layout` in the JDK 1.0.2), executes within an AWT synchronization lock. To avoid the risk of deadlock, you should not acquire any further synchronization locks in your `validate` or `layout` code (which, admittedly, is not always easy to ensure).

For reference, Table 5.1 lists the most common cases in which the AWT invokes `invalidate` or `validate` on your behalf. Note that this table presents implementation details of the JDK (1.0.2 and 1.1) that may change in future releases, but these are useful to know nevertheless.

Table 5.1: AWT Invocations of
invalidate **and** validate

Class	Method	Invokes
Container	add	invalidate
Container	remove	invalidate
Window	pack	validate
Window	show	validate

See also: Q5.1, Q5.2, Q5.6, Q5.7

Q5.6

Can I add new AWT components to objects already visible on the screen?

Yes, you can change your program's interface as the program is running.

Like other Java objects, AWT components can be created on the fly and connected to existing objects. To appear on screen, the component must be added to a container that is already on screen. You also need to invoke `validate` on the container so that it activates its layout manager to take the new component into account. The validate method lets you control when layouts are recalculated (Q5.5).

Following is a code fragment that adds or removes a button from a panel named centerPanel:

```
int buttonCount = 0;
Panel centerPanel = new Panel();
void addButton() {
    ++buttonCount;
    centerPanel.add(new Button("button " + buttonCount));
    centerPanel.validate();
}
```

CreateButtonsExample.html

See also: Q5.5, Q5.7

Q5.7

Can I add the same component to more than one container?

No; adding a component to a container automatically removes it from any previous parent (container).

The AWT automatically maintains the strict rule that a component can have only one parent. (This ensures that containment structures are always trees, in graph theory terms. Trees are easier to understand and easier to compute with than less-constrained graphs.) The JDK (1.0.2 and 1.1) source code for adding a component to a container includes the following lines:

```
/* in Container.java (JDK 1.0.2 and 1.1): */

// ... comp refers to the component being added
if (comp.parent != null) {
    comp.parent.remove(comp);
}
```

It is an easy mistake to add a component to more than one container, and then be left wondering why the original container is behaving strangely.

See also: Q5.1

Q5.8

How can I place an outline around a group of components to show explicitly how the components are grouped?

You can write your own Panel subclass that draws an outline and specifies appropriate inset values to ensure that the panel's components stay inside the outline.

Panel, as a subclass of Component, includes a paint method that draws the panel on the screen. Panels typically just draw a background color on which their components are placed, but you can define your own paint method to draw whatever you like in the panel. The drawRect method in the Graphics class provides a very simple means to draw an outline. The following paint method, for example, uses drawRect to provide a blue outline:

```
/* using JDK 1.1: */
public void paint(Graphics g) {
    Dimension size = getSize();
    g.setColor(Color.blue);
    g.drawRect(2, 2,
                size.width - 5, size.height - 5);
}
```

Anything you draw on a panel using paint, however, can be covered by components contained in the panel. Therefore, you need to inform the panel's layout manager that space at the margins should be left free for the outline. To do this, override the getInsets method to provide the necessary space, such as:

```
/* using JDK 1.1: */
public Insets getInsets() {
    return new Insets(5, 5, 5, 5);
}
```

To run in the JDK 1.0.2, these code samples would use the method names size and insets in place of getSize and getInsets.

BorderedPanelExample.html

See also: Q5.2, Q5.3

Q5.9

What are AWT peers?

Peers are native-platform on-screen counterparts to AWT components.

The AWT provides a cross-platform Application Programming Interface (API) for managing user-interface elements and behaviors. To provide a native look and feel, though, the AWT components rely on user-interface elements from the native-platform toolkits to draw themselves on screen and to provide an initial layer of event processing. These native counterparts are called *peers*. The java.awt.peer package defines interfaces through which Java components can control and otherwise communicate with their peers.

The AWT peer interfaces are implemented by platform-specific peer classes that access the platform's own toolkit using native methods (that is, methods implemented in a language other than Java). For example, an AWT button has three Java-language layers:

- Button, a class in the java.awt package

- ButtonPeer, an interface in the java.awt.peer package

- a platform-specific button peer class containing native methods

When you write a Java program, you typically only concern yourself with the AWT classes or your own subclasses of them. When the program is run, the AWT selects the appropriate peer objects and hooks them up to your AWT objects. This is the way that your Java program can create and control a Motif button when run on Solaris, a Win32 button when run on Microsoft Windows NT/95, or a Macintosh button when run on MacOS.

Java programmers should rarely have to deal directly with AWT peer objects, but knowing about them helps to avoid some subtle pitfalls:

- Some AWT components depend on their peer objects for information such as minimum and preferred sizes. In general, you should make sure a peer exists before you try to get size information about your component.

- Layout operations check component sizes; hence, they depend on peers.

- Some methods, such as getGraphics in the Component class, return null if the component doesn't yet have a peer.

See also: Q5.10

Q5.10

When are peers created and destroyed?

The creation and destruction of peers is in general triggered by add **and** remove **methods in class** Container**; but there are further complications.**

Creating an AWT component does not automatically create a peer for that component. Instead, the creation of peers waits until a component is rooted in a containment hierarchy that reaches up to a top-level window (more specifically, a Frame instance). This is necessary for some native toolkits—such as Motif—that require their interface components to be traceable to a top-level window. The AWT builds two well-formed component trees side by side—an AWT component tree and a peer component tree—and the AWT respects the constraints on both sides in the process.

There are two stages at which peers can be created. On the one hand, a component's peer can be created as soon as the component is added to a container, provided that the container itself already has a peer. This is the case where a peer tree descending from a frame (or other top-level window) already exists and is thus ready to grow further. The top-level window itself will get a peer when either pack or show is invoked on it. (The creation of peers is somewhat of a side effect of pack and show. Window's pack method resizes a window to the preferred size determined by the window's layout manager. Window's show method brings a window on screen if it wasn't visible, or brings the window to the front of other windows if the window is already on screen.)

Alternatively, a component can be contained, possibly many layers deep, in a Panel instance or other container that isn't yet linked into a frame. In this case, a whole subtree of AWT components exists without a corresponding peer subtree. This subtree is then subject to the first pattern described. As soon as it is added to a container with a peer, it will recursively descend through itself to create peers for all the subtree components.

The destruction of peers is simpler: a component's peer is destroyed when the component is removed from its container.

Note: The lifetime of AWT components is separate from that of any peers. For example, you can add and remove a component from a container several times, but each time you do, you create and destroy a separate peer.

AwtPeerExample.html

See also: Q5.9

WINDOWS, FRAMES, AND DIALOGS

Q5.11

How do I specify where a window is to be placed?

In the JDK 1.1, use `setBounds`, `setSize`, **or** `setLocation`; **in the JDK 1.0.2 use the older method names** `reshape`, `resize`, **or** `move`.

The `Window` subclasses, such as `Frame` and `Dialog`, all inherit from the AWT's `Component` class, which defines the basic methods for moving and sizing user-interface elements. The fundamental method for specifying both location and size of any component in the JDK 1.1 is `setBounds`, which takes either four `int` parameters or one `Rectangle` parameter:

```
setBounds(int x, int y, int width, int height)
setBounds(Rectangle r)
```

For convenience, `Component` provides additional methods for changing only the location or size of a component:

```
setSize(int width, int height)
setSize(Dimension d)
setLocation(int x, int y)
setLocation(Point p)
```

All of these method names were introduced in the JDK 1.1, as part of a broad effort to make AWT method names more systematic and property-like. They supersede the names in the JDK 1.0.2, as shown in Table 5.2.

Table 5.2: Sample AWT Renamings

JDK 1.1 name	JDK 1.0.2 name
setBounds	reshape
setSize	resize
setLocation	move

These methods use absolute coordinates specified in screen units. The origin, point (0, 0), lies at the top left of the screen, x values increase rightward, and y values increase downward. One screen unit equals one screen pixel.

You can also use information about the user's screen size and resolution when positioning your application's windows. The `java.awt.Toolkit` class provides methods for obtaining the current screen size (pixels) and resolution (pixels per inch):

```
/* methods in java.awt.Toolkit: */
getScreenResolution();
getScreenSize();
```

This allows positioning by inches, for instance, or by proportion of available screen space.

PlaceFrameExample.html, PlaceFrame11Example.html

See also: Q5.2, Q5.12

Q5.12

How can I draw at the top-left corner of a frame without it being covered by the frame's border?

Use the frame's inset values to figure out the top-left corner of usable space.

Frames are top-level windows that come with border material, such as a menu bar. The border material covers a portion of the frame's coordinate space, such that there are actually two notions of top-left corner that you could draw to:

- the true (0, 0) point in the frame, or

- the top-left corner of the frame's usable space.

Using (0, 0) will result in your image being partially covered by the frame's border material. Instead, you should query the frame for its `Insets` object:

```
Insets theInsets = myFrame.getInsets();  // using JDK 1.1
```

(The corresponding method name in the JDK 1.0.2 is `insets`.) The top-left corner of usable space is available as the point (`theInsets.left, theInsets.top`).

Note: Drawing directly on a frame is rarely necessary. Instead, you can place a canvas or a panel in the frame and draw on that. The frame's layout manager will ensure that the canvas or panel stays within the actual usable space.

Q5.13

How do I create a borderless window?

Create an instance of the Window **class, give it a size, and show it on screen.**

The JDK 1.0.2 includes the Window class, which creates borderless windows affiliated with some top-level frame. You can use a Window subclass, for example, to implement tool tips, warning panels, or popup menus. (The JDK 1.1 provides a ready-made PopupMenu class, but other uses for Window remain.)

The Window constructor requires one argument: a Frame instance. This frame is conceptually the anchor or owner of the window instance, although the window is not constrained to lie inside the frame. Windows by default are not visible. After creating one, you must give it a size and invoke its show method in order to bring it on screen:

```
Frame aFrame = ...
Window aWindow = new Window(aFrame);
aWindow.setLayout(new FlowLayout());
aWindow.add(new Button("Press me."));
aWindow.add(new Label("A Window instance"));
aWindow.reshape(50, 50, 200, 200);
aWindow.show();
```

WindowExample.html

See also: Q5.14

Q5.14

Several operations in the AWT, such as setting the cursor (in JDK 1.0.2) or creating a dialog box, require specifying a Frame *instance—how do I determine the* Frame *instance containing the current component?*

You can write your own method to search up the containment hierarchy and stop when it reaches a Frame **instance (or** null**).**

The JDK (1.0.2 and 1.1) API provides no direct way to ask for the top-level window that contains a given component. To find the `Frame` instance that contains your component, follow the parent chain upward until you reach a frame or you run out of parents:

```
public static Frame getFrame(Component comp) {
    for (Component c = comp; c != null; c = c.getParent()) {
        if (c instanceof Frame) {
            return (Frame) c;
        }
    }
    return null;
}
```

GetFrameExample.html

See also: Q4.15

Q5.15

How do I use a `FileDialog` *object in my applet or application?*

Create a `FileDialog` **instance, invoke** `show` **on it, and query it for values after** `show` **returns.**

The `FileDialog` class provides a window with which the user can browse the local file system to select a file for either loading or saving. The window is modal — once it is placed on screen, it will block all other AWT input until the window is dismissed.

To use a `FileDialog` in your program, you need to create a `FileDialog` instance, specify any default choices you wish it to present to the user, and then show it on screen:

```
Frame myFrame = ...;
FileDialog dialog = new FileDialog(myFrame,
                                   "Load File",
                                   FileDialog.LOAD);
dialog.setFile("FileDialogExample.java");
dialog.show();
```

When the dialog's `show` method returns, you know the user has either selected a file or canceled the entire operation. If the user cancels the operation, `getFile` returns `null`. Otherwise, a file and directory are selected, which your program can query and use:

```
String fileName = dialog.getFile();
String fileDirectory = dialog.getDirectory();
if (fileName != null && fileDirectory != null) {
    // ... process the given file name and directory
    // ... full path = fileDirectory + fileName
}
```

FileDialogExample.html

Q5.16

Can I create nonresizable windows?

Yes and no; the `setResizable` method (in class `Frame`) exists in the JDK 1.0.2 API but is not implemented until the JDK 1.1.

The AWT represents top-level bordered windows with the `Frame` class. The `setResizable` method is designed to control whether a top-level window can be resized under user control (that is, by dragging on the window boundary with the mouse). The `setResizable` method exists in the JDK 1.0.2 API but is unimplemented in that release (a bug). The JDK 1.1 contains a working version of `setResizable`.

MISCELLANEOUS

Q5.17

What does Component's `requestFocus` method do?

Invoking `requestFocus` on a component requests that the component be made the primary target of non-mouse input events.

A central task for the AWT is to direct events to specific components. Many events, such as mouse clicks, intrinsically select their targets. Keyboard events, however, are not inherently directed at any component on the screen. This is where focus comes in: focus designates which component will receive non-mouse input events.

A component uses the `requestFocus` method to attempt to obtain the focus. If the attempt succeeds, the component will be sent a `gotFocus` event.

FocusExample.html

See also: Q6.6, Q7.13

Q5.18

Does the AWT allow you to control the mouse location from within an application?

No; the AWT treats the on-screen mouse location as a pointer controlled directly by the user's actions.

It is a deliberate user-interface decision in the AWT that mouse locations on screen should directly reflect the user's physical actions. It is the experience of the AWT designers and others that breaking this link is significantly more confusing than helpful.

Q5.19

Does the AWT provide a standard way to signal a user error by flashing, beeping, or some other means?

The much-requested beep feature is not in the JDK 1.0.2, but has been added for the 1.1 release.

In the JDK 1.1, you can trigger the native platform's standard system beep by invoking the beep method in the `Toolkit` class:

```
/* using JDK 1.1: */
getToolkit().beep();
```

Beep11Example.html

Q5.20

What fonts are available to my AWT program?

A standard set of five fonts is available on all AWT implementations: Dialog, Helvetica, TimesRoman, Courier, and Symbol.

You can check if your system supports any other fonts by using Toolkit's getFontList method:

```
String[] availableFonts = getToolkit().getFontList();
```

See also: Q5.21

Q5.21

How can I dynamically change font attributes, for instance, rendering a string in successively larger font sizes?

Strictly speaking, you can't.

A Font object is created once and for all with fixed attributes, as specified in its constructor:

```
public Font(String name, int style, int size)
```

To get the effect of dynamically changing a font's size or style, you need to create a new Font object with the desired values. For example, the following paint method draws up to twenty characters from a string in successively larger sizes:

```
public void paint(Graphics g) {
    g.setColor(Color.blue);
    int maxLength = Math.min(20, inputString.length());
    for (int i = 0; i < maxLength; ++i) {
        g.setFont(new Font("Courier", Font.ITALIC, 12 + i));
        g.drawString(inputString.substring(i, i+1),
                    20 + 8*i + (int)(.2*i*i), 60);
    }
}
```

ChangingFontsExample.html

See also: Q5.20

CHAPTER 6

Events—JDK 1.0.2

Events—JDK 1.0.2 (Q6.1–6.11)

EVENTS—JDK 1.0.2

Q6.1

What information can be carried in the JDK 1.0.2 by an Event *object?*

Event **objects in the JDK 1.0.2 can carry information about the event's source, the event type, when and where the event occurred, the state of the keyboard for the event, and the state of the component affected by the event; this information is carried in a set of public fields, as listed in Table 6.1.**

Table 6.1: Public Fields in an Event object—JDK 1.0.2

target	the object targeted for the event, for example, a TextField instance receiving a mouse click
id	an integer indicating the type of event, for example, Event.ACTION_EVENT
when	the time stamp for the event, in milliseconds
x, y	the location of the event, in the coordinates of the component receiving the event
key	the key that was pressed or released to generate the event
modifiers	the state of the modifier keys, such as shift and control
arg	an additional, general purpose Object parameter

Q6.2

What information do specific event types in the JDK 1.0.2 carry?

Too much to answer in a single sentence, but just right for a couple of tables.

Table 6.2 lists the information carried in general component and window events. For these events, the result of the event is largely independent of the class of the target object. A key-press event, for example, conveys the time, key, and modifier status of the event, regardless of whether the key press was received by a text field, a button, or some other component.

Table 6.2: Information in Component and Window Events—JDK 1.0.2

Kind of event	Target class	Event ID and valid fields
Keyboard	Component (Q6.6)	KEY_PRESS: when, key, modifiers
		KEY_RELEASE: when, key, modifiers
		KEY_ACTION: when, key, modifiers
		KEY_ACTION_RELEASE: when, key, modifiers
Mouse	Component	MOUSE_DOWN: when, x, y, modifiers, clickCount
		MOUSE_UP: when, x, y, modifiers
		MOUSE_MOVE: when, x, y, modifiers
		MOUSE_DRAG: when, x, y, modifiers
		MOUSE_ENTER: when, x, y
		MOUSE_EXIT: when, x, y
Window	Window	WINDOW_DESTROY
		WINDOW_ICONIFY
		WINDOW_DEICONIFY
	Dialog	WINDOW_MOVED: x, y
	Frame	WINDOW_MOVED: x, y
Focus	Component	GOT_FOCUS
		LOST_FOCUS

Table 6.3 presents action and action-like events. These are events that convey the result of a user action in cases where the result depends very much on the class of the target object (Q6.5). For example, pressing on a button generates an action event conveying the string label of the button. Action and action-like events use the generic arg field to carry this variable information.

Table 6.3: Information in Action and Action-like Events — JDK 1.0.2

Kind of event	Target class	Event ID and valid fields
Action	Button	ACTION_EVENT: arg = target.getLabel()
	Checkbox	ACTION_EVENT: arg = new Boolean(state)
	Choice	ACTION_EVENT: arg = target.getItem(index)
	List	ACTION_EVENT: arg = target.getItem(index)
	TextField	ACTION_EVENT: arg = target.getText()
	MenuItem (Q6.8)	ACTION_EVENT: when, modifiers, arg = target.getLabel()
Action-like	List (Q6.9)	LIST_SELECT: arg = new Integer(index)
		LIST_DESELECT: arg = new Integer(index)
	Scrollbar (Q6.10)	SCROLL_LINE_UP: arg = new Integer(value), where value reflects the scroll bar's new position
		SCROLL_LINE_DOWN: arg = new Integer(value)
		SCROLL_PAGE_UP: arg = new Integer(value)
		SCROLL_PAGE_DOWN: arg = new Integer(value)
		SCROLL_ABSOLUTE: arg = new Integer(value)

The Event class defines two further event types, Event.LOAD_FILE and Event.SAVE_FILE, but these are not used by the JDK.

Note: Action and action-like events are delivered to the AWT components only after the native toolkit object (the peer; see Q5.9) receives them. This means that before your AWT component even has a chance to see the event, the peer object has already performed some default event processing, such as showing the button press for a button.

See also: Q5.9, Q6.3

Q6.3

What is the general model in the JDK 1.0.2 for distributing and handling events?

The event model in the JDK 1.0.2 propagates events up the containment hierarchy (Q5.1) and requires that you subclass a component to capture and handle its events.

The JDK 1.0.2 event model works well for small applets and applications. It was designed to:

- promote native look and feel by coordinating event handling between AWT components and their native-platform peers (Q5.9)

- promote extensibility and flexibility of AWT components by giving the AWT programmer choices in how and where to handle events

The basic process for handling an event runs as follows. The native windowing system receives the event (key press, mouse click, etc.) and determines which peer component should receive it. The chosen peer component converts the native event to an AWT Event object and passes the event on by invoking the postEvent method on its AWT counterpart.

The peer thus starts a chain of event passing, all managed by Component's postEvent method:

```
/* in Component.java (JDK 1.0.2): */
public boolean postEvent(Event e) {
    ComponentPeer peer = this.peer;
    if (handleEvent(e)) {
        return true;
    }
    Component parent = this.parent;
    if (parent != null) {
        e.translate(x, y);
        if (parent.postEvent(e)) {
            return true;
        }
    }
    if (peer != null) {
        return peer.handleEvent(e);
    }
    return false;
}
```

The gist of this code is to ascend the containment hierarchy recursively, looking for a component that is willing to consume the event. The main steps are as follows:

1. The `handleEvent` method is invoked on the current component. If this method returns `true`, the event is considered handled and goes no further.

2. If `handleEvent` returns `false`, and the component has a parent, `postEvent` starts over with the parent.

3. If repeating steps 1 and 2 leads to a top-level window, which also returns `false` from `handleEvent`, the event is finally passed to the peer of the original AWT component that started the upward chain. The peer can then take some platform-specific default action in response to the event, such as registering a key press in a text field.

The JDK 1.0.2 event model gives you three basic options when overriding an event-handling method in some `Component` subclass:

- consume the event by processing it and returning `true`

- filter the event by partially processing it and returning `false`

- pass on the event, untouched, by simply returning `false`

(Returning `false` is the default behavior inherited from class `Component`.)

The JDK 1.0.2 only partially implements this model. Keyboard events are passed on to all AWT components, but other events must occur in a `Canvas`, `Panel`, `Frame`, or `Window` for the AWT to see them.

Note: Text fields rely on their native peers for parts of their functionality. Your `TextField` subclass should therefore do whatever processing is necessary and then return `false` so that the event eventually reaches the text field's peer.

See also: Q5.1, Q5.9, Q6.2, Q6.4

Q6.4

What methods should I use in the JDK 1.0.2 to handle events?

Use an event-specific method, such as `keyDown` **or** `mouseDown`, **where possible; otherwise use the all-purpose** `handleEvent` **method.**

The Component class in the JDK 1.0.2 provides two kinds of methods for handling events. There are several methods that handle only specific events or event types, and one catch-all method, as shown in Table 6.4.

Table 6.4: Methods for Handling Events — JDK 1.0.2

Event-specific methods	`action`
	`keyDown, keyUp`
	`mouseDown, mouseUp`
	`mouseMove, mouseDrag`
	`mouseEnter, mouseExit`
	`gotFocus, lostFocus`
Catch-all method	`handleEvent`

Where possible, you should use the more specific event-handling methods. They often lead to simpler and clearer code. Instead of handling all the events in one large, ungainly method, you can write simple, separate methods for each of the event types your application needs. The method names themselves indicate which specific events your code is handling.

Overriding the `handleEvent` method is unavoidable for some event types, such as `Event.WINDOW_DESTROY`, because there is no specific method for catching them. If you override `handleEvent` but still want access to the event-specific methods, you must incorporate the superclass's version (Q1.17) of `handleEvent` as part of your own `handleEvent` method:

```
/* using JDK 1.0.2: */
public boolean handleEvent(Event evt) {
    if (evt.id == Event.WINDOW_DESTROY) {
        // ... window destroy handler code goes here
        return true;
    } else {
        return super.handleEvent(evt);
    }
}
```

Including the call to `super.handleEvent` accesses the version of `handleEvent` defined in the Component class. As can be seen from the following JDK 1.0.2

source code, this method dispatches events to appropriate event-specific methods where possible, or else it returns `false`, indicating that the event is unhandled:

```java
/* in Component.java (JDK 1.0.2) */
public boolean handleEvent(Event evt) {
    switch (evt.id) {
        case Event.MOUSE_ENTER:
            return mouseEnter(evt, evt.x, evt.y);
        case Event.MOUSE_EXIT:
            return mouseExit(evt, evt.x, evt.y);
        case Event.MOUSE_MOVE:
            return mouseMove(evt, evt.x, evt.y);
        case Event.MOUSE_DOWN:
            return mouseDown(evt, evt.x, evt.y);
        case Event.MOUSE_DRAG:
            return mouseDrag(evt, evt.x, evt.y);
        case Event.MOUSE_UP:
            return mouseUp(evt, evt.x, evt.y);
        case Event.KEY_PRESS:
        case Event.KEY_ACTION:
            return keyDown(evt, evt.key);
        case Event.KEY_RELEASE:
        case Event.KEY_ACTION_RELEASE:
            return keyUp(evt, evt.key);
        case Event.ACTION_EVENT:
            return action(evt, evt.arg);
        case Event.GOT_FOCUS:
            return gotFocus(evt, evt.arg);
        case Event.LOST_FOCUS:
            return lostFocus(evt, evt.arg);
    }

    return false;
}
```

See also: Q1.17, Q6.3, Q6.5

Q6.5

What is an action event?

An action event is the way some AWT components notify your program that they have been acted on and now have new information to report.

Table 6.5 shows the user-interface elements that generate action events in the JDK 1.0.2.

**Table 6.5: Components that Generate
Action Events — JDK 1.0.2**

Component	Generates action event for ___
Button	mouse click
Checkbox	mouse click
Choice	mouse click
MenuItem (Q6.8)	mouse click
List	double mouse click
List	return key press
TextField	return key press

See Q7.7 for corresponding information on action events in the JDK 1.1.

To catch and process an action event, you need to define your own Component subclass and override its action method. Remember to return true from your action method if you've handled it completely, or false if you want to pass it on for further processing (Q6.3).

ActionEventExample.html

See also: Q6.3, Q6.4, Q6.6, Q6.8, Q7.7

Q6.6

How does the JDK 1.0.2 handle events for function keys, arrow keys, and so on?

The JDK 1.0.2 delivers "action" key events like other key events — in either a keyDown or keyUp method — but the event id field is set to KEY_ACTION or KEY_ACTION_RELEASE.

The AWT has a broad category of action keys, which contains the function keys 1–12 together with the navigation keys UP, DOWN, LEFT, RIGHT, HOME, END, PGUP, and PGDN. An event generated by one of these keys will carry the information shown in Table 6.6.

Table 6.6: Information in an Action Key Event

Field	Possible value
id	Event.KEY_ACTION or Event.KEY_ACTION_RELEASE
key	Event.F1, Event.F2, ..., or Event.PGDN

To handle an action key event, you should override the keyDown or keyUp method in your component subclass and check that the event's id is KEY_ACTION or KEY_ACTION_RELEASE.

A common point of confusion about the Event class is how to interpret and how to use the public int class variables, such as Event.KEY_ACTION, Event.F1, and Event.SHIFT_MASK. Only *some* of these variables represent different event types (Q6.1, Q6.2). The rest, listed in Table 6.7, represent key types and key modifier bit masks.

Table 6.7: public int Class Variables in the Event Class that Are Not Event Types

Key types for KEY_ACTION events	F1, F2, F3, F4, F5, F6, F7, F8, F9, F10, F11, F12 HOME, END, PGUP, PGDN, UP, DOWN, LEFT, RIGHT
Bit masks for key modifiers	SHIFT_MASK, CTRL_MASK, META_MASK, ALT_MASK

If you see source code in which one of these key types or bit masks is compared to the event's id field, you know it's a mistake.

ActionKeyExample.html

See also: Q6.1, Q6.2, Q6.3, Q6.4, Q7.13

Q6.7

My frame doesn't close when I click on Quit/Close in the main menu — how do I fix this using JDK 1.0.2?

Override handleEvent **to process the** WINDOW_DESTROY **event.**

Clicking on Quit/Close (depending on the native windowing system) generates a window-destroy event in the JDK 1.0.2, which your application needs to catch and handle appropriately. You use Frame's dispose method to dispose of the frame along with any resources connected to it. If you want the frame's closing to terminate the application as well, you can invoke System's exit method.

Besides frames, the WINDOW_DESTROY event is also delivered to Dialog objects, which might choose to hide rather than dispose of themselves.

In the JDK 1.0.2, you catch the window-destroy event by subclassing Frame and overriding its handleEvent method; for example:

```
/* using JDK 1.0.2: */
public boolean handleEvent(Event e) {
    if (e.id == Event.WINDOW_DESTROY) {
        dispose();  // or hide();
        // Uncomment the following line to quit the application.
        // System.exit(0);
        return true;
    } else {
        return super.handleEvent(e);
    }
}
```

CloseFrameExample.html

See also: Q7.11

Q6.8

How is my program notified when a menu item is selected?

A menu item triggers an action event when it is selected; you need to catch and handle the event in the Frame object (that is, top-level window) containing the menu.

Menu items trigger action events (Q6.5), but their system for propagating and handling events is different from that used by regular components (Q6.3). Menu items (instances of the MenuItem class or its subclasses, including Menu) function as distant step-cousins of components—the two sides aren't really related, but for limited purposes they behave as if they belong in the same family. The MenuItem class inherits from MenuComponent rather than Component, and MenuComponent supports only a fraction of the functionality found in Component. The differences that impact event handling are summarized in Table 6.8.

Table 6.8: Event Handling—Component versus MenuComponent

Component	MenuComponent
Containment hierarchy is based on Component and Container classes (Q5.1)	Containment hierarchy is based on MenuComponent class and MenuContainer interface
Provides family of methods for handling events (Q6.4)	Provides no methods for handling events
postEvent method checks for event handler before propagating event up the component containment hierarchy (Q6.3)	postEvent method always propagates event up the menu containment hierarchy

Thus, menu items are event propagators but not event handlers. The action event generated by a menu item must propagate to a nonmenu container before it can be handled.

The AWT is designed to have each menu containment hierarchy rooted in a Frame object. The Frame class implements the MenuContainer interface (Q1.21), so that menu components can invoke menu container methods on Frame instances. In particular, invocations of postEvent, which propagate a menu item's action event upward, eventually reach the Frame object containing the whole menu hierarchy. Once there, they trigger Frame's version of postEvent (inherited from Component), which checks for an event handler by invoking handleEvent, which in turn invokes action (Q6.4, Q6.5). Thus, to handle the events generated by menu item selections, you must define a Frame subclass and override its action method to respond to the menu item events that can be generated within its menu system. The following code fragment shows the skeleton for this:

```
/* using JDK 1.0.2: */
import java.awt.*;
public class MyFrame extends Frame {

    public MyFrame() {
        // ... build up menu system and attach to frame
    }
    // ...
```

```
public boolean action(Event e, Object arg) {
    if (e.target instanceof MenuItem) {
        // ... determine which specific menu item was selected
        // ... return true if you've handled the event
    }
    return super.action(e, arg);
}
```

MenuItemEventExample.html

See also: Q5.1, Q6.3, Q6.4, Q6.5, Q7.8

Q6.9

How is my program notified in the JDK 1.0.2 when a list item is selected or deselected?

Your program receives a LIST_SELECT **or** LIST_DESELECT **event, which you must catch in your own** handleEvent **method.**

Instead of using the all-purpose action event (Q6.5), lists in the JDK 1.0.2 can send two kinds of events to distinguish between selecting and deselecting list items: Event.LIST_SELECT and Event.LIST_DESELECT. The event also reports the index of the selected or deselected item by means of its arg field.

The list events do not have a specific handler method (Q6.4). To catch them, you must override handleEvent, for example:

```
/* using JDK 1.0.2: */
public boolean handleEvent(Event evt) {
    if (evt.id == Event.LIST_SELECT) {
        // ... your event processing here
        // ... evt.arg = index of newly selected item (Q6.2)
        return true;
    } else if (evt.id == Event.LIST_DESELECT) {
        // ... your event processing here
        // ... evt.arg = index of newly deselected item
        return true;
    } else {
        return super.handleEvent(evt);
    }
}
```

ListEventExample.html

See also: Q6.2, Q6.4, Q6.5, Q7.9

Q6.10

How do I hook up a scroll bar in the JDK 1.0.2 so that it controls the scrolling of some other component?

Capture the scroll bar events in a `handleEvent` **method and use the scroll bar's changing position to control your other component(s).**

The `Scrollbar` class in the JDK 1.0.2 provides the basic support for controlling a slider on screen and for using the slider's position to control other objects. It may help to think of this class as providing a slider that has the potential for controlling scrolling.

Scroll bars provide five different ways of adjusting the value that the scroll bar represents: move forward by a small or large amount, move backward by a small or large amount, or move as dragged by the mouse. Each of these is expressed by a distinct constant in the `Event` class, as shown in Table 6.9.

Table 6.9: `id` **Constants in Class** `Event` **for** `Scrollbar` **Event Types**

`SCROLL_LINE_DOWN`	move forward (right/down) by one unit
`SCROLL_PAGE_DOWN`	move forward (right/down) by one page
`SCROLL_LINE_UP`	move backward (left/up) by one unit
`SCROLL_PAGE_UP`	move backward (left/up) by one page
`SCROLL_ABSOLUTE`	move to track mouse as it drags scroll bar knob

When a scroll event occurs, the `Event` object's `id` field will indicate which of the five types it was. (You can think of scroll bar events as a kind of action event that comes in five flavors.)

To use a scroll bar, you need to add it to a container and use its changing position to control some other object. When a scroll bar is moved, it sends out scroll-type events with information about the scroll bar's new position. To catch the event, you must override the `handleEvent` method in a `Scrollbar` subclass or in a parent of the scroll bar. For example:

```
/* using JDK 1.0.2: */
public boolean handleEvent(Event e) {
    if (e.target instanceof Scrollbar) {
```

```
        switch(e.id) {
            case Event.SCROLL_LINE_DOWN:
                // ... your event processing here
                // ... e.arg = new position (value) of scroll bar
                // ... return true if you've handled the event
                break;
            case Event.SCROLL_PAGE_DOWN:
                // ...
                break;
            // ... handle other scroll types
        }
    }
    return super.handleEvent(e);
}
```

The JDK 1.1 greatly simplifies scrolling for the developer by providing the ScrollPane class (Q7.10) with built-in connections to manage scrolling.

ScrollbarExample.html

See also: Q6.2, Q6.4, Q7.10

Q6.11

Does the AWT in the JDK 1.0.2 distinguish between mouse clicks made with different buttons on a two- or three-button mouse?

Yes; it makes the extra distinction by using the Event **object's** modifiers **field.**

All mouse clicks generate mouse-down and mouse-up events, but you can inspect the modifiers field in the Event object to determine which button was pressed. The JDK 1.0.2 uses the mapping shown in Table 6.10.

Table 6.10: modifiers **Field in Mouse Clicks—JDK 1.0.2**

If ___ mouse button click	then mouse event + ____
left	no modifier
right	meta key
center	alt key

The Event class provides a metaDown method to test the status of the meta key, but regrettably, no corresponding altDown method exists in the JDK 1.0.2. (The JDK 1.1 has regularized the modifier access methods; see Q7.14.) Therefore, you have to explicitly use the ALT_MASK bit mask provided by the Event class to test the event's modifiers field. For example:

```
/* using JDK 1.0.2: */
public boolean mouseDown(Event e, int x, int y) {
  if (e.modifiers == 0) {
      // ... handle plain (left) mouse click
      return true;
  }
  if (e.metaDown()) {
      // ... handle right mouse click
      return true;
  }
  if ((e.modifiers & Event.ALT_MASK) != 0) {
      // ... handle center mouse click
      return true;
  }
  return super.mouseDown(e, x, y);  // a good default response
}
```

MultiButtonMouseExample.html

See also: Q7.14

CHAPTER 7

Events—JDK 1.1

Event Classes, Listeners, and Methods (Q7.1–Q7.6)

Semantic Events (Q7.7–Q7.10)

Low-Level Events (Q7.11–Q7.14)

EVENT CLASSES, LISTENERS, AND METHODS

Q7.1

What information do specific event types in the JDK 1.1 carry?

JDK 1.1 event objects carry only the information relevant to their specific event class; you can tell what information is in an event object by the accessor methods of the event object's class.

Starting in the JDK 1.1, events in Java are organized by a class hierarchy rooted at `EventObject`, in package `java.util`. `AWTEvent`, an immediate subclass of `EventObject`, is the base class for all AWT-specific events. Table 7.1 shows the complete inheritance hierarchy of the 1.1 AWT event classes (all except `AWTEvent` are in the `java.awt.event` package).

The fields and methods of an event class are combined from the class itself and all the classes it inherits from. `WindowEvent`, for example, inherits from `ComponentEvent`, which inherits from `AWTEvent`, which inherits from `EventObject`. Table 7.2 (on pp. 154–155) shows the public methods supported by each of the event classes together with the information they yield.

Table 7.1: JDK 1.1 AWT Event Class Hierarchy

AWTEvent (in java.util)	ActionEvent		
	AdjustmentEvent		
	ItemEvent		
	TextEvent		
	ComponentEvent	ContainerEvent	
		FocusEvent	
		WindowEvent	
		PaintEvent	
		InputEvent	KeyEvent
			MouseEvent

Note regarding Table 7.2: All subclasses of `EventObject` inherit the `get-Source` method, which returns the object that emitted the event. Several of the AWT event classes, though, provide their own convenience accessor method, such as `getContainer` in class `ContainerEvent` and `getWindow` in class `WindowEvent`. These methods return a reference to the same object as `getSource` does, but in a class more specific to the event type.

See also: Q7.2, Q7.3

Q7.2

How do I catch events in the JDK 1.1 event model?

Determine which events you want to receive from a given component, provide one or more objects that implement the corresponding listener interfaces, and invoke the appropriate `add...Listener` **method to register your objects with the component.**

The JDK 1.1 event model for the AWT centers around event listeners — objects whose interface (or interfaces) allows them to be notified when specific event types occur. The AWT defines a set of eleven listener interfaces (Q1.20) that enable objects to catch specific event types. The `MouseMotionListener` interface, for example, contains two methods, `mouseMoved` and `mouseDragged`, that can notify your program of mouse-move and mouse-drag events.

There are two main parts to working with event listeners. First, you define a class that implements the interface. In the case of `MouseMotionListener`, for example, you could define the following class:

```
/* using JDK 1.1: */
class MouseTracker implements MouseMotionListener {
    // ...
    public void mouseDragged(MouseEvent e) {
        // ... handle mouse-drag event
    }
    public void mouseMoved(MouseEvent e) {
        // ... handle mouse-move event
    }
}
```

Second, you register an instance of the class with a component using the appropriate `add...Listener` method; for example:

```
Canvas aCanvas = ...
aCanvas.addMouseMotionListener(new MouseTracker());
```

From this point on, any mouse motion or mouse drag event generated over the aCanvas instance will trigger invocations of the `mouseMoved` and `mouseDragged` methods in your `MouseTracker` class.

Another new feature in the JDK 1.1, inner classes, makes it significantly easier to define small classes for local use. An inner class is defined inside another class, which has two primary benefits: proximity and access. You can define your inner class right beside the code that uses the class, and your inner class has direct access to methods, fields, and variables of the class and/or method within which it is defined. The following example shows `MouseTracker` from above rewritten as an inner class:

```
class Example {
    /** An inner class for tracking mouse motion. */
    class MouseTracker implements MouseMotionListener {
        public void mouseDragged(MouseEvent e) { /* ... */ }
        public void mouseMoved(MouseEvent e) { /* ... */ }
    }
    public void init() {
        // ...
        aCanvas.addMouseMotionListener(new MouseTracker());
    }
    // ...
}
```

The sample code in this chapter contains further examples of inner classes.

Table 7.2: Public Methods in each Event Class

Class	Method	Returns
EventObject	getSource	Object: object that emitted the event
	toString	String: string representing the event
AWTEvent	*2 methods inherited from* EventObject	
	getID	int: identification key for event type
	paramString	String: string representing event parameters
ActionEvent	*4 methods inherited via* AWTEvent	
	getModifiers	int: state of all modifier keys during action
	getActionCommand	String: command name for action
Adjustment-Event	*4 methods inherited via* AWTEvent	
	getValue	int: current value resulting from the event
	getAdjustmentType	int: type of adjustment that changed the value
	getAdjustable	Adjustable: object that emitted the event
ItemEvent	*4 methods inherited via* AWTEvent	
	getItem	Object: item changed by the event
	getStateChange	int: type of change—select or deselect
	getItemSelectable	ItemSelectable: object that emitted the event
TextEvent	*4 methods inherited via* AWTEvent	
Component-Event	*4 methods inherited via* AWTEvent	
Container-Event	*4 methods inherited via* ComponentEvent	
	getChild	Component: child that was added or removed
	getContainer	Container: object that emitted the event
FocusEvent	*4 methods inherited via* ComponentEvent	
	isTemporary	boolean: true for temporary focus loss (if focus will automatically return)

Table 7.2: Public Methods in each Event Class

Class	Method	Returns
PaintEvent	*4 methods inherited via* ComponentEvent	
	getGraphics	Graphics: Graphics object for the event
WindowEvent	*4 methods inherited via* ComponentEvent	
	getWindow	Window: object that emitted the event
InputEvent	*4 methods inherited via* ComponentEvent	
	isShiftDown	boolean: whether shift key is down
	isControlDown	boolean: whether control key is down
	isMetaDown	boolean: whether meta key is down
	isAltDown	boolean: whether alt key is down
	getWhen	int: millisecond timestamp for the event
	getModifiers	int: state of all modifier keys
	isConsumed	boolean: whether to prevent the source from processing the event in the normal manner
KeyEvent	*11 methods inherited via* InputEvent	
	getKeyCode	int: key code for the event
	getKeyChar	char: character associated with the event
	isActionKey	boolean: whether key for the event is action (noncharacter) key
MouseEvent	*11 methods inherited via* InputEvent	
	getX	int: x coordinate relative to the source object
	getY	int: y coordinate relative to the source object
	getPoint	Point: x, y location relative to the source object
	getClickCount	int: number of mouse clicks in the event
	isPopupTrigger	boolean: whether the event matches native platform's popup menu trigger

For truly simple and local class definitions, inner classes come in an anonymous flavor that defines a new class and creates an instance of it at the same time. Using this option, the `MouseTracker` example can be rewritten yet again:

```
/* using JDK 1.1: */
class Example {
    public void init() {
        Canvas aCanvas = ...
        aCanvas.addMouseMotionListener(new MouseMotionListener() {
            public void mouseDragged(MouseEvent e) {
                // ... handle mouse-drag event
            }
            public void mouseMoved(MouseEvent e) {
                // ... handle mouse-move event
            }
        });    /* end of aCanvas.add... statement */
        // ...
    }
}
```

This code defines an anonymous inner class that implements the `MouseMotion-Listener` interface with the two specified methods; it creates one instance of that anonymous inner class; and it registers that instance as a mouse motion listener for the canvas. The syntax takes a little getting used to—note that the method invocation expression beginning with "`aCanvas.add...`" ends several lines later with "`});`".

EventListener11Example.html

See also: Q1.20, Q7.3

Q7.3

What are the different kinds of event listeners, and what are their methods?

Each concrete subclass of `AWTEvent` (except `PaintEvent`) has a corresponding listener interface containing one or more methods, as described in Table 7.3.

Learning each of the listener interfaces is the easiest way to keep track of what events can be delivered to your application and what methods you must define to handle the events. Table 7.3 gives the full set of AWT listener interfaces and their methods in the JDK 1.1.

Table 7.3: AWT Listener Interfaces and Methods—JDK 1.1

ActionListener	actionPerformed(ActionEvent e)
AdjustmentListener	adjustmentValueChanged(AdjustmentEvent e)
ComponentListener	componentResized(ComponentEvent e)
	componentMoved(ComponentEvent e)
	componentShown(ComponentEvent e)
	componentHidden(ComponentEvent e)
ContainerListener	componentAdded(ContainerEvent e)
	componentRemoved(ContainerEvent e)
FocusListener	focusGained(FocusEvent e)
	focusLost(FocusEvent e)
ItemListener	itemStateChanged(ItemEvent e)
KeyListener	keyTyped(KeyEvent e)
	keyPressed(KeyEvent e)
	keyReleased(KeyEvent e)
MouseListener	mouseClicked(MouseEvent e)
	mousePressed(MouseEvent e)
	mouseReleased(MouseEvent e)
	mouseEntered(MouseEvent e)
	mouseExited(MouseEvent e)
MouseMotionListener	mouseDragged(MouseEvent e)
	mouseMoved(MouseEvent e)
TextListener	textValueChanged(TextEvent e)
WindowListener	windowOpened(WindowEvent e)
	windowClosing(WindowEvent e)
	windowClosed(WindowEvent e)
	windowIconified(WindowEvent e)
	windowDeiconified(WindowEvent e)
	windowActivated(WindowEvent e)
	windowDeactivated(WindowEvent e)

Note: The ubiquitous boolean return type in the JDK 1.0.2 event model (Q6.3) is nowhere to be seen in the JDK 1.1. All JDK 1.1 event-handler methods return no value (they are declared with void).

See also: Q6.3, Q7.1, Q7.2, Q7.4

Q7.4

When should I use an event adapter class?

Use one when it simplifies your code—the adapter classes are provided as a convenience, not a necessity.

The AWT event listener interfaces in the JDK 1.1 (Q7.3) contain from one up to seven event-handler methods. Even if you want to define only some of the event methods belonging to an interface, your listener object must still come from a class that implements the whole interface. (There is no way in the Java language to partially implement an interface.) As a convenience, the JDK 1.1 AWT provides an event adapter class as the default implementation for each listener interface that contains more than one method, shown in Table 7.4.

Table 7.4: Event Adapter Classes

ComponentAdapter	4 methods
ContainerAdapter	2 methods
FocusAdapter	2 methods
KeyAdapter	3 methods
MouseAdapter	5 methods
MouseMotionAdapter	2 methods
WindowAdapter	7 methods

Event adapters provide *empty* implementations for the methods in the corresponding interface. For instance, the JDK 1.1 source code for the MouseAdapter class is the following:

```
/* in MouseAdapter.java (JDK 1.1): */
public class MouseAdapter implements MouseListener {
    public void mouseClicked(MouseEvent e) {}
    public void mousePressed(MouseEvent e) {}
    public void mouseReleased(MouseEvent e) {}
    public void mouseEntered(MouseEvent e) {}
    public void mouseExited(MouseEvent e) {}
}
```

The empty implementations mean that events get delivered but are totally ignored.

When you subclass from an event adapter class, you only have to override methods for the event(s) you wish to handle. The remaining listener methods are inherited from the superclass. For example, to define a mouse listener class for handling just mouse-enter and mouse-exit events, you can define a subclass of MouseAdapter that overrides the mouseEntered and mouseExited methods:

```
class MouseTracker extends MouseAdapter {
    public void mouseEntered(MouseEvent e) {
        // ... handle mouse-enter event
    }
    public void mouseExited(MouseEvent e) {
        // ... handle mouse-exit event
    }
}
```

Because MouseTracker inherits from a class that implements the MouseListener interface, it too implements the interface. ClickTracker can define just the two methods it needs; it inherits empty methods from MouseAdapter to ignore the rest of the mouse events.

Event adapter classes are simply for your convenience. You could just as well define an equivalent MouseTracker2 class without the help of MouseAdapter:

```
class MouseTracker2 implements MouseListener {
    public void mousePressed(MouseEvent e) {}
    public void mouseReleased(MouseEvent e) {}
    public void mouseEntered(MouseEvent e) {
        // ... handle mouse-enter event
    }
    public void mouseExited(MouseEvent e) {
        // ... handle mouse-exit event
    }
}
```

See also: Q7.2, Q7.3

Q7.5

Do events propagate in the JDK 1.1 as they did in the older AWT event model?

No; events are sent only to the target component, and only if that component has a registered listener for the event type.

One of the central changes in the JDK 1.1 AWT event model (Q7.2, Q7.3) is that events do not propagate automatically from the event source up the containment hierarchy (Q6.3). Instead, events are delivered only to the listeners registered with the AWT component representing the source of the event. To catch an event, you must register an appropriate event listener with the specific source component (Q7.2).

If you want to catch events from all components in some container, you need to write code that recursively assigns listeners to that container's descendants. In other words, the approach shifts from propagating events up the tree to propagating listeners down the tree. The sample code in the `PropagateEvent11Example` class provides an illustrative implementation.

PropagateEvent11Example.html

See also: Q6.3, Q7.2, Q7.3

Q7.6

Will my code written for the older JDK 1.0.2 event model still run in the JDK 1.1?

Yes; the JDK 1.1 generates JDK 1.0.2 events (and propagates them) if it can detect that a program uses none of the JDK 1.1 event model.

Backward compatibility with code written for JDK 1.0.2 was a strong design goal and constraint for the JDK 1.1. The AWT event model in the JDK 1.1 (Q7.1, Q7.2, Q7.5) represents the most significant change from the previous API and programming model in the JDK 1.0.2. Nevertheless, AWT event code written exclusively for the JDK 1.0.2 can run in the JDK 1.1 environment.

The AWT decides which events to send based on the target component. The AWT dispatches JDK 1.1-style events for a component if it detects any signs of the JDK 1.1 event model associated with that component (e.g., an event listener is registered with the component). Otherwise, the AWT dispatches JDK 1.0.2-style events for that component via the `handleEvent` method (Q6.4), complete with propagation up the containment hierarchy (Q6.3).

See also: Q6.3, Q6.4

SEMANTIC EVENTS

Q7.7

How do I handle action events in the JDK 1.1?

Use the `addActionListener` **method to register an** `ActionListener` **object with the event source; the listener's** `actionPerformed` **method will be invoked when an action event occurs.**

An action event is the way some AWT components notify your program that they have been acted on and now have new information to report (Q6.5). The JDK 1.1 generates action events in the cases shown in Table 7.5.

Table 7.5: Action Events—JDK 1.1

Component	Generates JDK 1.1 action event for ___
`Button`	mouse click
`MenuItem`	mouse click
`List`	double mouse click
	return key press
`TextField`	return key press

Note that this list differs from the JDK 1.0.2 AWT by omitting `Checkbox` and `Choice` (Q6.5). These two classes now belong to a separate category of `Item-Selectable` objects—that is, objects from classes that implement the `ItemSelectable` interface. The `ItemSelectable` interface is intended to cover any class that has the semantics of a selection from a specific, finite set of choices. In addition to Checkbox and Choice, the List class implements the ItemSelectable interface as well.

To catch and handle an action event, you need to attach an ActionListener object to the source of the event. The listener's actionPerformed method is invoked for each action event on the source component. The following code fragment shows how to catch action events from three different components with the same listener:

```java
/* using JDK 1.1: */
class Example {
    /** An inner class that reports action events received. */
    class ActionReporter implements ActionListener {
        public void actionPerformed(ActionEvent e) {
            ++actionCount;
            actionEventLog.append("Action event #" + actionCount
                                    + ", e = " + e + "\n");
        }
    }

    ActionListener reporter = new ActionReporter();
    TextArea actionEventLog = new TextArea();
    int actionCount;

    public void init() {
        List animalList = new List(3, false);
        Button pushButton = new Button("Push Me");
        TextField text = new TextField(
                            "Type in me (and hit return).");
        /* Initialize event handlers. */
        animalList.addActionListener(reporter);
        pushButton.addActionListener(reporter);
        text.addActionListener(reporter);
    }
}
```

This sample code uses an inner class, ActionReporter, to define the Action-Listener. The inner class simplifies the event handling code by providing direct access to the Example class's instance variables, actionCount and ActionEvent-Log. Using a standard (non-inner) class would be much clumsier: you would have to set up extra methods or constructors to pass the necessary information between the Example instance and the ActionReporter instance.

ActionEvent11Example.html

See also: Q6.5, Q7.2, Q7.3

Q7.8

How do I catch menu item events in the 1.1 AWT event model?

Menu items emit an ActionEvent **when clicked, so you can catch menu item events the same way as other action events, with an** ActionListener **object.**

In the JDK 1.1 AWT event model, clicking on a menu item sends an action event to any ActionListener objects that have registered themselves with that menu item. There are two main strategies for how to assign listeners to the numerous menu items in a typical menu system: a unique listener for each menu item versus one large listener for all menu items. The code excerpt below illustrates the listener-per-item approach:

```
/* using JDK 1.1: */
class Example {
    /** Inner class for use as the "File Open" listener. */
    class MenuFileOpen implements ActionListener {
        public void actionPerformed(ActionEvent e) {
            openFile(e.getActionCommand());
        }
    }

    /** Inner class for use as the "File Save" listener. */
    class MenuFileSave implements ActionListener {
        public void actionPerformed(ActionEvent e) {
            saveFile(e.getActionCommand());
        }
    }

    public void init() {
        MenuItem openItem = new MenuItem("Open...");
        openItem.addActionListener(new MenuFileOpen());
        MenuItem saveItem = new MenuItem("Save");
        saveItem.addActionListener(new MenuFileSave());
        // ... assemble the menu system and show the main frame
    }

    // ... define openFile and saveFile
}
```

The one-large-listener approach, on the other hand, requires that you explicitly propagate that listener to all the menu items in your menu hierarchy. The following method, for example, recursively walks down the menu hierarchy in order to attach an ActionListener object to each menu item:

```
/* using JDK 1.1: */
static void addMenuListenerRecursively(MenuItem mi,
                                       ActionListener listener) {
    mi.addActionListener(listener);
    if (mi instanceof Menu) {
        Menu m = (Menu) mi;
        for (int i = 0; i < m.getItemCount(); ++i) {
            addMenuListenerRecursively(m.getItem(i), listener);
        }
    }
}
```

After you've built your entire menu structure, including the menu bar, you can invoke this method on each of the menus contained in menu bar:

```
for (int i = 0; i < myMenuBar.getMenuCount(); ++i) {
    addMenuListenerRecursively(myMenuBar.getMenu(i), tracker);
}
```

MenuItemEvent11Example.html

See also: Q6.8, Q7.7

Q7.9

In the JDK 1.1 AWT event model, how is my program notified when a list item is selected or deselected?

When an item in a list is selected or deselected, the AWT invokes itemState-Changed **on any** ItemListener **registered with that list; you can then query the** ItemEvent **for whether the state change is a select** (ItemEvent.SELECTED) **or a deselect** (ItemEvent.DESELECTED)**.**

The JDK 1.1 AWT event model makes a strong division between low-level events and semantic events. Low-level events represent raw input actions or window-system state changes, whereas semantic events represent meaningful happenings brought about by lower-level actions. Semantic events are defined in terms of a semantic model and can be generated by any user-interface element that supports that model. Thus, the semantic event generated by a List is not a ListEvent (no such event class exists) but an ItemEvent. An ItemEvent can in principle be generated by any class that supports a model of an item collection within which individual items are selected or deselected. If your class fits such a model, you are encouraged to use the `ItemSelectable` interface and `ItemEvent` class for your class's event behavior.

You catch item events from a `List` instance by registering one or more `Item-Listener` objects with that instance. The `ItemListener` interface contains a single method:

```
/* in Listener.java (JDK 1.1): */
public interface ItemListener extends EventListener {
    public void itemStateChanged(ItemEvent e);
}
```

Although the same event method is delivered whether the user selected or deselected an item, you can distinguish between the two by querying the `ItemEvent` object with its `getStateChange` method. A select event yields the `int` value `ItemEvent.SELECTED`, and a deselect event yields `ItemEvent.DESELECTED`. For example:

```
/* using JDK 1.1: */
if (e.getStateChange() == ItemEvent.SELECTED) {
    // ... handle select event
} else {
    // ... handle deselect event
}
```

`List` objects also produce action events, when the user either double clicks an item or presses the return key while an item has keyboard focus. You can catch these action events with an `ActionListener` object, the same as for other action events from other sources (Q7.7).

ListEvent11Example.html

See also: Q6.9, Q7.7

Q7.10

How do I control scrolling in the 1.1 AWT?

The JDK 1.0.2 forces you to handle scrolling on your own, but the JDK 1.1 provides the `ScrollPane` class as a ready-made container to handle scrolling automatically.

The ScrollPane class, new in the JDK 1.1, provides a ready-made scrolling container. ScrollPane is a subclass of Container that takes a single component as its child and manages horizontal and vertical scrolling for the child component. For basic scrolling behavior, using a ScrollPane can be as simple as creating a ScrollPane instance and adding your component to it. All the scrolling behavior is managed automatically by the scroll pane. The following simple class shows a scroll pane holding a panel, which contains 400 buttons in a 20-by-20 grid:

```
/* using JDK 1.1: */
class Example {
    /** Initializes the app, builds the interface. */
    public void init() {
        Frame mainFrame = new Frame("ScrollPane11Example");
        ScrollPane scrollPane = new ScrollPane();
        Panel buttonPanel = new Panel();
        buttonPanel.setLayout(new GridLayout(0, 20));
        for (int i = 0; i < 400; ++i) {
            buttonPanel.add(new Button("B" + i));
        }
        scrollPane.add(buttonPanel);
        mainFrame.add(scrollPane, "Center");
        mainFrame.pack();
        mainFrame.show();
    }

    /** Runs the class as a standalone application. */
    public static void main(String[] args) {
        Example example = new Example();
        example.init();
    }
}
```

As this example shows, if you want a collection of components to be scrollable as a group, place them in a panel and then place that Panel inside the scroll pane.

The ScrollPane class's default behavior is reasonable for many uses, but the class also provides programmatic control over the following aspects:

- scrollbar policy: can be set in the constructor; its possible values are SCROLLBARS_AS_NEEDED, SCROLLBARS_ALWAYS, and SCROLLBARS_NEVER

- scroll position: can be set programmatically via setScrollPosition(int, int) and can be queried with getScrollPosition()

- scrollbars: horizontal and vertical scrollbars of the ScrollPane instance can be inspected individually with getHAdjustable() and getVAdjustable()

You can also take internal measurements of the scroll pane with the following methods:

```
public Dimension getViewportSize()
public int getHScrollbarHeight()
public int getVScrollbarWidth()
```

ScrollPane11Example.html

See also: Q6.10

LOW-LEVEL EVENTS

Q7.11

My frame doesn't close when I click on Quit/Close in the main menu—how do I fix this using the JDK 1.1?

Define windowClosing **in a** WindowListener **object and use** addWindowListener **to register that listener to the frame.**

Clicking on Quit/Close (depending on the native windowing system) generates a window-destroy event, which your application needs to catch and handle appropriately. How you catch the event differs between the JDK 1.0.2 and 1.1, as will be discussed, but the code needed to respond to the event is essentially the same. You use the Frame class's dispose method to dispose of the frame along with any resources connected to it. Additionally, if you want the frame's closing to terminate the application, you can call System's exit method.

In the JDK 1.1, you catch the window-destroy event by attaching an appropriate WindowListener object to the frame. The key method to define is windowClosing:

```
/* using JDK 1.1: */
class Example extends java.applet.Applet {
    /** An inner class that closes the window and quits the app. */
    class WindowCloser extends WindowAdapter {
        public void windowClosing(WindowEvent e) {
            e.getWindow().dispose();
        }
    }
```

```
    public void init() {
        Frame f = new Frame("Closeable Frame");
        f.addWindowListener(new WindowCloser());
        // ...
    }
}
```

See also: Q6.7

Q7.12

Is there an event type that signals when a window is resized?

There is no event in the JDK 1.0.2 for window resizing, but the JDK 1.1 includes notification of window resizing by means of ComponentEvent.

The JDK 1.0.2 lacks a specific event type for window resizing. Some programmers noticed that Event.WINDOW_MOVED catches window resize events on Solaris, but this is a platform-specific coincidence that should not be relied on.

The JDK 1.1 event model in the AWT provides a general event type for signaling the resizing and relocating of any component, not just windows. You can detect window size and location changes by catching the component-resize and component-move events for your window. To do this, attach an appropriate ComponentListener object to the window(s) you wish to receive events from. The following simple class illustrates how:

```
public class Example {
    class ComponentReporter extends ComponentAdapter {
        public void componentMoved(ComponentEvent e) { /* ... */ }
        public void componentResized(ComponentEvent e) { /* ... */ }
    }
    ComponentListener reporter = new ComponentReporter();
    Frame mainFrame = new Frame("Resize and Move Events");
    public void init() {
        mainFrame.addComponentListener(reporter);
        // ...
    }
    // ...
}
```

WindowResizeEvent11Example.html

See also: Q7.11

Q7.13

How do I handle events for function keys, arrow keys, and so on in the JDK 1.1 event model?

Attach a `KeyListener` **object to the event source and check for the specific key types you want to catch.**

The JDK 1.1 event model divides key events into two types, as shown in Table 7.6. Lower-level events directly convey the user's actions on the keyboard, and higher-level events convey the input characters resulting from the user's typing.

Table 7.6: Key Events—JDK 1.1

Lower-level, key action	`keyPressed(KeyEvent e)`
	`keyReleased(KeyEvent e)`
Higher-level, key input	`keyTyped(KeyEvent e)`

For input characters directly supported by the user's keyboard, a single `keyTyped` event corresponds to a `keyPressed` event followed by a `keyReleased` event. For other input characters, more complex mappings from key actions are possible.

Function keys, arrow keys, and so on are *action keys*. The AWT reports any key presses or releases that occur on action keys, but it never generates key input events from the action keys. Therefore, to catch action key events, you need to supply a `KeyListener` object that handles the low-level events with its `keyPressed` and/or `keyReleased` methods.

Once you've caught the event, you can query the `KeyEvent` object to find out more specifically which key triggered the event. `KeyEvent`'s `isActionKey` method is useful for making the high-level split between action keys and content keys. To make finer distinctions among action keys, invoke `getKeyCode` on the event object, and test that value against the `KeyEvent` values shown in Table 7.7.

Table 7.7: Key Constants in `KeyEvent`—JDK 1.1

navigation keys	HOME, END, PGUP, PGDN, UP, DOWN, LEFT, RIGHT
function keys	F1, F2, F3, F4, F5, F6, F7, F8, F9, F10, F11, F12
other action-type keys	PRINT_SCREEN, SCROLL_LOCK, CAPS_LOCK, NUM_LOCK, PAUSE, INSERT

The following code excerpt shows a Canvas subclass that cares only about processing action keys, and that beeps the user as a reminder that content keys are not expected:

```
/* using JDK 1.1: */
class ExampleCanvas extends Canvas {

    /* An inner class listener for key pressed events. */
    class KeyTracker extends KeyAdapter {
        public void keyPressed(KeyEvent e) {
            if (e.isActionKey()) {
                drawXOR = e.isControlDown();
                switch (e.getKeyCode()) {
                    case KeyEvent.F1:
                        fullRepaint = true;
                        break;
                    case KeyEvent.LEFT:
                        translatePoint(-stepSize, 0);
                        break;
                    // ...
                    default:
                        break;
                }
                repaint();
                return;
            }

            /* Beep for any non-action key presses */
            getToolkit().beep();
        }
    }

    static int stepSize = 4;
    boolean drawXOR = false;
    boolean fullRepaint = true;

    public ExampleCanvas() {
        addKeyListener(new KeyTracker());
    }
    void translatePoint(int dx, int dy) { /* ... */ }
    // ...
}
```

ActionKey11Example.html

See also: Q6.6

Q7.14

How does the JDK 1.1 distinguish between mouse clicks made with different buttons on a two- or three-button mouse?

The JDK 1.1 `MouseEvent` class uses the `modifiers` field in the event object to distinguish between different mouse buttons; the `InputEvent` class provides modifier masks with which you can test the modifiers data.

Like the JDK 1.0.2, the JDK 1.1 generates mouse events for all mouse clicks on a multibutton mouse. The event methods are the same regardless of which button is used, but the `MouseEvent` object carries the distinction in its modifiers data. You can determine which button was used with the help of modifier masks in the `InputEvent` class (superclass of both `MouseEvent` and `KeyEvent`):

```
/* in InputEvent.java, JDK 1.1: */
public static final int BUTTON1_MASK = 1 << 4;
public static final int BUTTON2_MASK = 1 << 5;
public static final int BUTTON3_MASK = 1 << 6;
```

Below is a sample `MouseListener` that reports which mouse button was pressed, together with which modifier keys were down at the time:

```
class MouseReporter extends MouseAdapter {
    public void mousePressed(MouseEvent e) {
        int mod = e.getModifiers();
        if ((mod & InputEvent.BUTTON3_MASK) != 0) {
            System.out.print("button 3 ");
        } else if ((mod & InputEvent.BUTTON2_MASK) != 0) {
            System.out.print("button 2 ");
        } else {
            System.out.print("button 1 ");
        }
        System.out.println("pressed, "
                        + (mod == 0 ? "no modifiers "
                                    : "modifiers = ")
                        + (e.isAltDown() ? "alt " : "")
                        + (e.isMetaDown() ? "meta " : "")
                        + (e.isShiftDown() ? "shift " : "")
                        + (e.isControlDown() ? "control "
                                             : ""));
    }
}
```

MultiButtonMouse11Example.html

See also: Q6.11

CHAPTER 8

Drawing

Drawing AWT Components (Q8.1–Q8.8)

Loading and Drawing Images (Q8.9–Q8.19)

Images—JDK 1.0.2 (Q8.20–Q8.21)

Images—JDK 1.1 (Q8.22–Q8.24)

DRAWING AWT COMPONENTS

Q8.1

What is the paint *method for, when is it invoked, and by whom?*

The paint **method is usually invoked by the Abstract Window Toolkit (AWT), via the** update **method, in order to provide an up-to-date image on screen of the component.**

The paint method is the fundamental means by which an AWT component (Q5.1) draws itself on the screen. You need to define paint in your own code if you subclass from a Component class that does not already know how to draw itself—most commonly Canvas, Panel, or Applet. Other Component subclasses, such as Button and TextField, know how to draw themselves, and need no further help from you.

Typically, paint is invoked for you by update (Q8.5); but it can also be invoked directly, bypassing update, such as when a component is scrolled or resized, or when part of a window is exposed after being covered by another window (Q8.6).

Note: In the JDK 1.0.2 and 1.1, all component painting is run by a central AWT thread. If a component's `paint` method hogs time or blocks completely, it can stop the entire application from updating its appearance (Q8.5, Q9.17).

PaintExample.html

See also: Q5.1, Q8.2, Q8.3, Q8.5, Q8.6, Q9.17

Q8.2

What should I put in my `paint` *method?*

Put the minimum necessary to paint your component completely and quickly.

The purpose of `paint` is to provide a quick snapshot of what's happening in a program, rather than to make part of the action happen. In other words, `paint` should show state, not compute it. An applet displaying a bouncing ball, for example, should calculate the new ball position, spin, and so on outside of the `paint` method (hence, in a separate thread from `paint`); `paint` can then simply read the currrent coordinates for the ball and draw it accordingly.

A well-written `paint` method should execute quickly and should fully represent the component's visible state at any arbitrary time. There are handy tests for these requirements. First, watch how your component behaves when you scroll it into view. A speedy `paint` method allows a component to be repainted many times with little noticeable delay. Some existing applets fail this test spectacularly, often because they include lengthy state calculations in their `paint` methods. Second, cover your application's window and then re-expose it. Your components should show everything you want them to show.

SlowPaintExample.html

See also: Q8.18

Q8.3

What is `repaint` *for, when is it invoked, and by whom?*

You invoke `repaint` on a component whenever you want the component to be redrawn.

The `repaint` method issues a request that a component be redrawn within a specified time, or as soon as possible if the time is left unspecified. The JDK (1.0.2 and 1.1) organizes all drawing requests via a central drawing authority, run in a single thread. This ensures that different drawing requests don't interrupt each other and leave the screen in an inconsistent state. The central AWT thread responds to `repaint` requests by invoking `update` as needed on the components requesting a `repaint`.

You normally invoke `repaint` on a component when you know it no longer accurately reflects the internal state of your program. For example, if your program contains several graphing components connected to a data set, you can keep the graphs current by invoking `repaint` on each of them after any change to the data set.

For more complex programs, you need to be aware of the threaded implementation of `repaint`. First, `repaint` requests are asynchronous, which means that an invocation of `repaint` returns immediately rather than waiting for the drawing to complete. Second, if a component has two or more unfulfilled `repaint` requests waiting in the drawing queue, the AWT may merge them into a single request. Your code should not make assumptions about the number of actual `paint` or `update` calls that will occur in response to your `repaint` requests.

RepaintExample.html

See also: Q8.1, Q8.4

Q8.4

Why do my repeated calls to `repaint` *not have any effect?*

The `repaint` method issues drawing requests, but your code may be keeping the system too busy to fulfill those requests.

The `repaint` method issues a request for the component to be visually updated but relies on other methods to carry out the actual work. The underlying question is why these other methods are not doing their work.

The `repaint` method is asynchronous: it issues a request to the central drawing thread and returns immediately without waiting for the drawing work to finish. A common mistake is to keep the system (CPU) fully occupied in a tight loop by giving it nonstop repeated `repaint` requests. If the virtual machine implementation in your platform doesn't provide time-slicing for threads (Q9.15), the drawing thread may never get a turn to run. You can help the drawing thread by putting some breathing space in your `repaint` loop, by means of `Thread`'s `sleep` or `yield` method (Q9.5, Q9.13).

BusyRepaintExample.html

See also: Q9.5, Q9.13, Q9.15

Q8.5

What is update *for, when is it invoked, and by whom?*

In response to `repaint` requests for a component, the AWT invokes `update` to make the component bring its appearance up to date.

The `update` method works together with `Component`'s `paint` and `repaint` methods to keep a program's appearance up to date with any changes in its internal state. The key difference between `paint` and `update` is that `paint` must be able to draw the entire component from scratch, but `update` can be used for more selective and efficient drawing. Your `update` method needs to draw only enough to bring the component's appearance up to date from the last time it was drawn. For example, if a textual object deleted its last line, `update` could merely cover the space for the last line with the background color, whereas `paint` should redraw the entire object, unchanged and changed parts alike.

The AWT invokes `update` on components when it wants them to redraw themselves, typically in response to `repaint` calls made by your program. Note that the default implementation of `update` in the JDK (1.0.2 and 1.1) has no special knowledge of how to redraw the component selectively, so it does the safe thing and redraws the whole component from the ground up:

```
/* in Component.java (JDK 1.0.2 and 1.1): */
public void update(Graphics g) {
    g.setColor(getBackground());
    g.fillRect(0, 0, width, height);
    g.setColor(getForeground());
    paint(g);
}
```

In cases where you know more about how to optimize your drawing, you can, and should, override `update` to redraw only as much as needed. Some applets, for example, redefine `update` so that it simply paints on top of what's already present:

```
public void update(Graphics g) {
    g.setColor(getForeground());
    paint(g);
}
```

This step helps reduce flicker in simple animations where the applet redraws its entire area. Note that full-scale animation with moving parts over a constant background almost always requires a more sophisticated update method (Q8.5) and double buffering (Q8.18).

UpdateExample.html

See also: Q8.1, Q8.2, Q8.3, Q8.5, Q8.18

Q8.6

What drawing occurs if my applet or other component reappears after being covered by some other window?

The background is filled, and paint **is invoked.**

When an applet or other component is re-exposed after lying behind another window, your program must be able to redraw the re-exposed or "damaged" area. First, the damaged area is filled with the background color (often unpreventably by native platform itself); then the AWT invokes paint (Q8.1) on the affected components. Window re-exposure is one of a few cases in which your program receives a paint call directly without first going through the update method (Q8.5). Two other cases are when a component is first put on screen and when a component is scrolled.

See also: Q8.1, Q8.3, Q8.4, Q8.5

Q8.7

Can I implement an invisible or partly transparent component?

In the JDK 1.0.2 you can't, but the JDK 1.1 lays the groundwork to enable "lightweight" components that can be partly or totally transparent.

In the JDK 1.0.2, all components cover their space on screen with an opaque background color, on top of which you can draw. There is no way in the JDK 1.0.2 to have all or part of an AWT component be transparent.

Starting with the JDK 1.1, the AWT supports lightweight, peerless components that can draw themselves without the use of a native-platform peer (Q5.9). Peerless components can draw themselves as much or as little as they like, and whatever parts of their area they don't draw on remain transparent.

To define transparent Component subclasses, extend either Component or Container, and then define your subclass pretty much the same as you would any other Component:

```
/* using JDK 1.1: */
public class MyComponent extends Component {
    // ...
    public void paint(Graphics g) {
        // ... code to draw the component
    }
}
```

The code you put in paint can be just like paint code for nontransparent components. The difference is simply that the background is not automatically filled in. Any part of the component not covered by its paint method will be transparent.

Another key point about using lightweight components is to make sure that the parent of any lightweight component has an appropriate paint method itself that will invoke paint on the lightweight component. The default paint method inherited from Container manages this for you, so you get it for free if your container class doesn't override paint. If your container class must override paint, though, just be sure to include an invocation of super.paint in your class's paint method:

```
/* overriding paint in a container class: */
public void paint(Graphics g) {
    // ... do this class's special paint processing
    super.paint(g);  // invoke default paint to handle
                     // lightweight components
}
```

TransparentComponent11Example.html

See also: Q4.13, Q5.9

Q8.8

How does the XOR drawing mode work?

The XOR drawing mode flips pixel colors in a reversible fashion.

The Graphics class's setXORMode method allows your program to draw in a two-way reversible fashion. Instead of irrevocably covering previous colors with the Graphics instance's current color, setXORMode specifies a toggle color that will trade places with the current color on each drawing operation. XOR drawing has the following properties:

- performing the same draw twice restores all original colors
- the Graphics instance's current color switches exactly with the toggle color on each draw, and vice versa
- other color changes depend on the color model of the screen, but are also reversible

If you want to use XOR drawing, you must specifically request it. Otherwise, the Graphics class draws in its default "paint mode," which simply covers any pre-existing color with the current color.

XORDrawingExample.html

LOADING AND DRAWING IMAGES

Q8.9

How do I load an image from the net into my applet?

You first invoke getImage **to establish a pointer to the image's data source, and then invoke another method, such as** drawImage, **to actually start pulling the image data across the network.**

The primary function of the AWT Image class is to bridge the gap between a source of image data and a specific output format for rendering that data:

image data source $\Rightarrow$ Image instance $\Rightarrow$ rendering (pixels) in specific format

Correspondingly, loading an image from a network data source happens in two stages. You first create a connection to a source of image data via a URL. Then you fetch and convert the image data to match your rendering target.

For the simple case of displaying an image on screen in your applet, the two loading stages translate to the following method calls:

1. Invoke getImage (from the Applet class) to register a URL as the data source for the image.

2. Invoke drawImage on a Graphics instance to render the image at a given location, and optionally, scaled to a given size.

Step 1, invoking getImage, merely specifies a data source. The drawImage method in step 2 initiates the real work. It starts a combined process of transferring, converting, and rendering the image data. Because this process can take some time, the AWT handles it in a separate thread.

The following sample applet loads and displays an image file:

```
import java.awt.*;
public class LoadImageExample extends java.applet.Applet {
    Image myImage;
    public void init() {
        myImage = getImage(getDocumentBase(), "beach.gif");
    }
    public void paint(Graphics g) {
        g.drawImage(myImage, 0, 0, this);
    }
}
```

See also: Q4.12, Q8.15

Q8.10

How do I load an image from a file in a stand-alone Java application, rather than in an applet?

Use one of the getImage **methods in the AWT** Toolkit **class.**

Applet is the only Component subclass that provides its own getImage method. To load an image outside of an applet, you need the Toolkit class. Toolkit is an all-purpose utility class for AWT functionality not belonging to any component in particular. Toolkit provides two getImage methods, one taking a file name as an argument, and the other taking a URL instance:

- getImage(String)
- getImage(URL)

If the image file is on your local file system, you can invoke getImage with a string that represents the file name. For example:

```
myImage = getToolkit().getImage("beach.gif");
```

The getToolkit method returns a Toolkit instance, on which you can then invoke getImage to create an Image instance. That Image instance is connected to the specified file as its source of data.

To access a remote file, you need to invoke getImage with a URL argument. This requires the extra step of creating the URL instance:

```
String urlString = "http://somemachine.com/somedir/somefile.gif";
try {
    URL imageUrl = new URL(urlString);
    myImage = getToolkit().getImage(imageUrl);
} catch (MalformedURLException e) {
    // ... recover from bad URL string
}
```

AppGetImageExample.html

See also: Q4.12

Q8.11

When is an image actually loaded—why not immediately?

The AWT seeks smarter and more efficient data transfer by waiting as long as possible before starting to load images.

As mentioned in Q8.9, the two main steps for image loading are: (1) to associate an Image instance with its data source (using getImage) and (2) to fetch and convert the image data.

The AWT defers the second step until you invoke some method that specifically triggers the loading. These methods are listed in Table 8.1. The central idea is to wait to fetch the image data until the data is really needed. At this point, there is often enough information, such as target size, to make the process more efficient. The following scenarios illustrate the savings in time and space.

Scenario 1—loading a large image for use at a smaller scale. Suppose your source image is a GIF file that expands to 1 million pixels (1000×1000), each requiring 4 bytes of storage. If you automatically prefetch image data, your

Table 8.1: Methods that Trigger Image Loading

Class	Methods
Component	`prepareImage(Image, ImageObserver),` `prepareImage(Image, int, int, ImageObserver)`
Graphics	`drawImage` [family of four methods]
Image	`getWidth()`, `getHeight()`, `getProperty()`
PixelGrabber	`grabPixels()`, `grabPixels(long)`
MediaTracker	`wait`, `check`, and `status` family of methods (Q8.12)

program must hold the full 4 megabytes in memory before deciding what to do with it. If all you want is a 200×200 version of the image, you can call `drawImage` and pass in the desired width and height as arguments:

```
// ... set x and y as desired
g.drawImage(myImage, x, y, 200, 200, this);
```

This triggers the actual image loading. Your `Image` instance will rescale the image as it fetches it, and the image data takes only 160,000 bytes of final storage (1/25th of the full-scale image).

Scenario 2—loading/filtering a small portion of a large image. From the same-size image source as Scenario 1 (1 million pixels), you might want to display only a portion. The `CropImageFilter` class can extract a subarea from a larger source image, and it does so without requiring the full image data ever to be stored in memory.

Scenario 3—faster web-page loading. Since an applet is usually just one among many occupants on a web page, it is a good strategy to invoke only `getImage` in your applet's `init` method. This allows your applet to initialize quickly and not hinder the rest of the page from loading. Your applet should wait until its `start` method to initiate potentially lengthy image loads. By this point, the rest of the web page will be available to the reader, and waiting for images will be less irksome.

Delayed image loading provides substantial benefits, but also has its share of surprising twists that must be learned carefully. The `drawImage` method, for instance, returns immediately without waiting for the image to be completely loaded. Similarly, invoking `getWidth` or `getHeight` methods on an image before it is fully loaded will return the impossible value of −1. The AWT `MediaTracker` class (Q8.12) provides a key tool for overseeing the loading process and for ensuring that valid data is available from an image.

See also: Q8.12

Q8.12

How can I make sure that my images are completely loaded before I check for their data or parameters?

Use the `MediaTracker` class.

The AWT `MediaTracker` class lets you monitor how your program loads images. (As the class's name suggests, `MediaTracker` may handle other media objects in the future, such as sound.) `MediaTracker` supports four kinds of operations for tracking images:

- specifying groups of images to track
- waiting for images to finish loading
- checking for errors in the image-loading process
- checking the current status of images being loaded

A single `MediaTracker` instance can track any number of images, either all together or in separate groups. After creating a `MediaTracker` instance and as many `Image` instances as you need, you can add each image to a tracking group by invoking `addImage` on your `MediaTracker` instance. For example:

```
/* code in an Applet subclass: */
MediaTracker imageTracker = new MediaTracker(this);
Image smallImage = getImage(getDocumentBase(), "small.gif");
Image bigImage1 = getImage(getDocumentBase(), "big1.gif");
Image bigImage2 = getImage(getDocumentBase(), "big2.gif");
imageTracker.addImage(smallImage, 4);   // 1 image in group 4
imageTracker.addImage(bigImage1, 8);    // 2 images in a group 8,
imageTracker.addImage(bigImage2, 8);    //   e.g., for animation
```

This code fragment starts with a `MediaTracker` constructor, which requires that you specify a `Component` that will be the ultimate consumer of the image data. The next three lines create `Image` instances, and the final three lines specify that one image belongs to group 4 and the other two belong to group 8. You can choose whatever numbers you like for your image groups—MediaTracker merely uses the number as a tag for the group as a whole. Note that the JDK 1.0.2 provides methods only for adding images to tracking groups; the JDK 1.1 provides a matching set of methods for removing images from tracking groups.

The grouping of images allows other MediaTracker methods to apply to either a specific image group or to all images that the MediaTracker instance knows about. This distinction pervades the rest of the MediaTracker methods, as shown in Table 8.2.

Table 8.2: MediaTracker **Methods**

Method family	Apply to images in specified group	Apply to all images
wait for loading to complete	waitForID(int)	waitForAll()
	waitForID(int, long)	waitForAll(long)
check for loading errors	isErrorID(int)	isErrorAny()
	getErrorsID(int)	getErrorsAny()
check loading status	checkID(int)	checkAll()
	checkID(int, boolean)	checkAll(boolean)
	statusID(int, boolean)	statusAll(boolean)

Methods in the wait... family do not return until all images in the specified set of images have either finished loading or encountered an error. (The optional long parameter specifies a maximum number of milliseconds to wait, rather than waiting indefinitely.) These methods also trigger loading of any images that haven't already started loading. Continuing the example just started, you could use the following code to wait for all images in group 8 to complete loading:

```
try {
    imageTracker.waitForID(8);
} catch (InterruptedException e) {
    // ... handle exception
}
```

Note that waitForID, like several other methods that potentially suspend a thread's execution for a period of time, can throw an InterruptedException (Q2.23, Q9.5, Q9.12).

The isError... and getErrors... methods check whether any errors have yet occurred while loading the specified set of images. The isError... methods return a boolean value indicating whether an error occurred. The getErrors... methods return an Object array indicating specifically which images had errors (or null if none of the specified images had an error).

Finally, the loading status family of methods, check... and status..., report on the loading progress of the specified set of images. The check... methods return a boolean value indicating whether the images have finished loading. The status... methods report more specifically what states the images are in: not started, LOADING, COMPLETE, ERRORED, or ABORTED. The optional boolean parameter in the loading status methods specifies whether the method should also trigger loading for any images in the set that haven't yet started loading.

TrackImageExample.html, TrackErrorImageExample.html

See also: Q8.10, Q8.11, Q8.13

Q8.13

Why does my call to Graphics*'s* drawImage *method fail to show the image?*

The Graphics drawImage **method returns immediately, whether or not the image data is available; you need to check the image status by other means.**

The drawImage method in the Graphics class has two main tasks: it triggers the loading of image data across the network if the image data isn't already present, and it issues a request to start the drawing of the image. The method itself, however, is asynchronous — it issues requests to start this activity, but it returns immediately without waiting to see that everything has properly finished (Q8.11). If either the loading or drawing process goes astray, some other part of your program needs to detect and handle the situation.

Two different objects can track the progress of image loading and rendering. First, all versions of drawImage require an ImageObserver object, that is, an object that implements the ImageObserver interface (Q1.20). The AWT invokes the imageUpdate method on the ImageObserver object whenever the image's status changes — typically either additional data to render or trouble in loading.

Instances of any Component subclass, including an applet, can serve as an ImageObserver, by using their imageUpdate method to monitor images being drawn onto them. However, the default imageUpdate method in Component does not check for image errors; it merely repaints the component periodically to reflect any newly available image data. If you want to catch errors with an `ImageObserver` object, you need to override `imageUpdate` to check explicitly for error status in the method's `flags` argument.

Another way to catch image failures is to use a `MediaTracker` instance (Q8.12). After registering your images with a `MediaTracker` object, you can wait for the images to finish loading and then check whether any images were stopped with an error. For example:

```
Object[] imageErrorList;

public void start() {
    // ...
    try {
        imageTracker.waitForAll();
        imageErrorList = imageTracker.getErrorsAny();
    } catch (InterruptedException e) {
        // ... handle exception;
    }
}

public void paint(Graphics g) {
    g.drawImage(backImage, 0, 0, this);
    g.drawImage(foreImage, 130, 115, this);
    g.drawImage(bogusImage, 10, 10, this);
    if (imageErrorList != null) {
        String errors = imageErrorList.length
                        + " image(s) could not be loaded.";
        g.setColor(Color.red);
        g.drawString(errors, 10, 255);
    }
}
```

FailedDrawImageExample.html, TrackErrorImageExample.html

See also: Q1.20, Q8.12

Q8.14

Can I force `Applet`'s `getImage` *method to make a new connection for each image rather than reusing a cached version of the image?*

Yes; use the `flush` method in the `Image` class.

Although the default behavior for `getImage` is to try first to use a cached image copy, you can cancel this by invoking `flush` on the `Image` instance:

```
// ... myImage instance already created
myImage.flush();
// ... any use of myImage will now trigger a fresh download
```

This clears the Image instance so that it must be recreated from scratch or refetched across the net.

FlushImageExample.html

See also: Q8.15

Q8.15

How do I draw text over a background image?

Use the Graphics class's drawString method and draw the text directly on top of the image.

The drawString method in the Graphics class draws only the pixels that make up the letter shapes. All other space amidst the text is transparent and lets the underlying image show through.

You might be tempted to place a Label component on top of your image, but the effect will be quite unsatisfactory. Label instances always have a background color; the Label provides the text but also covers the image with an opaque background rectangle.

TextOnImageExample.html

See also: Q8.14, Q8.16

Q8.16

How do I load and display a transparent GIF image over a background image?

Use the same steps as for any other image.

Loading and displaying an image with transparency involves the same programming steps as a fully opaque image. The difference is just in how the image is rendered. The AWT doesn't paint anything for the transparent pixels of an image. Displaying a transparent image over a background image requires only that you draw the foreground image on top of the background image:

```
public void paint(Graphics g) {
    // ... set x and y to position foregroundImage
    g.drawImage(backgroundImage, 0, 0, this);
    g.drawImage(foregroundImage, x, y, this);
}
```

TransparentImageExample.html

See also: Q8.15

Q8.17

How can I create an image from a buffer of raw image data (red, green, and blue values for each pixel)?

Use the MemoryImageSource **class in the** java.awt.image **package.**

The MemoryImageSource class uses an array of ints to produce pixel values for an image. In the default color model, shown in Table 8.3, int values carry four channels of information:

Table 8.3: Default Color Model—32-bit int **Value**

top 8 bits (0xFF << 24)	alpha (opacity) value
2nd 8 bits (0xFF << 16)	red value
3rd 8 bits (0xFF << 8)	green value
bottom 8 bits (0xFF)	blue value

Each 8 bits is interpreted as an unsigned value (Q2.2) ranging from 0 to 255, with 255 indicating full presence of the color or full opacity.

The array of int elements provides one-dimensional storage for a conceptually two-dimensional grid of values. The array index progresses from left to right in a row and then back to the start of the next row down. For example, a grid with four rows by six columns would yield the following arrangement of indices:

```
 0  1  2  3  4  5
 6  7  8  9 10 11
12 13 14 15 16 17
18 19 20 21 22 23
```

Once you've created your `int` array, build a `MemoryImageSource` object from that, and then create an `Image` instance from the `MemoryImageSource` object:

```
int width, height;
int[] pixels;
// ... set values for width, height, and pixels as desired
Image myImage = createImage(new MemoryImageSource(width, height,
                                                  pixels, 0,
                                                  width));
```

Running animation from a `MemoryImageSource` object is clumsy in JDK 1.0.2, but significantly easier in JDK 1.1 (Q8.22).

MemoryImageExample.html

See also: Q8.22

Q8.18

What is double buffering—how can I create and draw to an offscreen image?

Double buffering is a drawing optimization in which you draw off screen first to create a complete image and then copy that image onto the screen all at once.

Using an offscreen image for drawing is only a little more complicated than drawing directly to onscreen components. The two extra steps are: (1) to create an offscreen `Image` instance and (2) to get a reference to its `Graphics` instance. For example:

```
int offscreenWidth = ...;
int offscreenHeight = ...;
Image offscreenImage = createImage(offscreenWidth, offscreenHeight);
Graphics offscreenGraphics = offscreenImage.getGraphics();
```

At this point you can draw or place images using this new `Graphics` instance the same way as with any other `Graphics` instance. The following code continues from the previous example and draws a series of green squares onto a black background within the graphics context of the offscreen image:

```
public void init() {
    // ...
    int offScreenSize = Math.min(offscreenWidth, offscreenHeight);
    offscreenGraphics.setColor(Color.black);
    offscreenGraphics.fillRect(0, 0,
                                  offscreenSize, offscreenSize);
    offscreenGraphics.setColor(Color.green);
    for (int i = 1; i < offscreenSize; i += 6) {
        int x = (offscreenSize - i) / 3;
        int y = (offscreenSize - i) / 3;
        offscreenGraphics.drawRect(x, y, i, i);
    }
}
```

Finally, you can render the offscreen image onto the screen:

```
public void paint(Graphics g) {
    // ... set x and y to position the top-left corner
    //     of the image
    g.drawImage(offscreenImage, x, y, this);
}
```

Using offscreen images has the main advantage that a complex image can be created once out of view of the user and then rendered on screen as many times as needed. This technique usually results in smoother animation, less flicker, and greater efficiency.

OffscreenImageExample.html

See also: Q8.5

Q8.19

How can I get at the raw data of an image, such as the pixel value at a given coordinate?

The PixelGrabber class (in the java.awt.image package) lets you extract pixel values from all or part of an image.

Creating an AWT Image instance does not immediately create an array of pixel values for the image; it specifies a connection to a data source for the image but defers loading the image data until some specific operation requires it (Q8.9, Q8.11). What an Image instance really represents, thus, is a conduit for obtaining image data rather than a stocked data repository. PixelGrabber is a convenience class that obtains pixel data from an Image instance and makes that data available for your inspection at the pixel level.

To use PixelGrabber, you specify all the important information up front in the PixelGrabber constructor. After that, you invoke grabPixels on the Pixel-Grabber instance (and provide for the InterruptedException that the method might throw; see Q2.23). For example:

```
// ... set width and height as desired
Image myImage = ...
int[] pixels = new int[width * height];
PixelGrabber pg = new PixelGrabber(myImage,
                               x, y, width, height,
                               pixels,
                               0, width);
try {
    pg.grabPixels();
} catch (InterruptedException e) {
    // ... handle exception
}
```

In this example, the x, y, width, and height arguments in the PixelGrabber constructor determine a rectangular region in the image: the region's top-left point (x, y) and its size (width, height). The grabPixels method pulls pixel values from this region and stores them as int values in the pixels array.

The int values in the pixel array encode colors following the AWT default color model, which allots 1 byte each for opacity (alpha), red, green, and blue values (Q8.17). To obtain Color instances corresponding to the extracted pixel values, use the Color(int) constructor:

```
// ... set index as desired
Color pixelColor = new Color(pixels[index]);
```

Unlike many other image-related methods, grabPixels is synchronous, so you can't be sure how long it takes to return. For robust applets, you should avoid calling grabPixels in any of the methods called within a system thread, such as init, start, and paint (Q9.16).

GrabPixelsExample.html

See also: Q2.23, Q8.17, Q9.16

IMAGES—JDK 1.0.2

Q8.20

Using the JDK 1.0.2, can I clear or reset a clipping rectangle that either I or the system has created?

In the JDK 1.0.2 you can't; for a given Graphics **instance, the drawable region represented by the clipping rectangle can only get smaller as new clipping rectangles are specified (this restriction is no longer true in the JDK 1.1).**

A Graphics instance provides a drawing space to your program in two parts:

- a coordinate space to locate the pixels affected by your graphics operations

- a clipping rectangle outside of which your graphics operations have no effect

You can change the coordinate space with the Graphics translate method, and you can change the clipping rectangle with the Graphics clipRect method.

The clipRect method, however, does not simply set a new clipping rectangle. Instead, the rectangle you specify as the argument to clipRect is intersected with the existing rectangle to yield the new drawable region. Each new clipping rectangle is contained wholly within the previous one. This ensures, for example, that components cannot draw outside the bounds of their containers, all the way up the containment chain. Similarly, no part of an applet can ever draw outside its bounds onto the rest of the web page.

If you need more freedom in using multiple clipping rectangles within your program, you can create separate "throwaway" graphics objects as children of your main Graphics instance. Below is an example of this cumbersome workaround:

```
/* using JDK 1.0.2: */
public void paint(Graphics g) {
    Graphics ng;
    int x, y, width, height;
    // ... set x, y, width, and height as needed
    ng = g.create(x, y, width, height);
    ng.drawSomething();
    ng.dispose();
```

```
    // ... set new values for x, y, width, and height
    ng = g.create(x, y, width, height);
    ng.drawSomethingElse();
    ng.dispose();
    // ... and so on
}
```

The Graphics create(x, y, w, h) method creates a new Graphics instance with the clipping rectangle (x, y, w, h) based on the old Graphics instance. The origin (0, 0) in the new Graphics instance corresponds to (x, y) in the parent Graphics context. Also, any clipping rectangle in the child will still be constrained to lie completely within the parent's clipping rectangle.

The JDK 1.1 provides direct support for resettable clipping rectangles, which removes the need for the above workaround (Q8.23).

SubgraphicsExample.html

See also: Q8.23

Q8.21

Using the JDK 1.0.2, can I copy a subarea of one image into another image?

Yes, but it's not as easy as it should be (and this is fixed in the JDK 1.1); the trick in the JDK 1.0.2 is to use the clipping rectangle of the receiving image to delimit the subarea of the source image.

Like all drawing methods in the Graphics class, drawImage honors the current clipping rectangle of the Graphics instance. In other words, the only part of the image that shows up is the part within the Graphics clipping rectangle. The following code fragment illustrates how to take advantage of this clipping behavior—it loads one image from a file, creates a second image that is one-half as long on each edge, and then draws a portion of the main image into the smaller image.

```
String srcImageName = ...;
int size = ...;
Image srcImage = getImage(getDocumentBase(), srcImageName);
Image dstImage = createImage(size/2, size/2);
```

```
Graphics dstImageGraphics = dstImage.getGraphics();
// ... select x, y to indicate the upper-left corner
//     of the subarea (e.g., size/4, size/4)
dstImageGraphics.drawImage(srcImage, -x, -y, this);
```

Understanding the last line of this code fragment is the key. That line tells the dstImageGraphics instance to render a copy of srcImage such that point (0, 0) of srcImage aligns with point (-x, -y) in the dstImage's coordinate space.

Now, which part of srcImage gets copied into dstImage? Only the part that falls within dstImageGraphics's clipping rectangle: from (0, 0) in the top-left corner to (size/2, size/2) in the bottom-right corner. Table 8.4 shows the key correspondences that map from dstImage's clipping rectangle into srcImage's coordinates:

Table 8.4: Coordinate Correspondences

dstImage	srcImage
(-x, -y)	(0, 0)
(0, 0)	(x, y)
(size/2, size/2)	(x + size/2, y + size/2)

Thus, in srcImage's coordinates, the subarea that gets copied ranges from (x, y) in the top-left corner to (x + size/2, y + size/2) in the bottom-right corner.

If you want to get fancier and draw the image subarea to a specific point in the second image, you need to restrict the clipping rectangle on the target rectangle. The following code, for example, copies srcImage's subarea (srcX, srcY, w, h) to point (dstX, dstY) in dstImage:

```
dstImageGraphics.clipRect(dstX, dstY, w, h);
dstImageGraphics.drawImage(srcImage, dstX - srcX, dstY - srcY,
                           this);
```

Q8.20 provides further information on setting clipping rectangles in conjunction with temporary Graphics objects.

Note: The JDK 1.1 provides a much simpler way to handle subarea copying; see Q8.24.

CopyImageSubareaExample.html

See also: Q8.20, Q8.24

IMAGES—JDK 1.1

Q8.22

How do I control animation with MemoryImageSource?

Use the new MemoryImageSource **methods in the JDK 1.1:** setAnimated, setFullBufferUpdates, **and** newPixels.

The MemoryImageSource class converts arrays of pixel values into a data source for Image instances (Q8.17). In the JDK 1.0.2, MemoryImageSource was designed for one-time image creation. Such images displayed quickly, but they did not automatically consult the original array data for each display. To update the image after the underlying array had changed required flushing the old image data (using Image's flush method; see Q8.14) and essentially creating an entirely new image. This model did not work well for animation.

The JDK 1.1 enhances MemoryImageSource with a family of methods designed for animation, as outlined in Table 8.5.

Table 8.5: Animation Methods in MemoryImageSource—**JDK1.1**

setAnimated(boolean)	specifies whether the image can receive dynamic updates for changes in the data
setFullBufferUpdates(boolean)	specifies whether the image updates should always send a full buffer of pixel data
newPixels() newPixels(int, int, int, int) ...	signals to any consumers of the image data that a new bufferful (or region) of pixel data is ready

The setAnimated and setFullBufferUpdates methods are used to prepare a MemoryImageSource instance for animation. The right place to invoke them is *before* you create an Image instance from the MemoryImageSource instance. For example:

```
int width = ...;
int height = ...;
int[] pixels = new int[width * height];
Image myImage;
MemoryImageSource imageSource;
```

```
Image buildAnimatedImage() {
    for (int i = 0; i < width * height; ++i) {
        pixels[i] = ...;
    }
    imageSource = new MemoryImageSource(width, height, pixels,
                                        0, width);
    /* Enable animation and subregion updates.*/
    imageSource.setAnimated(true);
    imageSource.setFullBufferUpdates(false);
    return createImage(imageSource);
}
```

These steps prepare the image for animation, but you must still invoke one of the newPixels methods to trigger an image update. The following code fragment continues from the above example:

```
Thread animation = ...;
public void run() {
    while (Thread.currentThread() == animation) {
        int x = ...;  // 0 <= x <= width
        int y = ...;  // 0 <= y <= height
        int index = y * width + x;
        pixels[index] = previousValue;  // change just one pixel
        imageSource.newPixels(x, y, 1, 1);
        // ... wait or sleep for a bit
    }
}
```

And, finally, the image itself must be displayed:

```
public void paint(Graphics g) {
    g.drawImage(myImage, 0, 0, 240, 240, this);
}
```

See also: Q8.14, Q8.17

Q8.23

Using the JDK 1.1, how do I reset a clipping rectangle?

Invoke one of the setClip methods; setClip establishes a new clipping region that is independent of previous calls to setClip.

The JDK 1.1 distinguishes between two kinds of clipping regions to limit your program's drawing space:

- a system-supplied clipping region set by the AWT as part of the Graphics argument in invocations of paint (Q8.1) and update (Q8.5)

- a user-defined clipping region, lying within the system-supplied region, determined by the most recent invocation of setClip on the current Graphics object

The overall drawable space is strictly bounded by the AWT-supplied clipping region, but you are free to set and reset a local clipping region within that space as much as you like. These temporary clipping regions are very useful for controlling individual rendering operations.

The new JDK 1.1 methods for controlling the clipping region are shown in Table 8.6.

Table 8.6: Methods for Getting and Setting the Clip Region — JDK 1.1

Shape getClip()	returns the current clipping region as a Shape object
Shape getClipBounds()	returns the smallest rectangle that completely encloses the current clipping region
void setClip(Shape)	sets the current clipping region to the specified Shape object (e.g., a Rectangle instance)
void setClip(int, int, int, int)	sets the current clipping region to a rectangle with the specified x, y, width, and height values

The JDK 1.1 supports only rectangular clipping regions, but, in anticipation of future implementations, the above methods are designed around the Shape interface (which has just one method, getBounds).

The following code fragment recasts the sample code of Q8.20 in terms of the JDK 1.1 methods:

```
/* using JDK 1.1: */
public void paint(Graphics g) {
    int x, y, width, height;
    // ... set x, y, width, and height as needed
    g.setClip(x, y, width, height);
    g.drawSomething();
    // ... set new values for x, y, width, and height
    g.setClip(x, y, width, height);
    g.drawSomethingElse();
    // ... and so on
}
```

You can also use the getClip method to save a clipping region so that you can restore it later. For example:

```
Shape originalClip = g.getClip();
g.setClip(x, y, width, height);
// ... draw using new clipping region
g.setClip(originalClip);
// ... draw using original clipping region
```

ResetClip11Example.html

See also: Q8.20

Q8.24

What's the best way in JDK 1.1 to draw just a subarea of an image?

Use the new drawImage methods (starting with JDK 1.1), which let you specify a rectangular subarea of the image to draw.

The JDK 1.0.2 provides drawImage methods that let you specify how a full image will be rendered into a target graphics context, but you have to work indirectly to achieve the effect of drawing just a portion of the image (Q8.21). The JDK 1.1 adds two new drawImage methods that let you specify a mapping from a rectangle in the image to a rectangle in the target graphics context. This mapping provides two capabilities not present in the JDK 1.0.2:

- you can specify a subarea of the source image to render

- you can flip the image horizontally, vertically, or both

Here's how it works. The two new drawImage methods specify rectangles differently from the rest of the AWT: they specify a logical top-left point and a logical bottom-right point for each rectangle, shown below as (x1, y1) and (x2, y2), respectively:

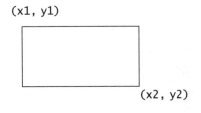

To draw a subarea of an image, provide the subimage rectangle in the two-point format just described. For example:

```
/* using JDK 1.1: */
Image myImage = ...;
public void paint(Graphics g) {
    g.drawImage(myImage,
                0, 0, 200, 100,     // points (0,0) and (200,100)
                                    // of destination rectangle
                50, 50, 150, 100,   // points (50,50) and (150,100)
                                    // of source rectangle
                Color.black,        // draw image on black background
                this);  // use this instance as the image observer
    // ...
}
```

This code takes an image subarea 100 units wide by 50 high, at location (50, 50), and draws it into the graphics area 200 units wide by 100 high, located at (0, 0). The following diagram shows the two rectangles, and how the two points defining the image source rectangle map to the two points defining the target graphics context rectangle:

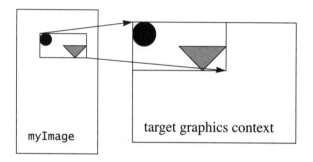

The drawImage methods also let you flip images vertically, horizontally, or both. The following drawImage invocation modifies the previous example to flip the image vertically:

```
g.drawImage(myImage,
            0, 0, 200, 100,     // points (0,0) and (200,100)
                                // of destination rectangle
            50, 100, 150, 50,   // points (50,100) and (150,50)
                                // of source rectangle
            Color.black,        // draw image on black background
            this);  // use this instance as the image observer
```

And the corresponding diagram:

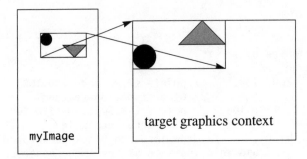

CopyImageSubarea11Example.html

See also: Q8.21

CHAPTER 9

Threads

Creating and Controlling Threads (Q9.1–Q9.5)

Thread Interactions (Q9.6–Q9.14)

User Threads versus System Threads (Q9.15–Q9.18)

CREATING AND CONTROLLING THREADS

Q9.1

What is a thread?

A thread is a sequence of executing instructions that can run independently of other threads yet can directly share data with other threads.

Threads let you organize your program into logically separate paths of execution. Multiple threads are like independent agents at your disposal. You give each one a list of instructions and then send it off on its way. From the individual thread's perspective, life is simple: it works on its own list of instructions until it either finishes the list or is told to stop. In this respect, a thread resembles a process, or a separately running program.

Data sharing among threads, however, can make the programmer's life quite complex. All memory for objects (that is, class instances and arrays) is allocated from system-managed memory shared by all Java threads. One thread could change the color of a Button instance, for example, and that change would be immediately visible to any other thread holding a reference to the same Button instance. (Not all data is shared between threads, though — Java threads each have their own execution stack, which keeps local variables and method arguments private to a thread.) Data sharing means that threads can interact with each other in surprising ways, and at the most unexpected times. Like a house of mirrors, unconstrained thread interactions can make objects suddenly appear or disappear, or values mysteriously change. You must work carefully to control how your threads access shared resources, so that each thread can read and write data accurately.

Despite the dangers, programming with threads typically provides significant advantages, including:

- reduced difficulty in writing highly interactive, multifaceted programs

- increased throughput of data

- improved performance on multiprocessor hardware

The main power of multithreaded programming lies in letting you tackle different tasks (very nearly) independently, leaving the worries of time sharing among tasks to the operating system or virtual machine. A web browser, for example, can use one thread to format and display the text of a web page as soon as it arrives, while other threads manage the slower downloading of large image or sound files. Without threads, the browser authors would have to pollute their text display code with periodic checks for new image data and with calls into the separate body of code to handle image data. What's more, adding a new operation to be performed while images are downloading would require yet more code intermingling, interruption, and greater potential for confusion and bugs.

Second, program throughput usually improves in multithreaded programs. Blocking one part of the program, such as the image fetch just mentioned, doesn't prevent other parts from getting their own work done.

Third, multiprocessor systems are becoming increasingly common and important. A program written with multithreading from the ground up can benefit directly and strongly from running different threads concurrently on different processors.

Integrated support for threads is a key facet of Java technology. As explained further on in this chapter, the Java platform provides synchronization (monitor) locks (Q9.6, Q9.7), the synchronized keyword (Q9.8), and classes like Thread (Q9.2) and ThreadGroup to make the multithreaded programmer's life more productive and less error-prone.

See also: Q9.2, Q9.6, Q9.7, Q9.8

Q9.2

How do I create a thread and start it running?

Create an instance of Thread **or of a** Thread **subclass, and invoke** start **on that instance.**

The Java programming language and virtual machine represent threads with instances of the Thread class. At the heart of every thread is a run method, which determines the body of code the thread will execute in its lifetime. The Thread class provides two ways to specify what run method the thread will execute:

- define a run method in a Thread subclass
- adopt the run method of an object that implements the Runnable interface

The first approach is to subclass Thread and override its run method. This approach is more straightforward, and works best when the data needed for running the thread is fairly self-contained. At a minimum, you can define a subclass of Thread with nothing more than a new run method. The following Thread subclass, for example, represents a thread of execution that can print out the square roots of integers from 1 to 1,000,000:

```java
public class SquareRootThread extends Thread {
    public void run() {
        for (int i = 1; i <= 1000000; ++i) {
            System.out.println("Math.sqrt(" + i + ") = "
                                + Math.sqrt(i));
        }
    }
}
```

This class definition merely specifies what the thread can do. To execute the thread's code, you create an instance of the class and invoke start on it:

```java
Thread t1 = new SquareRootThread();
t1.start();
```

Invoking start on a Thread instance starts a new, separately scheduled thread in the Java Virtual Machine, which then executes the code specified in the run method of that Thread subclass.

The second approach, using the Runnable interface, is less direct but often more useful. A new Thread instance can be created based on any object from a class that implements the Runnable interface (Q1.21). A Runnable object must include a definition for a run method that takes no parameters and has no return value: public void run() { /* ... */ }.

A Thread instance created from a Runnable object takes the run method of that object's class as its own code to execute. For example, Applet subclasses are commonly defined to implement Runnable so that their run methods can execute in a separate thread:

```
public class MyApplet extends java.applet.Applet
                        implements Runnable {
    public void run() {
        doThis();
        doThat();
    }
    // ...
}
```

You can create an instance of the Thread class using the Thread(Runnable) constructor. Once you have the Thread instance, you start it just like any other thread:

```
// ... "this" refers to the current applet instance
Thread t2 = new Thread(this);
t2.start();
```

A primary reason to create a thread from a Runnable object is to take advantage of full insider access to that object. Inside an applet, a run method has direct access to all the applet's data and methods. A Thread subclass, on the other hand, would be limited to only an outsider's view of the applet, which is typically just the public methods. In short, if your thread depends strongly on a certain object for its execution, you should should define that object's class to implement the Runnable interface, and construct a Thread instance from the object.

CreateThreadExample.html

See also: Q1.21, Q9.1, Q9.3

Q9.3

How does Thread's stop *method work—can I restart a stopped thread?*

Thread's stop **method stops a thread permanently—that thread cannot be run again.**

A Thread instance has three main phases in its existence:

1. prebirth: creation and configuration, before being started

2. life: execution of code, after being started and before terminating

3. death: postmortem, after terminating, but before being garbage collected

Creating and starting a Thread instance (Q9.2) brings a thread to life. A thread continues to execute code until it reaches the end of its run method or until stop is invoked on it. The Thread class's stop method could just as well be named *kill* or *terminate*. The method is not a hint, but a command—it irrevocably ends the execution phase of the thread. The thread may not die immediately, because it is in a sleep (Q9.5) or a wait (Q9.10), but in that case it is fated to die as soon as it awakes. Also, any synchronization locks (Q9.7) held by the terminated thread are automatically released. Once the Thread instance has reached this postmortem phase, you can no longer run code with it; you can only inspect its state.

Restarting a stopped thread is not possible, but you can achieve much the same effect by creating a new Thread instance to run the same code (Q9.4).

StopExample.html

See also: Q9.2, Q9.4, Q9.5, Q9.7, Q9.10

Q9.4

How should I stop a thread so that I can start a new thread later in its place?

Use the cooperative approach wherever possible: set a flag to indicate that the thread should stop, but let the targeted thread itself check for the flag and find a safe place to stop.

Early Java programs commonly used Thread's stop method (Q9.3) to terminate threads, especially in applet start and stop methods (Q4.18). For example:

```
/* common in applets, but NOT recommended: */
Thread myThread;
public void start() {
    if (myThread == null) {
        myThread = new Thread(this);
    }
    myThread.start();
}
```

```
public void stop() {
    myThread.stop();
    myThread = null;
}
```

This technique is simple but *dangerous!* Invoking stop on a thread is analogous to killing a process without warning: execution ceases, but there are no guarantees about what state the program is left in. Moreover, if another Thread instance is created to continue execution where the previous thread left off, an inconsistent state left by the earlier thread can inflict serious damage on your program.

In general, you should design your program so that a running thread can choose a safe place to stop itself. It's best to save the stop method for cases when you truly need to terminate an uncooperative thread. (While on the topic of methods to avoid, note also that suspend and resume are considered dangerous, or downright evil, by many Java developers.)

In normal cases, several conditions are desirable when starting and stopping a thread for an applet:

- Only one thread at a time can be running the applet code.

- Invoking start on the applet either starts a new thread for the applet or lets an existing thread continue running.

- Invoking stop on the applet registers a request that the running thread stop; a subsequent invocation of start can cancel that request.

The following code framework meets the conditions just specified:

```
boolean stopRequested = false;
Thread myThread;
/** Starts new thread for applet if applet doesn't have one. */
public synchronized void start() {
    if (myThread == null) {
        myThread = new Thread(this);
        myThread.start();
    }
    stopRequested = false;
}

/** Requests that this applet stop its activity. */
public synchronized void stop() {
    stopRequested = true;
}
```

```
/** Runs applet code in its own thread. */
public void run() {
    // ... thread activity
    /* At safe stopping point, check if thread should quit: */
    synchronized (this) {
        if (stopRequested) {
            // ... perform any quick cleanup necessary
            stopRequested = false;
            myThread = null;
            return;  // returning from run finishes current thread
        }
    }
    // ... further thread activity and flag checks
    }
}  // reaching end of run finishes current thread
```

HowToStopThreadExample.html

See also: Q9.2, Q9.3, Q9.16

Q9.5

How do I specify pause times in my program?

Use one of the sleep **methods in the** Thread **class.**

The Thread class's sleep methods let you time a thread's activities, or simply wait for a while, without wasting system resources. In the more commonly used version, you specify the number of milliseconds (thousandths of a second) that the current thread should cease execution. For example, to pause half a second between two portions of code, you could write:

```
// ... code before the pause
try {
    Thread.sleep(500);
} catch (InterruptedException e) {
    // ... handle exception
}
// ... code after the pause
```

Note that sleep can throw an InterruptedException, which your code must handle or explicitly ignore (Q2.23).

The sleep methods are class methods (Q1.6)—they belong to the Thread class but are not invoked on any particular Thread instance. Nevertheless, a sleep method knows which thread to pause: the thread that is currently executing.

Note: The wait methods in class Object provide an important alternative way to control a thread's pauses (Q9.10).

SleepExample.html

See also: Q1.6, Q2.23, Q9.10

THREAD INTERACTIONS

Q9.6

Why is thread synchronization important for multithreaded programs?

Thread synchronization provides the tool for ensuring that different threads take proper turns when using shared resources.

In general, multiple threads in a program run independently of one another. Each follows its sequence of commands, blithely ignorant of other threads or their activities. As long as a thread works with its own, separate data, the most it might suffer from other threads is to be slowed down because of sharing CPU time, if the number of threads is greater than the number of available processors.

A key property of threads, however, is their ability to directly access shared data. This ability is both a blessing and a curse because it allows threads to:

- communicate efficiently with each other by manipulating shared data

- interfere capriciously with each other by manipulating shared data

When threads act on shared data, timing is the crucial issue. You must always consider how one thread might disrupt the data used by another thread, by executing some of its instructions in between the instructions that the other is executing. (This potential for interleaved execution is true on both single-processor and multiprocessor platforms.) Even code that appears bullet-proof can be slain by an intervening thread. Consider, for example, the `getTitleLength` method in the following class definition:

```
public class SomeClass {
    String title = "Default Title";
    int getTitleLength() {
        if (title != null) {
            return title.length();
        }
        return -1;     // signal error condition
    }

    void setTitle(String s) {
        title = s;
    }

    void deleteTitle() {
        title = null;
    }
}
```

Suppose one thread (thread X) is about to run `getTitleLength`, and another thread (thread Y) is about to run `deleteTitle`. Thread X, entering `getTitleLength`, checks that the title string is non-null before invoking `length()` on it. Thread Y, however, can interpose between these two steps and invoke `deleteTitle`. The title string is now `null`, and thread X's next step will invoke the `length` method on a `null` reference — just what the `if` statement was supposed to prevent!

Safe multithreaded use of data requires that different threads must operate either on separate data or at different times. Since threads must often share data, the Java programming language provides the `synchronized` keyword to mark methods or blocks of code that cannot overlap each other in time (Q9.7, Q9.8).

See also: Q9.7, Q9.8

Q9.7

What is a monitor?

A monitor is a one-thread-at-a-time set of code-blocks and methods that also provides a wait-notify service.

When multiple threads access common, changeable data, you must regulate the timing of those threads to ensure that one thread doesn't interfere with another thread's assumptions of data integrity (Q9.6, Q9.8). The Java platform lets you restrict thread interactions by means of monitors. A monitor groups a set of code blocks into a single protected space, such that only one thread at a time can be *in the monitor,* that is, executing any of the code under the monitor's protection.

A monitor uses a mutual exclusion lock to protect its region of code. A thread must acquire/lock the lock in order to *enter* the monitor, and it relinquishes/unlocks the lock when it *exits* the monitor. While a monitor is locked, it blocks any other threads that attempt to enter it. Monitor locks also allow recursive access: once a thread has the lock, it can run other code that requires the same lock, effectively re-entering the monitor one level down. The lock is not released until the thread holding it completely exits the monitor at all levels. Only at that point can another thread enter the monitor.

A monitor also provides a wait-notify service to threads. A thread in the monitor can invoke `wait`, which releases the monitor lock and puts the thread to sleep until it is awakened by a `notifyAll` (or `notify`) method invocation (Q9.10).

You can use many different monitors in a single program to guard different parts of your data. Each monitor is associated with a specific class or object; this connection is often described in terms such as "each object has a monitor," or "each object has a lock." Keep in mind, though, that a monitor provides *no inherent protection* to its affiliated object. It's still up to you to choose carefully which code to include in monitors in order to protect your data.

Here's an alternate view of the preceding concept-heavy explanation. Let's call code that belongs to one or another monitor "protected code," and all other code "unprotected code." Imagine that each object in your program owns a unique, reusable ticket. Threads can execute unprotected code freely at any time—no tickets are required. Protected code, however, always requires a thread to have a ticket, and each synchronized statement or method specifies which object that ticket must come from. The thread holds on to the ticket while executing the protected code block or method, and hands the ticket back to its owner object immediately upon exiting the protected code. Because there is only one ticket per object, any other threads needing that ticket are forced to wait and then proceed in an orderly, one-by-one fashion through any protected portion of code.

See also: Q9.8, Q9.10

Q9.8

How does the synchronized *keyword work?*

The synchronized **keyword marks portions of code as belonging to a monitor: a protected portion of code that enforces a one-thread-at-a-time policy.**

The Java Virtual Machine provides monitors (Q9.7) as the fundamental concept for managing thread synchronization. Part of a monitor's function is to protect a set of code blocks and methods, such that only one thread at a time can execute any of the code belonging to the monitor. Each object is associated with a monitor, and you access a monitor by referring to its affiliated object.

You cannot directly inspect or manipulate monitors; instead, you define the scope of a monitor implicitly by specifying the code blocks and methods it contains. This is the job of synchronized statements and synchronized methods.

A synchronized statement specifies an object and a block of code: it flags the code block as belonging to the specified object's monitor. For example, much of the JDK 1.1 code for managing AWT (Abstract Window Toolkit) containment relationships (Q5.1) uses the Component.LOCK object in synchronized statements:

```
/* in Component.java (JDK 1.1): */
static final Object LOCK = new Object();
// ...
public void validate() {
    if (!valid) {
        synchronized (Component.LOCK) {
            valid = true;
        }
    }
}
```

A synchronized method is like a synchronized statement, except that it specifies only the block of code. The entire method body belongs to the target object's monitor (that is, the monitor of the object the method is invoked on). Following is the example from Q9.8, modified to contain one synchronized statement and two synchronized methods:

```
public class SomeClass {
    String title = "Default Title";
    int getTitleLength() {
        /* a synchronized statement */
        synchronized(this) {
            if (title != null) {
                return title.length();
            }
        }
        return -1;    // signal error condition
    }

    /* a synchronized method */
    synchronized void setTitle(String s) {
        title = s;
    }
```

```
        /* another synchronized method */
        synchronized void deleteTitle() {
            title = null;
        }
    }
```

This code specifies that each SomeClass instance has a monitor containing (at the least) the if statement inside of getTitleLength, the entire body of setTitle, and the entire body of deleteTitle.

Finally, the following are some key points to remember about the relation between monitors and the synchronized keyword. They were discussed earlier but deserve one more round of emphasis:

- Monitors define synchronization-protected sets of code blocks.

- Monitors are the fundamental unit of synchronization. Synchronized statements and synchronized methods merely serve to assign blocks of code to various monitors.

- Synchronized code is synchronized only with respect to other synchronized code in the same monitor. Unsynchronized code pays no attention to monitors, locks, etc.

- The monitor/lock associated with an object does *not* inherently lock the data in the object. Instead, it is like a per-monitor access ticket. Monitors fundamentally protect code, not data.

SynchronizationExample.html

See also: Q9.7, Q9.8

Q9.9

What objects do static synchronized *methods use for locking?*

Methods declared as static synchronized **are class methods; they must obtain a lock on the class object.**

All synchronized code is associated with one or another object for purposes of locking (Q9.7, Q9.8). Although synchronized methods don't explicitly indicate the object to use for locking, the rule is straightforward: a synchronized instance method obtains the lock for the object it's invoked on, and a synchronized class method obtains the lock for the class object (instance of class `Class`; see Q2.15) that represents the class.

Synchronized class methods (that is, static synchronized methods) give you a class object implicitly, but for static synchronized statements you must provide the class object explicitly. Two methods provide class objects for you:

- `Object`'s `getClass` method; this requires that you have an instance of the class on hand or are willing to create one

- `Class`'s `forName` method; this allows you to create a class object from a string representing the class's fully qualified name (Q1.30)

Starting with the JDK 1.1, you can also access class objects directly from a class's `class` field. For example, `Thread.class` is a reference to the class object for the `Thread` class.

Suppose that you have an instance `myTimer` of your `Timer` class; you can then use the first technique:

```
Timer myTimer = new Timer();
void myMethod() {
    // ...
    synchronized (myTimer.getClass()) {
        // ... code that requires synchronization
    }
}
```

Suppose next that you want to lock on the AWT's `Component` class. `Component` is an abstract class; therefore you cannot create instances of it. In the JDK 1.0.2, you have no choice but to use `Class`'s `forName` method (and deal with the `ClassNotFoundException` that `forName` can throw; see Q2.23):

```
void anotherMethod() {
    // ...
    try {
        synchronized (Class.forName("java.awt.Component")) {
            // ... code that requires synchronization
        }
    } catch (ClassNotFoundException e) {
        // ... handle the exception
    }
}
```

In the JDK 1.1, the preceding `Component` example can be simplified considerably:

```
/* using JDK 1.1: */
void anotherMethod() {
    // ...
    synchronized (Component.class) {
        // ... body of synchronized block
    }
}
```

See also: Q1.30, Q2.23, Q9.7, Q9.8

Q9.10

How do the wait *and* notifyAll/notify *methods enable cooperation between threads?*

They use a monitor as the middleman: wait **places the invoking thread on the monitor's waiting list for notifications, and** notifyAll (or notify) **instructs the monitor to reactivate all (or one) of the threads in its notification list.**

In contrast to the synchronized keyword, which helps threads stay out of each other's way, the wait and notifyAll/notify methods in class Object permit threads to cooperate actively. A thread invoking wait voluntarily suspends its activity, trusting that another thread will invoke notifyAll or notify to eventually reactivate the waiting thread. (Two versions of wait let you specify also a maximum waiting time, such that wait will return even if no notifications are received.) The working of these methods is personified in Table 9.1, from the point of view of a thread invoking the method on an object.

The wait and notifyAll/notify methods constitute a minimal framework of controlled interaction between threads. The service provided by these methods is:

- *mediated:* monitors must serve as middlemen between waiting threads and notifying threads; the threads never communicate directly.

- *anonymous:* a waiting thread can't specify which thread will notify/reactivate it, and a notifying thread can't specify which thread(s) it will reactivate.

- *contentless:* a reactivated thread receives no indication of what happened to trigger the notification. If the thread needs to know why it was reactivated, it must infer the cause from whatever data it has access to (Q9.11).

- *not guaranteed to be fair:* there is no required order in which to notify waiting threads. It is possible for a thread to remain on the wait queue arbitrarily long while other threads are chosen for notification. (Nevertheless, fairness is a desirable trait that virtual machine implementations should aim for.)

Table 9.1: `wait`, `notifyAll`, **and** `notify`

Method	Actions and constraints
`wait`	I deactivate myself, and ask this object's monitor to enter me on its notification waiting list.
	I must own the lock on this monitor at the point I invoke `wait`, but I release the lock as soon as I start waiting.
	When I wake up, I must reacquire the lock; this may take some time if one or more other threads beat me to it.
	When I acquire the lock, `wait` will return; I can then continue running.
`notifyAll`	I tell this object's monitor to reactivate all threads on its notification waiting list.
	I must own the lock on this monitor at the point I invoke `notifyAll`.
	None of the awakened threads can run until I release the lock.
`notify`	I tell this object's monitor to reactivate only one of its waiting threads (and I can't say which one).
	I must own the lock on this monitor at the point I invoke `notify`.
	The awakened thread can't run until I release the lock.

Finally, keep in mind that invoking `notifyAll` does *not* wake up all the threads in an application; it affects only those threads that are waiting on one specific monitor.

WaitNotifyExample.html

See also: Q9.11

Q9.11

How do I achieve the effect of condition variables if the Java platform provides me with only `wait` *and* `notifyAll`/`notify` *methods?*

Invoke `wait` **within a** `while` **loop that tests for the condition you're interested in, and make sure that other threads invoke** `notifyAll` **(or** `notify`**) at points where you think or know the condition will change.**

The idea behind a condition variable is that a waiting thread should be reactivated when a specified condition arises, but not otherwise. The Java language does not provide such a service—the interaction provided by the wait, notifyAll, and notify methods is anonymous and contentless (Q9.10), and no conditions are checked prior to reactivating a thread. When a waiting thread is awakened, it receives no information about who triggered the wakeup or why. The newly reactivated thread must determine for itself if the condition it's waiting for has arrived.

To achieve the effect of a condition variable, place your invocation of wait inside a while statement. (Do *not* use an if statement—the condition could change while the thread is waiting and it must be rechecked.) For example, the following Thread subclass waits until the amount of free memory drops below a predetermined level and then takes action:

```
class MemoryWatcherThread extends Thread {
    long lowMemoryLine = ...;

    public void run() {
        Runtime runtime = Runtime.getRuntime();
        while (true) {
            synchronized (Runtime.class) {
                while (runtime.freeMemory() >= lowMemoryLine) {
                    try {
                        wait(5000);   // wait up to 5 seconds
                    } catch (InterruptedException e) {
                    }
                }
            }
            // ... respond to low memory level
        }
    }
}
```

(If you're using the JDK 1.0.2, you need to replace the expression Runtime.class above with Runtime.getRuntime.getClass().) In this code, there are two ways a MemoryWatcherThread instance (call it a watcher thread) can become active. First, the invocation of wait specifies a maximum waiting time of five seconds (5000 milliseconds), after which wait will return. Second, any other thread invoking notifyAll (or notify) may wake up the watcher thread before that five-second time limit expires. For whichever reason the watcher thread reactivates, the thread (after acquiring the monitor lock) then goes back to the top of the while loop and checks the free memory level. If the level is not too low, the watcher thread goes into another wait; otherwise it runs its code to deal with the low memory level.

Continuing the example, objects from other classes can effectively request action from a watcher thread by notifying the monitor in which the watcher thread is waiting:

```
/* using JDK 1.1: */
    class Example {
    void checkMemory() {
        synchronized (Runtime.class) {
            Runtime.class.notifyAll();
        }
    }
    // ...
}
```

Using notifyAll ensures that all threads waiting on the monitor will be noti-fied — it lets each waiting thread decide for itself whether to reactivate or continue waiting. Using notify, on the other hand, would wake up only one waiting thread, and quite possibly the wrong one. In general, you shouldn't use notify unless you know precisely which single thread will be waiting for it, or you know that any of the waiting threads could respond equally well to the notification.

ConditionVariableExample.html

See also: Q9.10

Q9.12

How do I make one thread wait for one or more other threads to finish?

Use one of Thread's join **methods.**

Threads are designed for the most part to run independently of one another. Typically, one thread neither knows nor cares when another thread finishes executing. If you need one of your threads to wait for another thread to finish, however, you can use one of the join methods in the Thread class.

Invoking join involves two threads even though the method invocation only shows one, as in thatThread.join(). The second thread is implicit — it is the currently executing thread. The invocation of join causes the currently executing thread to suspend execution until the target thread (thatThread in the above exam-ple) finishes executing. In other words, invoking join on a thread is like waiting to be notified of that thread's death.

Also, like the `wait` methods, there is a family of `join` methods. The basic no-parameter method, `join()`, waits indefinitely until the target thread dies. You can also specify one or two arguments as a maximum duration to wait:

- `join(long millis)`: wait no more than the specified number of milliseconds (thousandths of a second).

- `join(long millis, int nanos)`: wait no more than the specified number of milliseconds and nanoseconds (billionths of a second).

A key difference from `wait` is that `join` need not and should not hold a monitor lock when it is invoked.

For reference, Table 9.2 summarizes the methods that can suspend a thread's execution (without irrevocably terminating it):

Table 9.2: Methods that can Suspend Thread Execution

Class	Methods
Thread	`sleep(long millis)`, `sleep(long millis, int nanos)`
	`join()`, `join(long millis)`, `join(long millis, int nanos)`
	`suspend()`
Object	`wait()`, `wait(long millis)`, `wait(long millis, int nanos)`

JoinExample.html

See also: Q9.5, Q9.10

Q9.13

What do I use the `yield` *method for?*

You invoke `yield` **in one thread to give other threads more chances to run.**

Any platform that runs more than one thread per processor needs to have a thread scheduler—a strategy for deciding when to switch execution from one thread to another, and which other thread to switch to. A thread scheduler typically regulates turn-taking according to thread states and thread priorities. The following thread states distinguish among which threads are executing or have the potential to execute:

- *running:* currently executing

- *runnable:* ready to run, but not currently executing

- *waiting:* not ready to run; must first be reactivated by a timer, a notification, or a `resume` method invocation

- *dead:* finished executing, cannot run anymore

By definition, only the running and runnable threads are considered when the scheduler picks the next thread to run.

Thread priorities further differentiate among the threads waiting to run. Whenever a thread scheduler has a choice between a lower- and higher-priority thread, it is supposed to prefer the higher-priority one. There are no guarantees, though. Thread priorities should be considered at best as hints, rather than as reliable tools for design.

The Java Virtual Machine specification leaves many details of thread scheduling open to the implementation. For example, the thread scheduler may or may not time-slice, that is, interrupt a currently executing thread after a given amount of time to give another thread a turn. In the JDK (1.0.2 and 1.1), for example, the Windows NT/95 implementation provides time-slicing, whereas the Solaris implementation does not (Q9.15).

The `yield` method gives you explicit control over a small piece of the thread-scheduling picture. By invoking `yield`, a thread voluntarily ends its turn at executing, so that the thread scheduler can choose which thread to run next. (That thread can even be the same one that just invoked `yield`, if the scheduler so chooses.) Using `yield` judiciously, such as in computation-intensive loops, enhances turn-taking and fairness among threads, especially when running on a virtual machine implementation that does not provide time-slicing. It also helps your program behave more consistently across platforms.

Moral: Time-slicing and thread priorities are dangerously variable across virtual machine implementations; for program correctness, design with synchronization and `yield`.

See also: Q9.15

Q9.14

Does the Java Virtual Machine protect me against deadlocks?

Yes and no: a Java Virtual Machine implementation should be designed to avoid deadlocks within its own code, but it cannot prevent your code from deadlocking.

A deadlock occurs when two or more threads each hold a resource that another is waiting for—neither thread can proceed to the point where it would free up the resource that the other one is waiting for. In Java code, the precious resource is usually a monitor lock needed for a synchronized method or synchronized block (Q9.7, Q9.8). If your code holds one lock and then tries to acquire another lock, you run the risk of getting deadlocked.

The prototypical scenario for a deadlock is the following:

1. Thread 1 includes code that acquires the lock for object X (call it lock X) and, while holding that lock, needs to acquire the lock for object Y (call it lock Y).

2. Thread 2 includes code that acquires lock Y and, while holding that lock, needs to acquire lock X.

3. Thread 1 runs, acquires lock X, and, before acquiring lock Y, gets put on hold by the thread scheduler, giving another thread a turn to run.

4. Thread 2 runs, acquires lock Y, and then tries to acquire lock X. Thread 2 blocks at this point because it can't get the lock—thread 1 is holding it. The thread scheduler tries to find another runnable thread.

5. Thread 1 runs up to the point it tries to acquire lock Y. Thread 1 then blocks because it can't get the lock—thread 2 is holding it. Threads 1 and 2 are now deadlocked. Neither can move forward because it needs a resource that the other is holding, and neither can release the resource it's holding until after it has moved forward.

The Java Virtual Machine does not attempt to prevent your program from deadlocking as it executes—that's simply too hard a problem to solve in general. A virtual machine implementation, however, can make it easier to diagnose and pinpoint cases of deadlock after they've happened. The JDK (1.0.2 and 1.1), for instance, lets you trigger full dumps of the threads and monitors currently used by the virtual machine. As your program is running, you can send a quit signal (ctrl-break on Win32, ctrl-backslash on Solaris) and get a current picture of the threads and monitors at work in your virtual machine. Following is an example triggered on Solaris while running a *DeadlockExample* class:

```
Full thread dump:
    "Thread-5" (TID:0xe6f009f8, sys_thread_t:0xe6a61de0) prio=5

DeadlockThread.grabSecondLock(DeadlockExample.java:100)

DeadlockThread.grabFirstLock(DeadlockExample.java:95)
        DeadlockThread.grabLocks(DeadlockExample.java:88)
        DeadlockThread.run(DeadlockExample.java:68)
    "Thread-4" (TID:0xe6f00998, sys_thread_t:0xe6a91de0) prio=5

DeadlockThread.grabSecondLock(DeadlockExample.java:100)

DeadlockThread.grabFirstLock(DeadlockExample.java:95)
        DeadlockThread.grabLocks(DeadlockExample.java:88)
        DeadlockThread.run(DeadlockExample.java:68)
    "Finalizer thread" (TID:..., sys_thread_t:...) prio=1
    "Async Garbage Collector" (TID:..., sys_thread_t:...) prio=1
    "Idle thread" (TID:..., sys_thread_t:...) prio=0 *current
thread*
    "clock handler" (TID:0xe6f00180, sys_thread_t:0xe6bf1de0)
prio=11
    "main" (TID:0xe6f00150, sys_thread_t:0x39990) prio=7
        DeadlockExample.main(DeadlockExample.java:31)
Monitor Cache Dump:
        unknown key (key=0xe6af1de0):        unowned
        Waiting to be notified:
            "Async Garbage Collector"
        java.lang.String@...:  monitor owner e6a61de0: "Thread-5"
        Waiting to enter:
            "Thread-4"
        java.lang.String@...:  monitor owner e6a91de0: "Thread-4"
        Waiting to enter:
            "Thread-5"
        unknown key (key=0x39990):        unowned
        Waiting to be notified:
                    "main"
```

This thread-and-monitor dump reveals that Thread-4 and Thread-5 are dead-locked. The Full thread dump section shows that Thread-4 and Thread-5 are each stuck in their own grabSecondLock method. The Monitor Cache Dump shows why: Thread-5 owns one lock (monitor owner) that Thread-4 is waiting for (Waiting to enter), and Thread-4 owns a lock that Thread-5 is waiting for.

When you suspect your program is deadlocked, trigger a thread-and-monitor dump and check first for this telltale waiting-to-enter, monitor-owner pattern. It would be nice if future implementations automated this check.

DeadlockExample.html

See also: Q9.7, Q9.8

USER THREADS VERSUS SYSTEM THREADS

Q9.15

Why does my multithreaded program run fine on Windows NT/95 but block on Solaris?

Most likely, you are seeing the difference between time-slicing on the Windows NT/95 JDK implementation versus no time-slicing on the Solaris JDK implementation; differing treatment of thread priorities may also be a factor.

Java technology places a premium on cross-platform compatibility and predictability, but some aspects of multithreaded behavior remain underspecified. Two key area where implementations vary are turn-taking and thread priorities.

The JDK (1.0.2 and 1.1) employs native, operating system-level threads in its Windows NT/95 implementation. This provides Java programs with time-slicing (guaranteed turn-taking) among equal-priority threads. The JDK (1.0.2 and 1.1) implementation on Solaris, on the other hand, runs on a user-level thread package, which is built on top of a single native process. In the Solaris implementation, equal-priority threads are *not* guaranteed to interrupt each other. The thread scheduler can switch among threads of equal priority, but it must be triggered by some event such as a blocking input/output call, a wait, or some change that could reactivate a higher-priority thread. Without such triggers (also called reschedule points), one thread can run to completion, or practically forever, before another equal-priority thread gets a turn.

In general, time-slicing gives the expected behavior in a multithreaded program: each thread gets some portion of time to execute, mixed in with the execution time given to other threads. Without time-slicing, you can get surprising results. A long-lived thread with no waits or sleeps, for example, can simply keep running, and other threads will be blocked out. Even more dramatically, the whole user interface can freeze up if your applet thread has the same priority as one of the AWT system threads. To avert such mishaps, your program can use Thread's yield method (Q9.13) to provide platform-independent turn-taking hints.

Remember: Do not depend on time-slicing and thread priorities for your program's correctness. To ensure that your various threads run according to your design, choose your synchronization strategy carefully and invoke yield wherever it makes sense to give another thread a turn at running.

See also: Q9.13

Q9.16

Why do so many applets run a copy of themselves in a separate thread rather than just running as they are?

Running a separate thread for much of your applet code is good defensive programming — otherwise your applet's errors can delay or hang an important system thread.

When you write a program, it is important to distinguish between threads that your program creates and controls (*user threads*) and threads that are created and controlled outside of your program, by the operating system or a browser (*system threads*). What you do with your (user) threads is your own business, because other programs do not depend on them. However, if your code misbehaves while a system thread is running it, not only is your program derailed, but so is any other program that is waiting to be run on that thread.

As mentioned in Q4.2, one of the special characteristics of an applet is that certain applet methods are invoked by the browser rather than the applet itself: the applet's flow of execution is partly determined by its browser context. The browser context will invoke several different methods that your applet should be prepared to handle: `init`, `start`, `stop`, and `destroy` (Q4.16).

System threads are an important resource on loan to your applet. Use them sparingly and responsibly. Write your system-called methods so that they can execute quickly and without surprises. Consider creating a new thread for operations that may take an indefinite amount of time to complete, or may otherwise be risky.

SystemThreadsExample.html

See also: Q4.2, Q4.16, Q9.4, Q9.17

Q9.17

How can it be that putting an applet thread to sleep in the wrong place can block other applets from running?

Some browser implementations employ a single thread to invoke special methods on their applets; if your applet runs in such a browser and blocks this thread, then it blocks all the other applets depending on the same thread.

How an applet runs in a browser is mostly platform independent. One of the areas in which browsers can differ, though, is in what system threads they use to run applets within them.

A browser might choose, for instance, to control each applet in a separate thread. In this case, if one applet accidentally blocks a thread for good, it wouldn't interfere with other applets. On pages with many, many applets, however, the overhead of one thread per applet can be prohibitive.

A different browser might choose to provide a single AWT (Abstract Window Toolkit) thread that runs all applets in the browser. If one applet blocks this thread, it prevents any other applets on the page from receiving window events.

As an applet writer, you should never invoke `sleep` in one of the *callback* methods, that is, one of the methods that the browser uses to call into your code. This includes the the applet life-cycle methods — `init`, `start`, `stop`, and `destroy` (Q4.16) — as well as `paint` (Q8.1), `update` (Q8.5), and any of the event-handler methods (Q6.4, Q7.3).

BlockAWTThreadExample.html

See also: Q4.16, Q6.4, Q7.3, Q8.1, Q8.5, Q9.16

Q9.18

Can I have a thread wait on an event from the operating system?

No; the standard Java classes are cross-platform; they do not provide direct access to any platform-dependent features.

CHAPTER 10

Input, Output, and Network

Basic Input and Output (Q10.1–Q10.6)

URL Connections (Q10.7–Q10.15)

Internet Addresses (Q10.16–Q10.18)

Sockets (Q10.19–Q10.27)

BASIC INPUT AND OUTPUT

Q10.1

How do I read a line of input at a time?

In the JDK 1.0.2, use the `readLine` **method in the** `DataInputStream` **class; in the JDK 1.1, use** `readLine` **in either** `BufferedReader` **or** `LineNumberReader`**.**

The `DataInputStream` class is a hidden workhorse in the Java input/output system. The class exists chiefly to read various data types in binary format from an input stream (Q10.3). It also provides a `readLine` method for reading one line of input at a time.

The `readLine` method reads from the current input position up to a line terminator. For cross-platform compatibility, `readLine` recognizes as line terminators the bytes for newline (\n), carriage return (\r), and the byte sequence newline-return (\n\r). Reaching the end of a file also counts as terminating an input line. Invoking `readLine` at the end of the input stream returns `null`.

The following sample code defines a method that calculates the average line length of text in the input stream:

```
/* using JDK 1.0.2: */
public static float getAverageLineLength(InputStream in)
                    throws IOException {
    DataInputStream dataIn = new DataInputStream(in);
    String currentLine;
    int lineCount = 0;
    int charCount = 0;
    while ((currentLine = dataIn.readLine()) != null) {
        ++lineCount;
        charCount += currentLine.length();
    }
    return (charCount / (float) lineCount);
}
```

DataInputStream's readLine method reads bytes, but it outputs a Java string containing 2-byte Unicode characters. Each input byte gets translated to a Unicode character by using the input byte as the output character's low byte and setting the output character's high byte to zero. Thus, DataInputStream's readLine method assumes that each input byte is a 8-bit character, which renders the method unfit for reading lines of Unicode text in general.

The JDK 1.1 fills in the Unicode input deficiency with a suite of ...Reader classes, which truly read Unicode input characters (Java's char type) rather than just byte streams. For line-oriented input, in particular, you can use the readLine method in either the BufferedReader or LineNumberReader classes. The sample method, rewritten to use LineNumberReader, follows:

```
/* using JDK 1.1: */
public static float getAverageLineLength(InputStream in)
                    throws IOException {
    LineNumberReader lineReader = new LineNumberReader(
                                    new InputStreamReader(in));
    String currentLine;
    int charCount = 0;
    while ((currentLine = lineReader.readLine()) != null) {
        charCount += currentLine.length();
    }
    return (charCount / (float) lineReader.getLineNumber());
}
```

This example also illustrates using the InputStreamReader class to convert from a byte-oriented input stream to a char-oriented Reader. The LineNumberReader instance is then constructed from that Reader object.

ReadLineExample.html, ReadLineExample11.html

See also: Q10.3

Q10.2

How do I read input from the user (or send output) analogous to using standard input and standard output in C or C++?

Use the standard system streams: `System.in`, `System.out`, **and** `System.err`.

C and C++ define standard input/output libraries (collections of compiled functions) that rely heavily on three input/output streams, called standard input, standard output, and standard error. The analogue in Java to a library in C or C++ is a Java language package (Q1.29). Completing the analogy, the `java.io` package defines essentially the same three streams, which you access as fields of the `System` class:

- `System.in`: standard input; the customary input stream for keyboard input when a program lacks a graphical user interface (GUI).

- `System.out`: standard output; the customary output stream for programs that lack a GUI.

- `System.err`: standard error; the customary output stream for error output in programs that lack a GUI.

`System.in` is an instance of `InputStream` and `System.out` and `System.err` are instances of class `PrintStream`.

If you want just string output (to either `System.out` or `System.err`), the `PrintStream` methods `print` and `println`, together with the string concatenation operator +, provide straightforward tools that get the job done (in the JDK 1.0.2). For example, the following code prints the value of one `int` variable and one `float` variable to `System.out`:

```
/* using JDK 1.0.2: */
int intValue = 3;
float floatValue = 3.1416F;
System.out.println("My int value = " + intValue + ".");
System.out.println("My float value = " + floatValue + ".");
```

For proper handling of Unicode text, the JDK 1.1 supersedes many of the byte-stream input/output classes with Unicode text-oriented classes: `Reader`, `Writer`, and their many subclasses. The `PrintStream` class, for example, is superseded by the `PrintWriter` class, with its own version of `print` and `println`. Thus, to use `println` to write to the standard output, you build a `PrintWriter` instance from the underlying `System.out` byte stream:

```
/* using JDK 1.1: */
int intValue = 3;
float floatValue = 3.1416F;
PrintWriter writer;
// Create a PrintWriter with autoflush set to true,
// so that each newline will automatically flush the output.
writer = new PrintWriter(System.out, true);
writer.println("My int value = " + intValue + ".");
writer.println("My float value = " + floatValue + ".");
```

Warning: When migrating code from 1.0.2 to 1.1, you may encounter some nasty surprises unless you carefully match the automatic flushing behavior of System.out. Use PrintWriter's two-parameter constructor, with the second argument set to true; this ensures that the output will be flushed once for each newline you send.

Reading from System.in is more complicated, depending on what format you're expecting to read the data in. System.in gives you a plain input byte stream, which has no idea of input formats and can read only one byte at a time. For more control over your input, you need to build a fuller-featured input stream around System.in, such as a DataInputStream instance. The following code fragment shows a DataInputStream instance reading one line of input at a time:

```
/* using JDK 1.0.2: */
String currentLine;
DataInputStream inStream = new DataInputStream(System.in);
try {
    while ((currentLine = inStream.readLine()) != null) {
        // ... process current line
    }
} catch (IOException e) { /* ... */ }
    // ... handle exception
}
```

Updating this code for JDK 1.1 primarily involves wrapping a BufferedReader instance around System.in (Q10.1):

```
/* using JDK 1.1: */
String currentLine;
BufferedReader reader;
reader = new BufferedReader(new InputStreamReader(System.in));
try {
    while ((currentLine = reader.readLine()) != null) {
        // ... process current line
    }
} catch (IOException e) { /* ... */ }
```

For further discussion of how to deal with input data in different formats, see Q10.1, Q10.3, and Q10.4.

StandardInputOutputExample.html, StandardInputOutput11Example.html

See also: Q10.1, Q10.3, Q10.4, Q10.5

Q10.3

Why do I get garbage results when I use DataInputStream*'s* readInt *or* readFloat *methods to read in a number from an input string?*

DataInputStream **methods such as** readInt **and** readFloat **are not for reading string input—they expect to read a** *binary* **representation of the specified numeric type in network byte order (high-end byte first).**

The DataInputStream and DataOutputStream classes are designed primarily for platform-neutral transport of binary data. Invoking DataOutputStream's writeInt method, for example, writes a four-byte binary representation of the int value to the output stream, high-order byte first. Correspondingly, DataInput-Stream's readInt method takes four bytes from the input stream and combines them into a single int value:

```
/* in DataInputStream.java (JDK 1.0.2 and 1.1): */
public final int readInt() throws IOException {
    InputStream in = this.in;
    int ch1 = in.read();
    int ch2 = in.read();
    int ch3 = in.read();
    int ch4 = in.read();
    if ((ch1 | ch2 | ch3 | ch4) < 0)
        throw new EOFException();
    return ((ch1 << 24) + (ch2 << 16) + (ch3 << 8) + (ch4 << 0));
}
```

If you mistakenly try to read a string representation of an integer value using readInt, the first four bytes from that string representation will be converted according to the formula just shown. The result will be systematic, predictable, and almost certainly wrong.

A simple rule for remembering the purpose of the read... methods in DataInputStream is that they exist to read the output of the corresponding

DataOutputStream write... methods. A notable exception to this naming pattern is readLine (Q10.1)—its counterpart is writeBytes.

Note: DataInputStream's readLine method has been deprecated starting with JDK 1.1. Its replacement is the readLine method in class BufferedReader.

ReadIntExample.html

See also: Q10.1

Q10.4

Is there a standard way to read in int, long, float, *and* double *values from a string representation?*

There is no one standard way, but there is a small group of methods and constructors that will do the job for you.

The java.lang package in the JDK 1.0.2 provides four classes for treating numbers as objects: Integer, Long, Float, and Double. Each of these classes provides constructors and methods that translate from a string to an instance of the class. You then need to invoke an additional *<type>*Value method to retrieve the numeric value of type *<type>* held in the numeric object. Alternatively, the Integer and Long classes provide additional parse*<type>* methods that make the conversion in one step. These techniques are arrayed in Table 10.1.

Table 10.1: Converting from Strings to Numerical Values

Target type	Code to convert from a String instance (JDK 1.0.2)
int	new Integer(String).integerValue()
	Integer.valueOf(String).integerValue()
	Integer.parseInt(String)
long	new Long(String).longValue()
	Long.valueOf(String).longValue()
	Long.parseLong(String)
float	new Float(String).floatValue()
	Float.valueOf(String).floatValue()
double	new Double(String).doubleValue()
	Double.valueOf(String).doubleValue()

Note: the valueOf methods in Integer and Long can also take a second argument specifying the radix for interpreting the string (e.g., base 8 for octal numbers).

This picture is expanded considerably in the JDK 1.1. As shown in Table 10.2, new classes Short and Byte parallel Integer and Long, and there is an additional decode method in Integer, Short, and Byte (but not Long, curiously):

Table 10.2: Additional Conversions from String to Number—JDK 1.1

int	Integer.decode(String).intValue()
short	Short.parseShort(String)
	new Short(String).shortValue()
	Short.valueOf(String).shortValue()
	Short.decode(String).shortValue()
byte	Byte.parseByte(String)
	new Byte(String).byteValue()
	Byte.valueOf(String).byteValue()
	Byte.decode(String).byteValue()

The decode methods add the convenience of understanding conventional prefixes such as 0x and # for hexadecimal and 0 for octal.

All of the above number-parsing expressions throw a NumberFormatException if the String argument does not parse correctly for the desired numerical type. Correct parsing requires that the string is well formed as a number representation *and* that the value it represents lies within the range covered by the numerical type. The string "128", for instance, fails to parse as a byte. Your code must handle the possible NumberFormatException explicitly, either by catching the exception or declaring it (Q2.22, Q2.23). For example:

```
String someString = ...;
double value;
try {
    value = Double.valueOf(someString).doubleValue();
} catch (NumberFormatException e) {
    // ... handle exception
}
// ... now use value
```

Finally, note that the valueOf and parse*<type>* methods each have a counterpart taking a second parameter—the radix to use for interpreting the string numerically. For example, the following code parses a `long` value from a string in hexadecimal format:

```
String hexString = "cafebabe";  // cannot have leading 0x
long value = 0;  // int isn't big enough to hold "cafebabe"
try {
    value = Long.parseLong(hexString, 16);
} catch (NumberFormatException e) { /* ... */ }
```

ReadNumberExample.html, ReadNumber11Example.html

See also: Q4.19

Q10.5

When do I need to flush an output stream?

Invoke `flush` on a stream whenever you want your output to be sent to the other end of the output connection (file, remote socket, etc.) as soon as possible.

Some methods of the input/output system buffer their output and input. In other words, they read or write data in relatively large chunks — usually larger than required by individual method calls — and they keep any excess material in a buffer (temporary storage area) until required to move the data. The `flush` method in the `OutputStream` class instructs the system to send any pending material without further delay.

Besides invoking `flush` explicitly, you should be aware of flushing that can occur automatically. In the JDK 1.0.2, instances of the `PrintStream` class can be created with automatic flushing (`autoflush`) turned on or off. When `autoflush` is on, the output is flushed whenever a newline occurs in the output stream. Using `PrintStream`'s one-parameter constructor, `PrintStream(OutputStream)`, gives the default: `autoflush` off. To create a `PrintStream` instance with `autoflush` on, use the two-parameter constructor, with a second argument of `true`:

```
OutputStream outStream = ...;
PrintStream out = new PrintStream(outStream, true);
```

In the JDK 1.1, `PrintStream` is superseded by the `PrintWriter` class, which provides the same autoflushing controls and defaults. However, a `PrintWriter` instance does *not* inherit the autoflushing properties of the underlying output stream it is build on top of. In particular, `System.out` is a `PrintStream` instance autoflush set to `true`, but you must still explicitly set autoflush to `true` for a `PrintWriter` instance built on top of `System.out`:

```
PrintWriter writer;
writer = new PrintWriter(System.out, true);
```

FlushOutputExample.html

See also: Q10.2

Q10.6

Why do I see no output when I run a simple process, such as `r.exec("/usr/bin/ls")`*?*

You need to get an input stream from the process, so that output from the process becomes input for your program.

The `Runtime` class connects a Java application to the native environment in which the application is running. Among other things, it allows you to start independent processes on the host system, via one of the exec methods. The following code fragment would work on a UNIX system to start a local process that lists the files in the current directory:

```
Runtime r = Runtime.getRuntime();
Process p = r.exec("/usr/bin/ls");
```

To communicate with a process you've started, you need to hook up the process's standard input and output streams to output and input streams in your Java program. The `Process` class provides three methods for making such connections, shown in Table 10.3.

Table 10.3: Methods for Communicating with a `Process` Instance

`getInputStream()`	returns an `InputStream` object for reading from the process's standard output
`getOuputStream()`	returns an `OutputStream` object for writing to the process's standard input
`getErrorStream()`	returns an `InputStream` object for reading from the process's standard error output

Remember that what you call input versus output depends on which side of the connection you view it from: the process's output is your program's input, and your program's output can be the process's input. Also, be aware that if you use the exec method, your program forfeits the cross-platform advantage central to Java technology.

The following code fragment presents a simple example:

```
/* using JDK 1.0.2, on Solaris: */
Process p;
Runtime r = Runtime.getRuntime();
try {
    p = r.exec("/usr/bin/wc");      // UNIX word count program

    /* Send lines of text to the subprocess. */
    out = new PrintStream(p.getOutputStream());
    out.println("This is line 1.");
    out.println("This is line 2.");
    out.println("And this is a somewhat long line 3.");
    out.close();    // important

    /* Read in the output from the subprocess. */
    in = new DataInputStream(p.getInputStream());
    while ((currentLine = in.readLine()) != null)
        System.out.println(currentLine);
    }
} catch(IOException e) {
    // ... handle exception
}
```

The corresponding code for the JDK 1.1 uses the same Runtime and Process methods, but wraps appropriate Reader or Writer subclass instances around the underlying byte streams:

```
/* using JDK 1.1, in Solaris: */
Process p;
Runtime r = Runtime.getRuntime();
try {
    p = r.exec("/usr/bin/wc");   // UNIX word count program
    PrintWriter outWriter = new PrintWriter(System.out, true);

    /* Send lines of text to the subprocess. */
    writer = new PrintWriter(p.getOutputStream(), true);
    writer.println("This is line 1.");
    writer.println("This is line 2.");
    writer.println("And this is a somewhat long line 3.");
    writer.close();  // important
```

```
            /* Read in the output from the subprocess. */
            reader = new BufferedReader(new InputStreamReader(
                                        p.getInputStream()));
            while ((currentLine = reader.readLine()) != null) {
                outWriter.println(currentLine);
            }
    } catch(IOException e) {
        // ... handle exception
    }
```

ProcessOutputExample.html, ProcessOutput11Example.html

See also: Q10.2

URL CONNECTIONS

Q10.7

What's the difference between a URL *instance and a* URLConnection *instance?*

A URL **instance represents the location of a resource, and a** URLConnection **instance represents a link for accessing or communicating with the resource at that location.**

The URL class provides an abstraction of a Uniform Resource Locator (URL), the World Wide Web's basic type of pointer. A URL specifies where and how (by which protocol) to reach a resource; it does not specify the contents at that location.

The URLConnection class represents a connection to the resource specified by a URL. It provides general connection support both for the well-known protocols such as http and for custom protocols that you might create. You can use a URLConnection instance to inspect and set properties of the connection (e.g., whether the connection can be used for output in addition to input), to get information from the URL (e.g., content length and header fields), and to get input and output streams for moving data through the connection.

Q10.8

How do I make a connection to a URL?

You obtain a URL **instance and then invoke** openConnection **on it.**

URLConnection is an abstract class, which means you cannot directly create instances of it using a constructor. Nor would you want to, because the type of connection you need depends on the protocol specified in the URL. The URL class's openConnection method manages these details for you. When you invoke openConnection on a URL instance, you automatically get the right kind of connection (subclass of URLConnection) for your URL.

When you create a URL instance or invoke openConnection, remember to handle the exceptions that might be thrown (if not, the compiler will remind you; see Q2.23, Q2.24):

```
URL url;
URLConnection connection;
try {
    url = new URL (...);
    connection = url.openConnection();
} catch(MalformedURLException e) {
    // ... handle exception from URL constructor
} catch(IOException e) {
    // ... handle exception from URL.openConnection
}
```

Obtaining a URLConnection instance is merely the first step. To inspect or communicate with the resource at the other end, you need to set up input or output streams for the connection (Q10.9).

Example: URLConnectionExample.html

See also: Q2.23, Q2.24, Q10.9

Q10.9

How do I read from a remote file if I have its URL?

Get a URL connection from the URL, get an input stream from the connection, and then read from that stream according to the type of data you expect.

A `URLConnection` instance manages the connection between your program and a URL, but it delegates much of the actual work to other objects. For example, you do not directly send data to or receive data from a `URLConnection` instance. Instead, you ask the connection for an input stream or output stream and then transfer data through that stream. To obtain finer control over the data flow, you can wrap a stream filter (an instance of a subclass of `FilterInputStream` or `FilterOutputStream`) around the basic input or output stream.

Below are the typical steps for reading from a file:

1. Create a `URL` instance that points to the file you want to read.

2. Invoke `openConnection` on that `URL` instance.

3. Invoke `getInputStream()` to get an `InputStream` object from the connection.

4. Wrap an instance of an appropriate `FilterInputStream` subclass around the basic input stream and read from it.

5. Close the `InputStream`.

For convenience, `URL`'s `openStream` method combines steps 2 and 3. The code fragment below exemplifies the process:

```
/* using JDK 1.0.2: */
URL url = null;
URLConnection connection;
String urlString = "http://java.sun.com/";
String currentLine;
DataInputStream inStream;
try {
    url = new URL (urlString);
} catch(MalformedURLException e) { /* ... */ }

try {
    connection = url.openConnection();
    inStream = new DataInputStream (connection.getInputStream());
    while (null != (currentLine = inStream.readLine())) {
        System.out.println(currentLine);
    }
    inStream.close();
} catch (IOException e) { /* ... */ }
```

To write equivalent code using the JDK 1.1, perform the standard conversion from byte-oriented input streams to character-oriented readers, as illustrated in Q10.1, Q10.2, and Q10.6.

Note: In an applet, similar code could read data only from the host that originally delivered the applet code. In general, applets loaded over the net can make network connections only back to the host they were loaded from.

ReadFromURLExample.html, ReadFromURLAppletExample.html

See also: Q10.1, Q10.2, Q10.6

Q10.10

Why do I get a null *result when I use the* getHeader... *methods in the* URLConnection *class?*

There are two main sources of null **results from** getHeader... **methods: you requested a specific header field that doesn't exist for the present connection, or you used a** getHeader... **method that is not fully implemented in the JDK 1.0.2 (in other words, a bug).**

The URLConnection class provides two different ways to request header information: by specific header type and by position in the overall header list. The general way to request the value of a specific header field is to ask for it by name, using the getHeaderField(String) method:

```
public String getHeaderField(String name)
```

If the named header field exists, this method returns a String instance representing the field's value; otherwise the method returns null. For convenience, the URLConnection class also provides methods to access standard header fields and return digested numerical values where appropriate:

- `public String getContentEncoding()`
- `public int getContentLength()`
- `public String getContentType()`
- `public long getDate()`
- `public long getExpiration()`

The second approach is to retrieve the header fields by position rather than by name. For this you use the pair of methods that index the header fields starting with one (*not* zero):

- `public String getHeaderFieldKey(int index)`
- `public String getHeaderField(int index)`

For example, the following method iterates through all the header fields for the given URLConnection instance:

```
public void printHeaders(URLConnection connection) {
    for (int i = 1; true; ++i) {
        String headerKey = connection.getHeaderFieldKey(i);
        if (headerKey == null) {
            break;
        }
        System.out.println("    Header " + i + ":   "
                        + headerKey + ": "
                        + connection.getHeaderField(i));
    }
}
```

In the JDK 1.0.2, the two methods for retrieving headers by index always return null — this is a bug, not a feature. The JDK 1.1 has fixed this bug, as you can verify by running the GetHeaderExample sample code within the JDK 1.1 virtual machine.

GetHeaderExample.html

Q10.11

What is URLConnection's getOutputStream *method intended to work with on the server side?*

The output stream you get from a URL connection usually hooks up with an http-related process on the server side, such as a CGI script.

Intermachine (network) communication requires cooperating processes at the two ends. With a URL connection, one end is a Java Virtual Machine running your application or applet, and the other end is some server process — using http, ftp, or some other protocol specified in your URL. Reading from a URL connection's input stream is the common and simple case. A general-purpose server process, such as a web or ftp server, can locate and send back a copy of the resource you request.

Writing to a URL connection's output stream, however, is more restricted, because of the actions required on the server side. Http servers, for example, can't simply create or write to arbitrary files specified in a URL. They must use special processes that have been configured explicitly to accept input across the net. When you send data through a URL connection, you will most likely be sending it to a CGI (Common Gateway Interface) process. (A telltale "cgi-bin" in a URL usually gives away that you are communicating with a CGI process.)

Note: The default behavior for URL connections is to disallow output streams. The current JDK implementations (1.0.2 and 1.1) define `getOutputStream` in the `URLConnection` class to throw an `UnknownServiceException`:

```
/* In URLConnection.java (JDK 1.0.2 and 1.1) */
public OutputStream getOutputStream() throws IOException {
    throw new UnknownServiceException(
            "protocol doesn't support output");
}
```

To enable output, a `URLConnection` subclass must override `getOutputStream`, as Sun's JDK implementation does in its `HttpURLConnection` class in order to allow posting to http servers (Q10.12).

See also: Q10.12

Q10.12

How do I send data from my Java program to a CGI program?

You can use an http GET request by packing your data into the query string of the URL, or you can use an http POST request by sending your data through an output stream obtained from the URL connection.

The way you send data to a particular CGI (Common Gateway Interface) program depends on what that program has been written to handle. CGI programs generally expect to receive their data either as an http GET request or as an http POST request. In Java, `URLConnection` instances support sending data through both mechanisms.

GET requests are the basic http mechanism for fetching material from the World Wide Web. On the server side, a GET request typically causes the server to locate the resource indicated by the URL and send it back to the client. CGI programs can piggyback on the GET mechanism by looking for a query string at the tail of the URL:

```
http://<machine-name>/<path-to-cgi-program>?<query-string>
```

The information in the query string is made accessible to the program as the value of an environment variable called QUERY_STRING. The CGI program then generates its output and sends that to the client.

To use a GET request from the client side, a Java program must create an appropriate `URLConnection` instance (Q10.8), obtain an input stream from the connection, and then read from that stream. The following code fragment, for example, simply reads and prints the CGI program's output:

```
/* http GET + query string -- using JDK 1.0.2: */
DataInputStream inStream;
String urlString = "http://hoohoo.ncsa.uiuc.edu/cgi-bin/test-cgi"
String queryString = "arg1=val1"
                    + "&arg2=val2"
                    + "&arg3=val3"
                    + "&arg4=val4"
                    + "&arg5=val5";
urlString += ("?" + queryString);
try {
    String currentLine;
    URL url = new URL(urlString);
    URLConnection connection = url.openConnection();
    inStream = new DataInputStream(connection.getInputStream());

    /* Read the server's response and close up. */
    while (null != (currentLine = inStream.readLine())) {
        System.out.println(currentLine);
    }
    inStream.close();
    inStream = null;
} catch (Exception e) {
    // ... handle exception
} finally {
    if (inStream != null) {
        inStream.close();
    }
}
```

GET requests are appropriate when the CGI program needs relatively little information per interaction.

Alternatively, a client program can make an http POST request. A POST lets you send an arbitrary amount of information to the CGI program, separate from the URL used to initiate the connection. The URL thus has no query string; it specifies only the path to the CGI program:

```
http://<machine-name>/<path-to-cgi-program>
```

After creating a `URLConnection` instance, your program needs to prepare the connection for a POST (`setDoOutput(true)`), obtain an output stream from the connection, write data to it, and close it. After that, reading the output from the CGI program works the same as for the GET request just described. The following code fragment illustrates these steps:

```
/* http POST -- using JDK 1.0.2: */
DataInputStream inStream;
PrintStream outStream;
String urlString = "http://hoohoo.ncsa.uiuc.edu/cgi-bin/test-cgi"
String dataString = "arg1=val1"
                + "&arg2=val2"
                + "&arg3=val3"
                + "&arg4=val4"
                + "&arg5=val5";

try {
    URL url = new URL(urlString);
    URLConnection connection = url.openConnection();
    connection.setDoOutput(true);
    outStream = new PrintStream(connection.getOutputStream());
    outStream.println(dataString);
    outStream.println();
    outStream.close();
    outStream = null;

    /* Read the server's response and close up. */
    inStream = new DataInputStream(connection.getInputStream());
    while (null != (currentLine = inStream.readLine())) {
        System.out.println(currentLine);
    }
    inStream.close();
    inStream = null;
} catch (Exception e) {
    // ... handle exception
} finally {
    if (outStream != null) {
        outStream.close();
    }
    if (inStream != null) {
        inStream.close();
    }
}
```

PostExample.html

See also: Q10.8

Q10.13

Can I write (from my applet) to an external file on a URL?

No; the standard URLConnection **classes allow you only to send data to a CGI program on the server (from which your applet was loaded), but not to write directly to a file URL.**

The JDK URLConnection classes — the abstract URLConnnection class and its various implementation subclasses — support writing output to a URL only in the form of http POST requests (Q10.12). Thus, there is no direct way to write to a file specified by a URL; you need to have (or write) a CGI program at the receiving end that can take the data in your POST request and save it to a file.

See also: Q10.12, Q10.13

Q10.14

How can my Java stand-alone application fetch documents in the same fashion as (partially simulating) a browser?

Fetching is easy enough, with the assistance of java.net **classes (Q10.9), but you would also need to parse, format, and display what you fetch, which requires substantial extra work on your part.**

See also: Q10.9

Q10.15

Why do I get a security exception when I try to connect to an external URL from an applet? (If I run equivalent code as an application, it works fine.)

As part of the Java security model, applets are quite restricted in the network connections they can make: applets can typically make network connections only back to the URL host they were fetched from, whereas stand-alone applications do not have this restriction.

For more details, including the latest status of all known security-related bugs, see JavaSoft's security FAQ web page (http://java.sun.com/sfaq/).

INTERNET ADDRESSES

Q10.16

The API doesn't list any constructors for InetAddress—*how do I create an* InetAddress *instance?*

Use InetAddress**'s** getByName(String) **class method.**

The InetAddress class's getByName method translates from host names to InetAddress instances. By delivering InetAddress instances with a method rather than a constructor, the InetAddress class gains in flexibility and efficiency. It can create new InetAddress instances if it needs to, but it also has the option of returning a reference to an InetAddress instance it has already created and saved. This kind of caching is hidden from you as an implementation detail, but it is important for efficiency and performance.

getByName is a class method (Q1.6), which means you invoke it on the InetAddress class. You provide a String argument that represents either the symbolic name of the host or its numeric address. This method can throw an UnknownHostException, so your code must either handle or declare that exception (Q2.23). The following code fragment illustrates:

```
InetAddress address1;
InetAddress address2;
try {
    address1 = InetAddress.getByName("java.sun.com");
    address2 = InetAddress.getByName("192.9.9.100");
} catch (UnknownHostException e) { /* ... */ }
```

InetAddressExample.html

See also: Q1.6, Q1.7, Q2.23

Q10.17

Is it possible to get the real local host IP?

Yes; use InetAddress**'s** getLocalHost **method.**

InetAddress's getLocalHost method returns the address of the local host, if the method can find it; if not, the method throws an UnknownHostException. The following code fragment obtains an `InetAddress` instance representing the local host, from which it then gets the local host's name and IP address:

```
InetAddress localHost = null;
String localHostName;
byte[] byteAddress;
try {
    localHost = InetAddress.getLocalHost();
} catch (UnknownHostException e) { /* ... */ }
localHostName = localHost.getHostName();
byteAddress = localHost.getAddress();
```

LocalHostExample.html

See also: Q10.16

Q10.18

How can I create an `InetAddress` *instance from an IP address that has no DNS entry?*

A bug in the JDK 1.0.2 implementation prevents this from working, but in the JDK 1.1 you can use `InetAddress`**'s** `getByName` **method (using a** *number.number.number.number* **address; see Q10.16) even if no DNS entry exists for the address.**

See also: Q10.16, Q10.20, Q10.27

SOCKETS

Q10.19

How do I create and use sockets in Java?

Create `Socket` **instances on the client side by specifying a host and port number to connect to, and create** `ServerSocket` **instances on the server side by specifying a port number at which to wait for new connections.**

Sockets work in pairs, with a built-in asymmetry between *client* and *server*. The Socket class in the java.net package represents a client socket. It is always created with a communication target: a communications port number on a specific host machine. The client socket typically initiates interactions. It sends messages over the net to its target, expecting that the right kind of program will be waiting at the specified port, ready to respond to the client's message.

The server socket, represented by the ServerSocket class, plays this second, wait-and-respond role. A server socket need only specify a port number to listen at; it doesn't have to know in advance to where it will send messages. For each incoming message, it sends its reply back to the source address indicated in the message. In this way, a single process at a server socket can reply to many different clients on different machines.

The key to using sockets is to keep in mind that they provide only a low-level abstraction of a communication channel as a stream of bytes. The SocketExample sample code, for instance, shows how to pack a Java String instance into an array of bytes and then write that array to the output stream of the socket. To receive data from the server, a useful strategy is to wrap a DataInputStream instance around the client socket's input stream and then use an appropriate read method for the data type(s) you expect (Q10.3).

SocketExample.html, Socket11Example.html

See also: Q10.3

Q10.20

How can I get a server socket and client socket going on a stand-alone machine, not on a network?

In the JDK 1.1 (but not 1.0.2, due to a bug), you can use the loopback interface — IP address 127.0.0.1 — for socket communication without a network.

Creating a Socket instance requires that you specify the host to connect to, either by name or as an InetAddress instance. Standard TCP/IP practice reserves a special IP address — 127.0.0.1 — as the *loopback interface*. Data packets sent to this address don't actually leave the machine; they are passed by software to the same machine's receiving ports, as if they had come in off the network. Thus, you can use this loopback address to test or run network code, even if your machine is not on a network.

Using the loopback interface affects code only for the client socket. It must create a Socket instance using "127.0.0.1" as the target address:

```
InetAddress loopback = InetAddress.getByName("127.0.0.1");
connection = new Socket(loopback, SERVER_PORT);
```

No special code is needed for a server socket. As always, it uses whatever address the client socket is connecting from.

The above code works in the JDK 1.1, but a bug in the JDK 1.0.2 implementation prevents loopback connections from working if your machine isn't on a network. In particular, InetAddress's getByName method in 1.0.2 requires that domain name lookup succeed before it returns an InetAddress instance. This is a bug, not a feature, and it prevents you from creating an InetAddress instance by means of the "127.0.0.1" address.

SocketWithoutNetworkExample.html, SocketWithoutNetwork11Example.html

See also: Q10.19

Q10.21

Will raw sockets ever be introduced—and if not, how can I create ICMP messages so that I can do operations like 'ping'?

Raw sockets are not currently scheduled for an upcoming release, and without them, your only option for such low-level network access is to write your own native methods.

The socket operations provided by the java.net classes deliberately shelter you from the lower layers of the TCP/IP protocol stack. Once you create a socket, you only have to worry about sending and receiving data through it. The nitpicky details of the lower transport layers, such as IP addresses, packet sequence numbers, and packet checksums are managed by system code. For the great majority of applications, this division of labor is desirable.

For a small set of applications, though, the higher-level abstraction provided by sockets shields the very data—the header bytes in an individual packet—that the application needs to control. The UNIX "ping" program, for instance, manipulates individual packets at the level of IP headers, in order to send packets conforming to the Internet Control Message Protocol (ICMP). You simply can't write a ping program using Java socket-related classes. For network control at this level, you need to write native methods.

Q10.22

How do I detect if an input stream belonging to a socket has been terminated by the remote host?

Check the return value of your read **(or** readLine, **etc.) method; if the remote host has terminated the socket input stream from its end, your invocation of** read **should return an end-of-stream value.**

Like other input streams, a socket's input stream signals the end of its data by returning the standard end-of-stream value, -1, from its read methods. The end of a socket's input stream is determined by the remote host: the remote host marks the end of its data by closing the connection (either the data stream or the whole socket) at its end. On the local side, your program may not detect the closing right away because it may still read in some buffered data first, but your program will eventually detect the end-of-stream mark.

The base InputStream class returns -1 from its read methods to signal end-of-stream. Because you can build other types of input streams or readers on top of the basic input stream, you need to check for the appropriate end-of-stream marker for the specific type you're using: -1 for read methods that return int and null for readLine methods that return String.

Note: InputStream's available method cannot detect the closing of an input stream — it merely reports how many bytes can be read from the input stream without blocking. In other words, it basically tells you how many bytes are in the TCP buffer on the local receiving end of the current connection; it does not indicate the state of the remote host.

DetectSocketClosureExample.html

See also: Q10.19

Q10.23

If the Socket *class has no support for firewalls, how can I get my Java program with sockets to work through different firewalls?*

Define a SocketImpl **subclass that can work through your firewall, and use** Socket's setSocketImplFactory **method to configure your application with that** SocketImpl **subclass.**

The Socket class provides a front-end interface for socket operations. It lets you open and close socket connections, obtain input and output streams from the socket, and so on. Although you invoke methods on a Socket object, that object does very little of the work. Instead, it delegates practically all of the implementation details to a separate implementation object, which belongs to a subclass of SocketImpl. The Socket getOutputStream method in the JDK (1.0.2 and 1.1), for example, shows how simple the delegation can be:

```
/* in Socket.java (JDK 1.0.2 and 1.1): */
public OutputStream getOutputStream() throws IOException {
    return impl.getOutputStream();
}
```

Building in the back-end know-how for communicating through firewalls requires several steps:

- define your own SocketImpl subclass; override methods like bind, listen, accept, and connect

- define a class that implements the SocketImplFactory interface; this interface contains a single method createSocketImpl(), which returns a SocketImpl instance

- invoke Socket's setSocketImplFactory method, providing your SocketImpl-Factory object as the argument

If you don't specify a SocketImplFactory, the JDK (1.0.2 and 1.1) provides an instance of PlainSocketImpl (a nonpublic class in java.net) for you. This implementation class does not conduct security checks and knows how to handle only SOCKS firewalls.

See also: Q10.19

Q10.24

How do I create a nonblocking server socket in Java?

You can't, exactly, but you can achieve the same affect by using a separate thread to run ServerSocket's accept **method.**

A ServerSocket instance has only one way to wait for incoming connections: by invoking the ServerSocket accept method. The accept method is defined to be a blocking call, which means that the thread invoking it will block further execution until a connection is made. If you want to avoid blocking some central thread in your server code, you should have a separate thread run the accept method. The following code fragment illustrates one approach:

```
class ServerThread extends Thread {
    ServerSocket listenSocket;
    Socket acceptSocket;

    /**
     * Creates a new server thread that will listen for a connection
     * at the specified socket.
     */
    public ServerThread(ServerSocket socket) {
        listenSocket = socket;
    }

    /**
     * Accepts a connection and then starts another server thread
     * to wait for the next connection while this thread runs
     * to completion.
     */
    public void run() {
        acceptSocket = listenSocket.accept();
        new ServerThread(listenSocket).start();
        // ... handle current connection
    }
    // ...
}
```

NonblockingServerExample.html, NonblockingServer11Example.html

See also: Q10.19

Q10.25

Is there a standard Java way to specify the address of the host doing the listening when instantiating a ServerSocket*?*

In the JDK 1.0.2, you can't specify a local address for a server socket to listen at, but the JDK 1.1 fills this gap by providing an additional ServerSocket **constructor taking an** InetAddress **parameter.**

The JDK 1.0.2 provides two public constructors for the ServerSocket class. When creating a ServerSocket instance, you must specify the port number to listen at for connections, and you can optionally specify a maximum size for the waiting list of connect requests waiting to be accepted:

```
ServerSocket(int port)
ServerSocket(int port, int backlog)
```

In the JDK 1.0.2, there is no way to specify that the server socket should listen on a specific IP address. This restriction can be an issue on "multihomed" machines, that is, machines with more than one IP address.

Thanks to strong demand, the JDK 1.1 filled this gap by providing one further constructor in the ServerSocket class:

```
ServerSocket(int port, int backlog, InetAddress bindAddr)
```

The third argument specifies a local IP address for the server socket to listen at. For example, the following (admittedly silly) code fragment defines a server that only allows connections on its loopback interface:

```
// ... SERVER_PORT defined elsewhere
listenSocket = new ServerSocket(SERVER_PORT, 50,
                    InetAddress.getByName("127.0.0.1"));
```

The second argument, 50, provides the default value for the request backlog allowed by a server socket. You can set this to another value more appropriate for your program if you wish.

See also: Q10.19, Q10.24

Q10.26

How do I send and/or receive datagram packets?

Create an appropriate datagram socket and datagram packet, then send or receive the packet via the socket.

The java.net package supports two fundamentally different ways to send data over the network: normal sockets and datagram sockets. Normal sockets provide a model of reliable data transport as a stream of bytes (or a matched pair of streams) that connects two network locations. You first establish the connection, and then send (and receive) data through it (Q10.19). The socket implementation hides from you all the gory details of splitting the stream into addressed data packets, ensuring that the packets all arrive at their destination, and reassembling the stream in correct order from the packets. The protocol underlying this model is the Transmission Control Protocol (TCP).

Datagram sockets, in contrast, provide a more rudimentary, lightweight service for sending out or receiving individual data packets. There is no ongoing connection or data stream, and the delivery mechanism specifically does *not* guarantee that the data reaches its destination. Instead, for each packet, you have to manage the details of providing a data buffer and appropriate destination address and port number. The protocol underlying this model is the User Datagram Protocol (UDP).

Using datagrams thus centers around packets: either composing and sending them, or receiving and unpacking them. To send a packet, the standard steps are:

1. Create a `DatagramSocket` instance.

2. Allocate and fill a data buffer (a `byte` array).

3. Create a `DatagramPacket` instance that combines the data buffer with address information.

4. Send the packet through the socket.

The following code fragment exemplifies these steps:

```
InetAddress destination = ...;
int destinationPort = ...;
byte[] dataBuffer = ...;
DatagramSocket socket;
DatagramPacket packet;
try {
    socket = new DatagramSocket();
    packet = new DatagramPacket(dataBuffer, dataBuffer.length,
                                destination, destinationPort);
    socket.send(packet);
    socket.close();
} catch (Exception e) {
    // ... handle exception
}
```

Notice that the `DatagramSocket` instance created for sending does not require that you specify a port number, since the `DatagramPacket` instance itself conveys all the necessary routing information. The socket still uses a port number, but it takes one that the system assigns automatically. Another noteworthy point is that the `try-catch` statement is needed because several of the `DatagramSocket` methods and constructors throw exceptions.

Receiving a packet involves many of the same components as sending, except you are preparing an empty packet to be filled:

1. Create a datagram socket.

2. Allocate a data buffer, but don't fill it.

3. Create a datagram packet with that buffer, but with no address information.

4. Invoke `receive` on the socket to wait for data to arrive and fill the packet.

The following sample code illustrates each of these steps:

```
int MAX_BYTES = 576;
int SERVER_PORT = ...
DatagramSocket socket;
DatagramPacket packet;
byte[] dataBuffer = new byte[MAX_BYTES];
try {
    socket = new DatagramSocket(SERVER_PORT);
    packet = new DatagramPacket(dataBuffer, dataBuffer.length);
    socket.receive(packet);
    socket.close();
} catch (Exception e) {
    // ... handle exception
}
// ... process contents of packet
```

Datagram sockets distinguish most strongly between the sender and the receiver, but they also distinguish weakly between client and server:

- A client must know the server's address and port in advance, in order to make the initial contact.

- A server can read the client's address and port from the datagram packet it receives.

DatagramExample.html

See also: Q10.19

Q10.27

When will I be able to create a broadcast datagram packet?

Starting with the JDK 1.1, you can create broadcast datagram packets.

Creating a broadcast datagram packet is like creating other datagram packets for sending (Q10.26), except that you use the reserved broadcast address 255.255.255.255. The following code fragment illustrates how:

```
InetAddress destination;
int destinationPort = ...
DatagramSocket socket;
DatagramPacket packet;
byte[] dataBuffer = { 3, 1, 4, 1, 5, 9, 2, 6, 5, 3, 5 };
try {
    destination = InetAddress.getByName("255.255.255.255");
    socket = new DatagramSocket();
    packet = new DatagramPacket(dataBuffer, dataBuffer.length,
                                destination, destinationPort);
    socket.send(packet);
    socket.close();
} catch (Exception e) { /* ... */ }
```

The reason this doesn't work in pre-1.1 JDK releases is that they contain a bug in their getByName method that prevents broadcast packets from working. Looking up an IP address that lacked a Domain Name Service (DNS) entry generates an UnknownHostException, even in cases (like the broadcast address) where the IP address has a useful, well-established meaning independent of DNS.

BroadcastExample.html

See also: Q10.18, Q10.26

CHAPTER 11

Miscellaneous

Classes in java.lang **and** java.util **(Q11.1–Q11.4)**

Audio (Q11.5–Q11.10)

Miscellaneous (Q11.11–Q11.14)

CLASSES IN java.lang AND java.util

Q11.1

Why doesn't String's replace *method have any effect when I apply it to a string?*

String's replace **method, like other** String **methods, doesn't alter the original string; instead, it creates a new** String **instance with the specified properties.**

The String class creates read-only (*immutable*) strings. Once you create a String instance, you can inspect it and use it to build other strings, but you cannot alter that instance itself. Any String method that sounds like it would change the string actually creates a new string with the properties required by the method. The replace method, for instance, performs character replacement in a new string copy rather than the original string:

```
String oldString = "java.lang.Thread";
String newString = oldString.replace('.', '/');
```

After this code executes, newString has the value "java/lang/Thread" and the value of oldString remains unchanged.

Table 11.1 shows all the `String` methods that look like they could alter a string (but instead create a new string with the alterations shown there).

Table 11.1: `String` **Methods with the Appearance of Mutating a String**

Method	Creates new string based on target string by ___
`concat(String)`	appending the argument string
`replace(char, char)`	replacing all occurrences of the first argument character with the second argument character
`toLowerCase()`	converting all uppercase characters to lowercase
`toUpperCase()`	converting all lowercase characters to uppercase
`trim()`	removing any whitespace from both ends of string

If you need editable strings, use the `StringBuffer` class—it provides several methods, shown in Table 11.2, that directly modify a `StringBuffer` instance.

Table 11.2: `StringBuffer` **Methods that Modify a** `StringBuffer` **Instance**

Method	Modifies the target `StringBuffer` instance by ___
`append` [many varieties]	appending a string representation of a primitive type or object
`insert` [many varieties]	inserting a string representation of a primitive type or object at the specifed buffer location
`reverse()` [in JDK 1.1]	reversing the characters in the buffer
`setCharAt(int, char)`	setting the character at the specified buffer location
`setLength(int)`	setting the length of the buffer, possibly truncating characters stored in the buffer

StringReplaceExample.html

Q11.2

How can I access native operating system calls from my Java program?

You get some cross-platform access to operating system calls via the standard Java API; for fuller access, you can either use the `Runtime` and `Process` classes in the `java.lang` package, or you can write your own native method implementations (but then your program will be captive to your specific platform).

The Java platform — virtual machine, language, and standard class libraries — is designed to be strongly independent of specific software/hardware platforms. This guideline confers a tremendous benefit in "write once, run everywhere," but it also entails restricted access to powerful but platform-specific functionality. Java technology aims at a robust, practical balance — a workable middle ground between the grand sum of all platforms and the lowest common denominator.

Many operations performed by native-platform operating system calls are reflected in the standard Java API. For example:

- file and network IO: packages `java.io` and `java.net`

- file system operations: `File` class in the `java.io` package

- socket operations: `Socket` and other classes in the `java.io` package

- multithreading: `Thread` and `Object` classes in the `java.lang` package

Wherever possible, you should aim to express your functionality in terms of these classes so that your Java program will be truly cross-platform.

Alternatively, the `Runtime` class in package `java.lang` provides a set of `exec` methods with which you can start a process on the native platform (modeled after the UNIX exec system call). The exec methods take a variety of `String` parameters and return a `Process` instance:

- `Process exec(String command);`

- `Process exec(String command, String[] envp);`

- `Process exec(String[] commandArray);`

- `Process exec(String[] commandArray, String[] envp);`

The Process instance returned by exec lets you interact with the executing native-platform process in a variety of ways, as shown in Table 11.3.

Table 11.3: Methods in the Process Class

destroy	kills the process
waitFor	returns when the process has completed or has been terminated
exitValue	returns the process's int exit value
getErrorStream	returns an InputStream reference with which you can read from the process's error output stream
getInputStream	returns an InputStream reference with which you can read from the process's standard output stream
getOutputStream	returns an OutputStream reference with which you can write to the process's standard input stream

Finally, native methods allow you to provide the implementation of the method in another language, such as C. You can then access any native operating system calls that the language and its libraries support.

See also: Q10.6

Q11.3

Does Java provide standard iterator functions for inspecting a collection of objects?

Sort of; the Enumeration interface in the java.util package provides a bare-bones framework for stepping once through a collection of objects.

The Enumeration interface in the java.util package lets you extract elements one by one from a collection without needing to know how the collection is implemented. The interface comprises just two methods:

```
/* in Enumeration.java (JDK 1.0.2 and 1.1): */
public interface Enumeration {
    boolean hasMoreElements();
    Object nextElement();
}
```

The `hasMoreElements` method determines whether the enumeration has more elements to offer. The `nextElement` method returns the next element in the enumeration, if there is one. The first invocation of `nextElement` on a fresh `Enumeration` object returns the first element.

Enumerations are consumed as you use them; each invocation of `nextElement` should yield a new element from the underlying collection—one that you haven't seen yet. To borrow a phrase from probability theory, the `nextElement` method constitutes sampling without replacement.

In addition to their simplicity, enumerations are very flexible. An enumeration can provide all types of Java objects. The `nextElement` method is defined as returning objects of type `Object`, which automatically extends to all subclasses of `Object` as well as all arrays. What's more, a single enumeration can even yield objects of different types on different calls to `nextElement`, although the usual case is for the elements in an enumeration to all belong to the same class (or have some common superclass that is more specific than `Object`).

The most common way to use an enumeration is for inspecting the collection of elements returned from some object. Several collection classes in the standard Java packages include methods that return an enumeration of the collection's elements. For example, the `keys` method in the `Hashtable` class (in `java.util`) returns an enumeration of all the keys in a given hashtable; you can loop through this enumeration to print out all the keys as follows:

```
Hashtable symbols = ...;
Enumeration symbolKeys = symbols.keys();
System.out.println("Keys in symbol table:");
while (symbolKeys.hasMoreElements()) {
    System.out.println("    " + symbolKeys.nextElement());
}
```

EnumerationExample.html

See also: Q1.20

Q11.4

The `Math.random` *method is too limited for my needs—how can I generate random numbers more flexibly?*

The `random` method in the `Math` class provides quick, convenient access to (pseudo-)random numbers, but for more power and flexibility, use the `Random` class in the `java.util` package.

The core Java packages provide two ways to generate pseudo-random (that is, nearly or apparently random) numbers. The `random` method in the `Math` class is primarily a convenience method for easily generating random numbers. It requires no preparation in advance — you merely invoke `Math.random()` each time you want a new random value:

```
for (int i = 0; i < 10; ++i) {
    double doubleVal = Math.random();
    System.out.println("doubleVal = " + doubleVal);
}
```

The `random` method returns a `double` value greater than or equal to `0.0` and less than `1.0`.

If you need greater flexibility, then consider using the `java.util.Random` class. The `Random` class provides methods returning `float`, `double`, `int`, and `long` values; it also provides random numbers from a Gaussian ("normal," or "bell-shaped") distribution. Table 11.4 summarizes the relevant methods.

Table 11.4: Methods in the Random Class

Method	Returns
nextFloat	type `float`; `0.0 <= value < 1.0`
nextDouble	type `double`; `0.0 <= value < 1.0`
nextInt	type `int`; `Integer.MIN_VALUE <= value <= Integer.MAX_VALUE`
nextLong	type `long`; `Long.MIN_VALUE <= value <= Long.MAX_VALUE`
nextGaussian	type `double`; has Gaussian ("normal") distribution with mean 0.0 and standard deviation 1.0

Each (non-Gaussian) random value method returns a value within a standard range for the data type in question. If you want random numbers representing some other range, take the output from the method with the correct return type and scale and shift its output. For example, the following code fragment generates `float` values ranging from `-10.0` to just under `10.0` (`9.9999...`):

```
Random r = new Random();
for (int i = 0; i < 10; ++i) {
    float floatVal = r.nextFloat() * 20 - 10;
    System.out.println("floatVal = " + floatVal);
}
```

The return value of nextFloat is scaled and shifted as follows. Multiplying by 20 expands the output range to be from 0.0 to just under 20.0; subtracting 10 then shifts that range to be from -10.0 to just under 10.0.

If you want to be more precise and exclude both endpoints, you need to complicate the nextFloat line a little:

```
do {
    floatVal = r.nextFloat() * 20 - 10;
} while (floatVal == -10.0)
```

RandomExample.html

AUDIO

Q11.5

How do I play sounds in an applet?

Invoke one of Applet's getAudio **methods to get an** AudioClip **object, then invoke** start **and** stop **on that object.**

The java.applet package provides bare-bones support for playing sounds. Using the Applet and AudioClip classes, you can load sound files over the network, start them playing, and stop them in midstream. Using audio well in an applet is challenging, and requires that you understand the details of the different audio-related methods. The following discussion includes implementation details, especially concerning threads, that hold in the JDK 1.0.2 and 1.1.

Applet's getAudioClip method is synchronous: it fetches data for the audio clip and returns when the data is fully loaded and ready to play. (This is the opposite of Component's getImage method, which returns immediately without loading its data; see Q8.11.) After a call to getAudioClip, invoking play on the AudioClip object should should start the sound immediately:

```
/* code in an applet ... */
String filename = ...
AudioClip currentSound = getAudioClip(getCodeBase(), "gong.au");
currentSound.play();
```

AudioClip objects are usually cached, so that subsequent calls to getAudioClip for the same clip do not incur the delay of fetching the data over the net.

AudioClip's play method is asynchronous: it issues a request to another thread to play the sound, and it returns almost immediately. In other words, it does *not* wait for the sound to actually start playing, let alone finish playing. Unfortunately, the current JDK implementations, 1.0.2 and 1.1, do not provide any direct way for your program to find out when an audio clip has finished playing.

AudioClip's stop method is also asynchronous, but its effects are pretty much immediate, so you can think of it as stopping the sound as soon you invoke it. Invoking start on an audio clip that is already playing first stops the clip and then starts it again from the beginning.

For the simplest uses, the Applet class also provides convenience methods, play(URL) and play(URL, String), which combine the work of fetching and starting an audio clip. Applet's play(...) methods are functionally equivalent to getAudioClip(...).play().

PlayAndStopExample.html

See also: Q8.11, Q11.6, Q11.7

Q11.6

How do I play several audio clips simultaneously?

You can play several audio clips almost simultaneously by creating distinct AudioClip objects and then starting them all at roughly the same time.

AudioClip's start method works asynchronously: it sends a request to another thread, which manages the actual playing of sounds through the native platform's audio device. Because start returns almost immediately, you can start several different audio clips almost simultaneously simply by preloading the clips and then invoking start on them in sequence:

```
/* ... in an applet ... */
AudioClip clip1 = getAudioClip(getCodeBase(), "bass.au");
AudioClip clip2 = getAudioClip(getCodeBase(), "guitar.au");
AudioClip clip3 = getAudioClip(getCodeBase(), "drums.au");
clip1.play();
clip2.play();
clip3.play();
```

See also: Q11.5, Q11.7

Q11.7

Can I tell when an audio clip has finished playing?

No — the best you can do for now is estimate when the audio clip will finish; the current audio API (JDK 1.0.2 and 1.1) does not provide any notification when an audio clip finishes playing.

The audio support in the JDK 1.0.2 and 1.1 is quite limited, and one glaring gap is that there is no way to notify your program when an audio clip has finished playing. If you have actions whose timing depends on when a clip finishes, you have to estimate the timing yourself.

As an example, consider the problem of playing two sound clips in succession. If you know in advance the length of the first audio clip, you can predict when to start the second one, as follows:

```
/* ... in an applet ... */
AudioClip firstClip = getAudioClip(...);
AudioClip secondClip = getAudioClip(...);
long playLength = ...;   // length of firstClip in milliseconds
                         // (somehow we know this from elsewhere)
firstClip.play();
try {
    Thread.sleep(playLength);
    secondClip.play();
} catch (InterruptedException e) {
    // ... handle exception
}
```

The forthcoming Java Media Framework will provide a much richer foundation for controlling the capture and playback of media streams (audio and video). Notification of playback completion is one of the planned capabilities.

See also: Q11.5, Q11.6

Q11.8

How can I play audio in a stand-alone application?

Stand-alone applications can't yet play audio in a cross-platform manner; the current API (JDK 1.0.2 and 1.1) requires the support of a browser or other applet context.

In the current JDK releases (1.0.2 and 1.1), the java.applet package contains the only cross-platform Java support for playing audio. However, this functionality is ultimately backed up by the applet's execution context—either the Applet Viewer or a Java-enabled browser. For example, when you invoke the getAudio-Clip method on an Applet instance, the call gets forwarded to an AppletContext object:

```
/* in Applet.java (JDK 1.0.2 and 1.1): */
public AudioClip getAudioClip(URL url) {
    return getAppletContext().getAudioClip(url);
}
```

AppletContext is an interface; the applet's execution context has the role of providing an actual object from a class that implements this interface. If you merely define an Applet subclass and place instances of it in your application, you haven't actually provided your applets with the proper context to support audio.

The upcoming work on the Java Media Framework will provide a much richer set of cross-platform capabilities for both applets and applications.

See also: Q4.2

Q11.9

What audio formats does the JDK support besides Sun's .au *format?*

No other ones; the JDK 1.0.2 (and 1.1) supports only the .au **format.**

The current releases of the JDK (1.0.2 and 1.1) support only the .au audio file format:

- 8 bits per sample

- 8000 samples per second (8000 Hz)

- one channel (mono)

- mu-law encoding of amplitude (nonlinear, quasi-logarithmic)

This format represents sound with approximately telephone-voice quality. It is commonly used to compress the dynamic range of a 16-bit linear format into half as many bits.

Sound files in other formats can be converted to the .au format with varying degrees of difficulty. The easiest is NeXT's .snd format, which is practically identical to the .au format. If you have a NeXT .snd file, you can simply rename it from XXX.snd to XXX.au and it should work. The two formats differ slightly in their sampling rate—8000 samples per second (.au) versus 8012 samples per second (.snd)—but this 0.15 percent difference should be negligible for many uses.

Sound files in other audio formats require more work to convert to the .au format. The best-known tool for this is the free SoX program; for further information, see http://www.spies.com/Sox/.

Q11.10

Is there a method for generating sounds of a given frequency, something along the lines of playTone(int frequency, int duration)*?*

No; the current JDK (1.0.2 and 1.1) does not provide any methods for sound generation.

The audio capabilities provided by the JDK (1.0.2 and 1.1) have focused on basic support for applet audio. You can load and play audio files specified by URLs, but there is no way to generate sounds directly from within your program. The JavaMedia APIs and implementation under development at JavaSoft will provide stunningly improved sound capabilities in upcoming releases.

MISCELLANEOUS

Q11.11

What's the difference between Java and JavaScript?

Java is a general-purpose object-oriented programming language developed at Sun; Javascript is a web-page scripting language developed at Netscape.

Java and JavaScript have little in common beyond the similarity in names. Table 11.5 enumerates several of the main differences.

Table 11.5: Java versus JavaScript

Java	JavaScript
is a full-featured programming language for applications and applets	is a scripting language for web pages
can run as a stand-alone application or as an applet within a browser	has no existence outside of browsers and html
code does not occur in web pages, only an APPLET tag	code is written entirely inside of web pages
is compiled into class files, which a browser can download via the URL specified in an APPLET tag	is interpreted directly from the web page by the browser
can execute on any Java Virtual Machine implementation	can execute in a Netscape browser
enforces strong security constraints to prevent code loaded over the net from damaging your system	provides minimal security constraints
was developed at Sun Microsystems	was developed at Netscape
was originally named Oak	was originally named LiveScript

See also: Q4.1, Q4.2, Q4.4

Q11.12

How can I obtain a performance profile of my Java program?

In the JDK (1.0.2 and 1.1) you can use the Java interpreter's `-prof` option; this creates a `java.prof` file with information about which methods call which, and how much time is spent executing a given method.

The JDK implementation of the Java Virtual Machine supports simple performance monitoring of Java methods. If you specify the -prof option when running the java command (e.g., java -prof MyClass), the virtual machine executes your code and produces a file named java.prof when it exits. (Starting with the JDK 1.1, you can also specify an alternate name for the profile file using -prof: *<file>*, e.g., java -prof:MyClass.prof MyClass.) java.prof is a plain text file that you can inspect with any text editor, or process further with a separate analysis program.

The java.prof file primarily traces method execution. It reports on which methods invoked which other methods, how many times, and how long each method spent executing. This information is organized by pairs of methods: the callee (the method whose execution is measured) and the caller (the method invoking the callee). For each callee–caller pair, java.prof provides a line with four fields, as shown in Table 11.6.

Table 11.6: Fields in a java.prof **Method Line**

count	the number of times this caller invoked this callee
callee	the method whose execution time is reported
caller	the method that invoked the callee
time	the total time (in milliseconds) that the callee spent executing when invoked by this caller

How to use the information in a java.prof file is best seen by example. Consider the following source file, Foo.java, as a starting point:

```java
class Foo {
    void m1() {  m2();  m3();  }
    void m2() {  m3();  }
    void m3() {}
    public static void main(String[] args) {
        Foo foo = new Foo();
        for (int i = 0; i < 100000; ++i) {
            foo.m1();
            foo.m2();
            foo.m3();
        }
    }
}
```

After compiling `Foo.java`, run `java -prof Foo` and then inspect the resulting `java.prof` file. One pass on a 140 MHz Sun UltraSparc (using the JDK 1.1.1) produced the following data:

```
count callee caller time
200000 Foo.m3()V Foo.m2()V 258
100000 Foo.m2()V Foo.m1()V 490
100000 Foo.m3()V Foo.m1()V 129
100000 Foo.m2()V Foo.main([Ljava/lang/String;)V 532
100000 Foo.m3()V Foo.main([Ljava/lang/String;)V 156
100000 Foo.m1()V Foo.main([Ljava/lang/String;)V 1241
...
...
```

From these lines, you can extract information for specific callee–caller pairs, or for combinations of such pairs. The `m3` method, for instance, was invoked a total of 400,000 times: 200,000 times by `m2`, 100,000 times by `m1`, and 100,000 times by `main`. As another example, the `m2` method spent a total of 532 milliseconds in 100,000 calls by `main` (about 5 microseconds per call) and 490 milliseconds in 100,000 in calls by `m1`.

Note: the JDK 1.0.2 attempted to format the information in `java.prof` using aligned columns, truncating method names if necessary. This made the data somewhat easier to view, but at the expense of sometimes removing crucial parts of method names. The JDK 1.1 simply presents the full information, and leaves any formatting work to be handled separately.

ProfileExample.html

See also: Q3.9

Q11.13

What is the purpose of the executable files that have an extra _g at the ends of their names (e.g., `java_g`*)?*

The XYZ_g **executables are significantly more debuggable than their plain** XYZ **counterparts (but run significantly slower); they are useful when you need to submit a bug report to JavaSoft concerning the executable itself rather than one of the class libraries.**

Q11.14

If Java is platform-independent, why doesn't it run on all platforms?

The Java language, standard class libraries, and compiled class files are platform-independent, but the Java Virtual Machine underneath them must be ported to specific native platforms one by one.

Java technology spans several levels. Closest to the developer is the source code. Pure Java source code is written in the Java language and uses the standard Java class libraries. Java is designed to be wholly platform-independent at this level. For example, the Java language fully specifies the order of evaluation in expressions and in method argument lists; other languages, such as C, allow a compiler to implement its own platform-specific order. Similarly, the standard Java class libraries define cross-platform capabilities and behaviors, which get mapped onto specific native platforms. Apart from execution speed and multi-threaded timing, your Java program should give essentially identical behavior independent of the native platform (Windows NT/95, Solaris, Macintosh, or other) that you run it on.

At the next level, Java source code is compiled to Java class files, which embody an architecture-neutral binary format for executable code. Like the Java language, the class file format is defined independent of any specific hardware platform. Its "machine instructions" are designed for one specific target, the Java Virtual Machine.

The Java Virtual Machine constitutes the foundation layer of Java technology. Java programs, compiled to class files, must finally execute in some machine, and the Java Virtual Machine provides that machine entirely in software. The Java Virtual Machine is itself a program that runs on the native platform. It bridges the gap between the platform-neutral intended behavior of a Java program and the actual execution of code on a specific platform.

Java's target for platform independence is that an application writer needs to write an application only once, and then it can run identically on all platforms that support the Java Virtual Machine. Thus, Java applications are not ported from one platform to another; only the underlying virtual machine is. The leverage in this model is tremendous and unmistakable: one porting effort per platform, the virtual machine, immediately enables the world of pure Java applications to run on the new platform.

Index

& (logical-and) operator
preventing sign extension of `byte` value with;
44 (Q2.2)
+ (plus) operator
addition as use of; 49 (Q2.7)
as only overloaded operator; 49 (Q2.7)
string concatenation as use of; 49 (Q2.7)
>>> (right shift) operator
preventing sign extension of `byte` value with;
44 (Q2.2)
127.0.0.1 (IP address)
as loopback interface; 246 (Q10.20)
255.255.255.255 (IP address)
as reserved broadcast address; 254 (Q10.27)

A

abstract
abstract class
concrete class compared with; 28 (Q1.24)
interface compared with; 27 (Q1.24)
(table); 28 (Q1.24)
interface implemented by; 26 (Q1.21)
interfaces and; 25–32 (Q1.20–Q1.28)
obtaining lock for; 213 (Q9.9)
term definition and characteristics; 10 (Q1.9)
`abstract` keyword
abstract class defined with; 11 (Q1.9)
abstract method defined with; 9 (Q1.8)
interface need not include; 27 (Q1.23)
nonmatch permitted in method overriding;
19 (Q1.16)
as reserved keyword; 46 (Q2.4)
abstract method
term definition and characteristics; 9 (Q1.8)
accept method
run in separate thread; 249 (Q10.24)
(code example); 250 (Q10.24)
access
See also protections; security
accessor methods
for event information; 151 (Q7.1)
`getSource`; 152 (Q7.1)
(table); 154–155 (Q7.1)

access (*continued*)
levels
for classes and interfaces; 36 (Q1.32)
for methods, constructors, and fields;
36 (Q1.32)
package support for; 33 (Q1.29)
`protected` access; 37 (Q1.33)
for public methods and fields within nonpublic classes; 38 (Q1.34)
modifiers
for classes and interfaces; 36 (Q1.32)
for methods, constructors, and fields;
36 (Q1.32)
packages and; 33–40 (Q1.29–Q1.34)
as part of class declaration; 3 (Q1.2)
accessing
applet data from thread
advantage of `Thread(Runnable)` constructor; 204 (Q9.2)
limited in `Thread` subclass; 204 (Q9.2)
class information; 58 (Q2.15)
class objects; 213 (Q9.9)
files via `FileDialog` class; 130 (Q5.15)
image data; 190 (Q8.19)
local host IP address; 244 (Q10.17)
monitor locks; 210 (Q9.7)
objects returned by `forName`; 85 (Q3.7)
operating system calls; 257 (Q11.2)
public methods, fields, and constructors at run
time; 60 (Q2.16)
superclass with `super` keyword
for constructors; 20 (Q1.17)
for methods; 21 (Q1.17)
for variables; 22 (Q1.17)
versus inheritance; 20 (Q1.17)
URL information
with `getHeader`; 238 (Q10.10)
(code example); 239 (Q10.10)
with `URLConnection`; 235 (Q10.7)
WWW information
with http GET request; 240 (Q10.12)
action events
`ActionEvent` class
objects generated by menu items, (code
example); 163 (Q7.8)

action events (*continued*)

  ActionEvent class (*continued*)

    position in JDK 1.1 class hierarchy, (table);
      152 (Q7.1)

    public methods, (table); 154 (Q7.2)

  ActionListener interface

    for catching action events, (code example);
      162 (Q7.7)

    public methods, (table); 157 (Q7.3)

  generated

    in JDK 1.0.2, (table); 142 (Q6.5)

    in JDK 1.1, (table); 161 (Q7.7)

  handled

    in JDK 1.0.2 with action method, (table);
      140 (Q6.4)

    in JDK 1.1 with actionPerformed method;
      161 (Q7.7)

  information

    in JDK 1.0.2, (table); 137 (Q6.2)

    in JDK 1.1, (table); 154 (Q7.1)

  registering listener for; 161 (Q7.7)

  term definition; 141 (Q6.5)

activating

  web pages from applets; 112 (Q4.21)

adapter

  when to use for events; 158 (Q7.4)

addImage method

  for adding images to tracking group, (code
    example); 183 (Q8.12)

add method

  assigning components to containers, (code
    example); 123 (Q5.6)

  removing component from previous parent;
    123 (Q5.7)

  invalidate invoked by, (table);
    122 (Q5.5)

  peer creation triggered by; 126 (Q5.10)

add...Listener methods

  addActionListener method

    for action events; 161 (Q7.7)

  addWindowListener method

    for window events; 167 (Q7.11)

  registering event listeners; 153 (Q7.2)

addition

  as use of plus (+) operator; 49 (Q2.7)

address(es)

  accessing local host; 244 (Q10.17)

  internet; 244–245 (Q10.16–Q10.18)

adjustment events

  AdjustmentEvent class

    position in JDK 1.1 class hierarchy, (table);
      152 (Q7.1)

    public methods, (table); 154 (Q7.2)

  AdjustmentListener interface

    public methods, (table); 157 (Q7.3)

agents

  threads as independent; 201 (Q9.1)

algorithm

  garbage collection, in JDK; 83 (Q3.5)

align attribute (APPLET tag)

  characteristics; 96 (Q4.4)

  from JDK README file; 98 (Q4.7)

allocation

  of arrays dynamically; 65 (Q2.19)

alt attribute (APPLET tag)

  characteristics; 96 (Q4.4)

  from JDK README file; 98 (Q4.7)

animations

  controlled with MemoryImageSource;
    195 (Q8.22)

  preparing for, (code example); 195 (Q8.22)

  reducing flicker in; 177 (Q8.5)

  starting; 109 (Q4.18)

  stopping; 109 (Q4.18)

  triggering updates in, (code example);
    196 (Q8.22)

anonymous inner classes

  (code example); 156 (Q7.2)

anononymous interaction

  characteristic of wait-notify; 214 (Q9.10)

API (Application Programming Interface)

  characteristics; 75 (Q2.26)

  cross-platform in AWT; 125 (Q5.9)

  inter-applet communication as part of;
    112 (Q4.20)

  reflection API (JDK 1.1); 61 (Q2.17)

append method

  (table); 256 (Q11.1)

applet(s)

  See also AWT (Abstract Window Toolkit); key
    themes; networks

  activating web pages from; 112 (Q4.21)

  Applet class

    containing main method to function as appli-
      cation; 93 (Q4.3)

    overriding update, (sample code);
      16 (Q1.14)

applet(s) (*continued*)
APPLET tag (HTML)
attributes; 95 (Q4.4)
class file location syntax; 101 (Q4.9)
code attribute as pointer to class file;
100 (Q4.8)
as HTML applet enabler; 92 (Q4.1)
naming applets in; 112 (Q4.20)
syntax and component description;
98 (Q4.7)
AppletContext interface
used to handle audio clips, (code example);
264 (Q11.8)
implementation required for linking in
applets; 115 (Q4.23)
AppletStub interface
implementation required for linking in
applets; 115 (Q4.23)
applications compared with; 91–95 (Q4.1–4.3),
92 (Q4.2)
(table); 93 (Q4.2)
background
setting color; 104 (Q4.12)
transparent not possible; 104 (Q4.13)
capabilities compared to applications, (table);
95 (Q4.3)
characteristics, components, and requirements;
91 (Q4.1)
class file location specified in URL; 101 (Q4.9)
communication; 111–114 (Q4.20–Q4.22)
components of; 99 (Q4.8)
constructors not used by; 109 (Q4.17)
context
methods invoked by; 107 (Q4.16)
requirements for; 92 (Q4.1)
data access from thread
advantage of Thread(Runnable) constructor; 204 (Q9.2)
limited in Thread subclass; 204 (Q9.2)
determining applet size; 103 (Q4.11)
DTD URL; 99 (Q4.7)
image loading; 179 (Q8.9)
including information for non–Java-enabled
browsers; 97 (Q4.6)
including multiple applets on web page;
97 (Q4.5)
installing; 95–103 (Q4.4–Q4.10)
inter-applet communication
different web pages; 114 (Q4.22)
same web page; 111 (Q4.20)

applet(s) (*continued*)
life cycle managed by applet context and AWT;
107 (Q4.16)
loading
into applications; 114 (Q4.23)
with forName method; 86 (Q3.7)
menus workaround; 105 (Q4.14)
miscellaneous topics; 114–116 (Q4.23–Q4.24)
playing sounds in; 261 (Q11.5)
simultaneous play of mulitple audio clips;
262 (Q11.6)
program structure; 107–111 (Q4.16–Q4.19)
re-exposure handled by AWT; 177 (Q8.6)
restrictions
on reading remote files; 238 (Q10.9)
on writing to URL-specified files;
243 (Q10.13)
security exception for external URL connection
attempt; 243 (Q10.15)
TAG page URL; 99 (Q4.7)
term definition; 91 (Q4.1)
threads interacting with system threads;
223 (Q9.16)
user interface; 103–107 (Q4.11–Q4.15)
writing applications that can run as; 93 (Q4.3)
application(s)
See also key themes
applets compared with; 91–95 (Q4.1–Q4.3)
security exception differences; 243 (Q10.15)
(table); 93 (Q4.2), 95 (Q4.3)
builder tools supported by reflection API;
62 (Q2.17)
fetching documents in; 243 (Q10.14)
loading
applets into; 114 (Q4.23)
images into; 180 (Q8.10)
playing sounds in; 263 (Q11.8)
starting, by invocation of main; 77 (Q3.1)
terminating; 144 (Q6.7)
writing applets that can run as; 93 (Q4.3)
archives attribute (APPLET tag)
characteristics from JDK README file;
99 (Q4.7)
arg field
meaning in JDK 1.0.2 AWT, (table); 135 (Q6.1)
arguments
passed by value in method invocations;
54 (Q2.12)
array(s); 65–68 (Q2.10–Q2.21)
See also data
allocated dynamically; 65 (Q2.19)

array(s) (*continued*)
ArrayIndexOutOfBoundsException
    meaning of; 69 (Q2.22)
classes compared with, (table); 67 (Q2.20)
creating; 66 (Q2.19)
determining size of; 68 (Q2.21)
dynamic
    allocation at run time; 65 (Q2.19)
    extension requires Vector class; 66 (Q2.19)
fixed size after creation; 65 (Q2.19)
holding function pointer equivalents;
        64 (Q2.18)
initializer
    in array declaration; 66 (Q2.19)
    in JDK 1.1 array creation expression;
        66 (Q2.19)
initializing; 66 (Q2.20)
as object; 3 (Q1.2)
as reference type; 41 (Q2.1)
variables, have object references as value;
        12 (Q1.10)
arrow keys
handling arrow key events
    in JDK 1.0.2; 142 (Q6.6)
    in JDK 1.1; 169 (Q7.13)
assignment
compatibility tested with instanceof
    operator; 30 (Q1.26)
conversion triggered by byte to int
    promotion; 43 (Q2.2)
of listeners to menu items, (code example);
        163 (Q7.8)
asynchronous execution
of drawImage method
    impact on image loading; 185 (Q8.13)
    rationale for; 181 (Q8.11)
of repaint method
    managed by AWT; 175 (Q8.3)
    overwhelmed by repreated invocations;
        175 (Q8.4)
audio; 261–265 (Q11.5–Q11.10)
See also http://www.spies.com/Sox/; media
.au as only supported audio format;
        264 (Q11.9)
AudioClip class
    getAudio method; 261 (Q11.5)
    simultaneous start of mulitple clips;
        262 (Q11.6)
estimating audio clip completion, (code exam-
    ple); 263 (Q11.7)

audio (*continued*)
formats
    conversion; 265 (Q11.9)
    supported; 264 (Q11.9)
planned capabilities in Java Media Framework;
        263 (Q11.7), 264 (Q11.8)
playing in applet; 261 (Q11.5)
playing in application; 263 (Q11.8)
simultaneous play of multiple clips;
        262 (Q11.6)
sound generation not supported; 265 (Q11.10)
AWT (Abstract Window Toolkit)
See also applet(s); browser; component(s);
        containers; frame(s); key themes;
        menu(s); windows
applet methods invoked by; 107 (Q4.16)
applet must work with; 93 (Q4.3)
AWTEvent class
    as base class for all AWT-specific events;
        151 (Q7.1)
    position in JDK 1.1 class hierarchy, (table);
        152 (Q7.1)
    public methods, (table); 154 (Q7.2)
(chapter); 117–133 (Q5.1–5.21)
components
    Component class
        as abstract superclass; 11 (Q1.9)
        as base class for AWT user-interface
            elements; 117 (Q5.1)
        drawing; 173–179 (Q8.1–Q8.8)
        peers as native platform counterpart;
            125 (Q5.9)
dynamically adding components; 122 (Q5.6)
event
    class hierarchy in JDK 1.1, (table);
        152 (Q7.1)
    model compatibility between JDK 1.0.2 and
        1.1; 160 (Q7.6)
layout manager; 119 (Q5.2)
    assignment by default; 118 (Q5.2)
listener interfaces and methods in JDK 1.1,
        (table); 157 (Q7.3)
paint invoked by; 173 (Q8.1)
single drawing thread, as consistency mecha-
    nism; 175 (Q8.3)
synchronization
    avoiding deadlock in validate or layout;
        122 (Q5.5)
    managing containment relationships, (code
        example); 211 (Q9.8)
thread blocked by applets; 224 (Q9.17)

B

background

filling as re-exposure action; 177 (Q8.6)

setting color of; 104 (Q4.12)

setting image as; 104 (Q4.12)

transparent

not possible for applets; 104 (Q4.13)

supported in JDK 1.1; 177 (Q8.7)

beep method

signaling errors with; 132 (Q5.19)

behavior

modified by subclasses; 13 (Q1.11)

platform-dependent because of thread scheduling; 222 (Q9.15)

bell-shaped distribution

generating random numbers from; 260 (Q11.4)

binary

nature of class files; 116 (Q4.24)

input methods; 229 (Q10.3)

binding

See also virtual methods

dynamic; 23 (Q1.18)

static; 23 (Q1.18)

blocking threads

by interaction between applet thread and browser thread; 223 (Q9.17)

system thread; 223 (Q9.16)

strategies to prevent; 224 (Q9.17)

boolean

boolean keyword

as reserved keyword; 46 (Q2.4)

Class instance corresponding to, (table); 63 (Q2.17)

literal, (table); 50 (Q2.8)

borders

BorderLayout class; 119 (Q5.2)

creating windows without; 129 (Q5.13)

drawing covered by frame; 128 (Q5.12)

reserving border space with inset values; 119 (Q5.3)

break

break keyword

as reserved keyword; 46 (Q2.4)

statement, limited goto-like power; 46 (Q2.4)

broadcast

datagram packets; 253 (Q10.27)

(code example); 254 (Q10.27)

IP address; 254 (Q10.27)

browser

See also AWT (Abstract Window Toolkit)

applet thread interaction issues; 223 (Q9.17)

context as controller of applet execution, (table); 93 (Q4.2)

document fetch simulated by stand-alone application; 243 (Q10.14)

requesting web page display from; 113 (Q4.21)

buffer(ing)

BufferedReader class

enhancing System.in with, JDK 1.1, (code example); 228 (Q10.2)

Unicode input handling; 226 (Q10.1)

double

drawing offscreen images with; 189 (Q8.18)

(code example); 190 (Q8.18)

flushing output; 232 (Q10.5)

buttons

adding and removing from panel, (code example); 123 (Q5.6)

action events generated

in JDK 1.0.2, (table); 142 (Q6.5)

in JDK 1.1, (table); 161 (Q7.7)

Button class

constructor example; 21 (Q1.17)

events associated with, (table); 137 (Q6.2)

as subclass of Component; 14 (Q1.12)

bytecodes

characteristics; 78 (Q3.2)

interpreted; 81 (Q3.4)

term definition; 78 (Q3.2)

bytes

See also data

byte keyword

as reserved keyword; 46 (Q2.4)

Byte class

converting string to byte value, (table); 231 (Q10.4)

byte type

Class instance corresponding to, (table); 63 (Q2.17)

treating as unsigned value; 43 (Q2.2)

as stream for sockets; 246 (Q10.19)

Unicode incompatible with; 226 (Q10.1)

C

C/C++ language

capabilities omitted from Java

enumerated types; 45 (Q2.3)

C/C++ language (*continued*)

  capabilities omitted from Java (*continued*)

    operator overloading; 48 (Q2.7)

    preprocessor macros; 48 (Q2.7)

    `typedefs`; 48 (Q2.7)

  code migration help in error message; 46 (Q2.4)

  equivalents in Java

    case sensitivity; 47 (Q2.5)

    data structures; 52 (Q2.10)

    standard input, output, and error; 227 (Q10.2)

    virtual methods; 23 (Q1.18)

  `include` versus Java `import`; 35 (Q1.30)

  program speed compared with Java; 88 (Q3.9)

callback methods

  `sleep` not welcome in; 224 (Q9.17)

canvas

  as drawing surface placed in frame; 129 (Q5.12)

capitalization

  conventions for identifiers; 47 (Q2.5)

carriage return

  as line terminator; 225 (Q10.1)

case

  `case` keyword

    as reserved keyword; 46 (Q2.4)

  conversion methods in the `String` class, (table); 256 (Q11.1)

  sensitivity and capitalization conventions; 47 (Q2.5)

casting

  conversionof `byte` to `int`; 43 (Q2.2)

  `double` literal to `float`; 51 (Q2.8)

  references, not objects; 51 (Q2.9)

  references returned by `newInstance` method; 85 (Q3.7)

  returned value to more specific type; 20 (Q1.16)

catch

  `catch` keyword

    as reserved keyword; 46 (Q2.4)

  catching events

    action, (code example); 162 (Q7.7)

    JDK 1.1 versus JDK 1.0.2; 160 (Q7.5)

    from menu items, JDK 1.1; 163 (Q7.8)

  catching exceptions

    catcher; 68 (Q2.22)

    code for; 69 (Q2.22)

    method execution compared with, (table); 69 (Q2.22)

CGI (Common Gateway Interface)

  scripts as target of URL connetcion; 239 (Q10.11)

  sending data to; 240 (Q10.12)

  tell-tale inclusion of "cgi-bin" in URL; 240 (Q10.11)

chain of initialization

  `super` keyword used in; 20 (Q1.17)

char

  `char` keyword

    as reserved keyword; 46 (Q2.4)

  character conversion methods in

    `String` class, (table); 256 (Q11.1)

    `StringBuffer` class, (table); 256 (Q11.1)

  `Class` instance corresponding to, (table); 63 (Q2.17)

  literal, (table); 50 (Q2.8)

  as Unicode character data type; 226 (Q10.1)

check... methods

  as trigger for image loading, (table); 182 (Q8.11)

  (table); 184 (Q8.12)

Checkbox class

  action event generated

    in JDK 1.0.2, (table); 142 (Q6.5)

    not in JDK 1.1; 161 (Q7.7)

  information in action event, (table); 137 (Q6.2)

checked exceptions

  advantages of; 71 (Q2.24)

  handling; 70 (Q2.23)

  as part of API contract; 75 (Q2.26)

  term definition; 70 (Q2.23)

  unchecked exceptions compared with, (table); 72 (Q2.24)

Choice class

  action event generated by, JDK 1.0.2, (table); 142 (Q6.5)

  events associated with, (table); 137 (Q6.2)

  JDK 1.1 changes; 161 (Q7.7)

  not included in JDK 1.1 action events list; 161 (Q7.7)

class files

  as applet components; 99 (Q4.8)

  corrupted by http server; 115 (Q4.24)

  disassembled by `javap`; 79 (Q3.3)

  interpreted by virtual machine; 81 (Q3.4)

  maximum identifier size in; 48 (Q2.6)

  specified in applet URL; 101 (Q4.9)

  verified by `javap`; 88 (Q3.8)

class(es)

See also object-oriented concepts

abstract

concrete classes compared with; 28 (Q1.24)

interface compared with, (table); 28 (Q1.24)

interfaces and; 25–32 (Q1.20–Q1.28)

term definition and characteristics; 10 (Q1.9)

access modifiers; 36 (Q1.32)

accessing information about; 58 (Q2.15)

arrays compared with, (table); 67 (Q2.20)

`ClassCastException` as result of illegal downward cast; 52 (Q2.9)

`Class` class

accessing Java data type information at run time; 58 (Q2.15)

automatic import of; 35 (Q1.31)

instances corresponding to primitive data types, (table); 63 (Q2.17)

class constants; 45 (Q2.3)

class hierarchy

interfaces independent of; 29 (Q1.24)

`class` keyword

as reserved keyword; 46 (Q2.4)

`class` literal

obtaining `Class` instance with; 59 (Q2.15)

class loader

identity obtained from `Class` class; 58 (Q2.15)

processes managed by; 87 (Q3.8)

term definition; 86 (Q3.7)

verification options; 88 (Q3.8)

class methods

declared as `static synchronized` for locking on class object; 212 (Q9.9)

declared with `static` keyword; 8 (Q1.6)

instance methods compared with; 7 (Q1.6)

overriding not permitted with; 23 (Q1.18)

relation to class; 4 (Q1.3)

static reference to nonstatic variable, error; 57 (Q2.14)

class objects

methods that obtain; 213 (Q9.9)

synchronization of; 212 (Q9.9)

class variables

definition of; 57 (Q2.14)

instance variables compared with; 6 (Q1.5)

object references as value of; 12 (Q1.10)

classes, interfaces, and packages, (chapter); 1–40 (Q1.1–Q1.34)

designed to support cloning; 32 (Q1.28)

class(es) *(continued)*

`final` class

characteristics and use; 24 (Q1.19)

inner classes

creating function pointer equivalents with; 64 (Q2.18)

event handling simplification with, (code example); 162 (Q7.7)

term definition; 65 (Q2.18), 153 (Q7.2)

instances compared with, (table); 3 (Q1.2)

See instance(s);

interfaces compared with; 25 (Q1.20)

interfaces implemented by; 26 (Q1.21)

nonpublic containing public members; 38 (Q1.34)

objects, and methods; 1–12 (Q1.1–Q1.10)

as reference type; 41 (Q2.1)

term definition; 2 (Q1.1)

characteristics and; 2 (Q1.2)

cleaning up

system resources; 84 (Q3.6)

client

See also network(s); servers

creating `Socket` instance; 245 (Q10.19)

datagram handling by; 253 (Q10.26)

GET request used by; 241 (Q10.12)

clipping rectangle

See also drawing

handling, JDK 1.0.2; 192 (Q8.20)

methods to get and set, (table); 197 (Q8.23)

narrowed by `clipRect` method; 192 (Q8.20)

resettable in JDK 1.1; 196 (Q8.23)

(code example); 197 (Q8.23)

used in JDK 1.0.2 image copying, (code example); 193 (Q8.21)

cloning

characteristics and restrictions; 31 (Q1.27)

`clone` method

error messages; 31 (Q1.27)

reasons for overriding; 31 (Q1.28)

`Cloneable` interface

implementation required for cloning; 31 (Q1.27), 31 (Q1.28)

no methods in; 32 (Q1.28)

deep versus shallow copying; 32 (Q1.28)

designing class for; 31 (Q1.28)

closing windows

in JDK 1.0.2 by catching `WINDOW_DESTROY` event; 143 (Q6.7)

in JDK 1.1 by registering window listener; 167 (Q7.11)

code

characteristics and tradeoffs, *See* efficiency,
extensibility, flexibility, portability,
robustness, safety, usability

code attribute (APPLET tag)

characteristics from JDK README file;
98 (Q4.7)

codebase attribute (APPLET tag)

characteristics from JDK README file;
98 (Q4.7)

encapsulation in classes; 64 (Q2.18)

examples, *See* example(s), code

not added by import declaration; 35 (Q1.30)

protected by monitor; 212 (Q9.8)

style for creating instances; 9 (Q1.7)

color(s)

background; 104 (Q4.12)

Color objects created from extracted pixel
values; 191 (Q8.19)

default model, (table); 188 (Q8.17)

reversal with XOR drawing mode; 178 (Q8.8)

communication

applet; 111–114 (Q4.20–Q4.22)

on different web pages; 114 (Q4.22)

on the same web page; 111 (Q4.20)

interface specification of; 25 (Q1.20)

through socket without network; 246 (Q10.20)

compatibility

of JDK 1.0.2 event code within JDK 1.1 event
model; 160 (Q7.6)

compilation

See also Java language; Java Virtual Machine
(JVM)

exception checking

advantages of; 71 (Q2.24)

conditions enforced by; 72 (Q2.24)

of Java source code into bytecodes; 81 (Q3.4)

JIT (just-in-time)

characteristics; 82 (Q3.4)

speed impact of; 88 (Q3.9)

optimization as source of problems with verification; 87 (Q3.8)

type checking

advantage lost by dynamic method invocation; 64 (Q2.17)

use of instanceof operator; 30 (Q1.26)

units, package declaration for; 33 (Q1.29)

component(s)

See also AWT (Abstract Window Toolkit)

Component class

as abstract superclass; 11 (Q1.9)

component(s) *(continued)*

Component class *(continued)*

as base class for AWT user-interface
elements; 117 (Q5.1)

characteristics; 117 (Q5.1)

events associated with, (table); 136 (Q6.2)

imageUpdate method for tracking images;
185 (Q8.13)

information in event types, (table);
136 (Q6.2)

methods for positioning; 127 (Q5.11)

methods that trigger image loading, (table);
182 (Q8.11)

requestFocus method; 131 (Q5.17)

setBackground method inherited by
Applet; 104 (Q4.12)

Component.LOCK synchronization object;
211 (Q9.8)

ComponentAdapter class

strategies for use; 158 (Q7.4)

ComponentEvent class

position in JDK 1.1 class hierarchy, (table);
152 (Q7.1)

public methods, (table); 154 (Q7.2)

window resizing notification; 168 (Q7.12)

ComponentListener interface

methods, (table); 157 (Q7.3)

used for window resizing, (code example);
168 (Q7.12)

containers, peers, and; 117–126 (Q5.1–Q5.10)

drawing; 173–179 (Q8.1–Q8.8)

outlines around groups; 124 (Q5.8)

grouped in container; 117 (Q5.1)

integration frameworks supported by reflection
API; 62 (Q2.17)

layout manager

disadvantages of not using; 120 (Q5.4)

layout controlled by; 118 (Q5.1)

lightweight components, in JDK 1.1; 178
(Q8.7)

notification in JDK 1.1

for relocating; 168 (Q7.12)

for resizing; 168 (Q7.12)

peers as native platform counterparts to;
125 (Q5.9)

re-exposure actions taken by AWT; 177 (Q8.6)

redrawing with repaint method; 174 (Q8.3)

setting

cursor in JDK 1.1; 107 (Q4.15)

focus on; 131 (Q5.17)

single container requirement for; 123 (Q5.7)

computation
as applet capability; 92 (Q4.1)
concatenation of strings
as use of plus (+) operator; 49 (Q2.7)
with concat method, (table); 256 (Q11.1)
concrete classes
abstract classes and interfaces compared with, (table); 28 (Q1.24)
implemented by abstract class; 11 (Q1.9)
term definition; 10 (Q1.8)
condition variables
obtaining effect of; 215 (Q9.11)
connection
to network managed with URLConnection; 235 (Q10.7)
to URLs; 236 (Q10.8)
conservative
mark-and-sweep garbage collection; 83 (Q3.5)
term definition; 83 (Q3.5)
constants
See also final keyword
class constant
near match for enum; 45 (Q2.3)
term definition; 45 (Q2.3)
const keyword
not allowed in Java; 46 (Q2.4)
as reserved keyword; 46 (Q2.4)
expressions and; 41–53 (Q2.1–Q2.10)
f suffix on float constants, reasons for; 49 (Q2.8)
in KeyEvent class, (table); 169 (Q7.13)
static final variables as; 25 (Q1.20)
constraint-based layout managers
JDK 1.1 support for; 119 (Q5.2)
constructors
See also object-oriented concepts
accessing superclass with super keyword; 20 (Q1.17)
creating class instances with; 8 (Q1.7)
Class class information available in JDK 1.1; 59 (Q2.15)
class method in place of, in InetAddress class; 244 (Q10.16)
Constructor class
for inspecting constructors; 60 (Q2.16)
default superclass constructor; 21 (Q1.17)
not used by applets; 109 (Q4.17)
for specifying listening address in Server-Socket class; 250 (Q10.25)

containers
See also AWT (Abstract Window Toolkit)
border space specified for; 119 (Q5.3)
components, peers and; 117–126 (Q5.1–Q5.10)
Container class; 117 (Q5.1)
ContainerAdapter class
strategies for use of; 158 (Q7.4)
ContainerEvent class
position in JDK 1.1 class hierarchy, (table); 152 (Q7.1)
public methods, (table); 154 (Q7.2)
ContainerListener interface
methods, (table); 157 (Q7.3)
containment hierarchy
events propagated up in JDK 1.0.2; 138 (Q6.3)
finding Frame instance in; 106 (Q4.15)
inheritance hierarchy compared with; 118 (Q5.1)
for menu, rooted in frame; 145 (Q6.8)
as strict tree structure; 123 (Q5.7)
term definition; 117 (Q5.1)
layout
dynamic; 121 (Q5.5)
handled by layout manager; 118 (Q5.2)
process split between validate and invalidate; 121 (Q5.5)
ScrollPane class
for scrolling in JDK 1.1; 165 (Q7.10)
context
applet context
methods invoked by; 107 (Q4.16)
requirements for; 92 (Q4.1)
browser context
impact on applet execution, (table); 93 (Q4.2), 223 (Q9.16)
continue
continue keyword
as reserved keyword; 46 (Q2.4)
statement, limited goto-like power; 46 (Q2.4)
contract
API; 75 (Q2.26)
term definition; 2 (Q1.1)
control flow
See also exceptions; methods
in threads; 201–208 (Q9.1–Q9.5)
conventions
capitalization
in class constants; 45 (Q2.3)
in identifiers; 47 (Q2.5)

conventions (*continued*)

  names of `DataInputStream` read...
    methods; 229 (Q10.3)

conversion

  audio formats; 265 (Q11.9)

  `byte`-oriented input to `char`-oriented input;
    226 (Q10.1)

  character case in `String` methods, (table);
    256 (Q11.1)

  image data; 180 (Q8.9)

  of strings to numerical values; 110 (Q4.19)
    (table); 230 (Q10.4)

coordinates

  absolute

    window positioning with; 128 (Q5.11)

copying

  deep versus shallow

    (code example); 32 (Q1.28)

    term definitions; 32 (Q1.28)

  images

    JDK 1.0.2, (code example); 193 (Q8.21)

    subareas; 198 (Q8.24)

      (code example); 199 (Q8.24)

creating

  arrays; 66 (Q2.19)

  broadcast datagram packets; 253 (Q10.27)
    (code example); 254 (Q10.27)

  class types from dynamic names; 86 (Q3.7)

  images from raw image data; 188 (Q8.17)

  `InetAddress` instances; 244 (Q10.16)

  instances; 8 (Q1.7)

    returned by `forName`; 86 (Q3.7)

    at run time; 62 (Q2.17)

  `java.prof` files; 266 (Q11.12)

  nonblocking server sockets; 249 (Q10.24)

  peers; 126 (Q5.10)

  sockets; 245 (Q10.19)

  threads; 201–208 (Q9.1–Q9.5), 203 (Q9.2)

  windows

    nonresizable; 131 (Q5.16)

    without borders; 129 (Q5.13)

creation

  applet

    managed by applet context; 108 (Q4.16)

CropImageFilter class

  image loading impact; 182 (Q8.11)

cursors

  setting in JDK 1.0.2; 106 (Q4.15)

  setting in JDK 1.1; 107 (Q4.15)

D

data

  See also array(s); bytes; key themes; list(s);
    numbers; stacks; string(s)

  `DataInputStream` class

    characteristics and use; 225 (Q10.1)

    enhancing `System.in` capabilities in JDK
      1.0.2, (code example); 228 (Q10.2)

  files as applet components; 99 (Q4.8)

  not protected by monitors; 212 (Q9.8)

  pixel data

    creating images from; 188 (Q8.17)

  primitive data types

    advantages of; 42 (Q2.1)

    `Class` instances and class literals corre-
      sponding to, (table); 63 (Q2.17)

    obtaining Class instances for; 62 (Q2.17)

    reference types versus; 41 (Q2.1)

  shared data among threads

    added complexity; 201 (Q9.1)

    importance of synchronization; 208 (Q9.6)

  structures and types;

  tranferring from remote files; 237 (Q10.9)

datagram

  See also networks; sockets

  broadcast datagram packets

    creating; 253 (Q10.27)

    (code example); 254 (Q10.27)

    sending and receiving; 251 (Q10.26)

  `DatagramSocket` class

    receiving datagrams, (code example);
      253 (Q10.26)

    sending datagrams, (code example);
      252 (Q10.26)

  sockets

    characteristics and use; 251 (Q10.26)

dead state

  used for thread scheduling; 219 (Q9.13)

deadlocks

  See also threads

  detection, solution, and prevention;
    220 (Q9.14)

  precautions against, in container layout
    management; 122 (Q5.5)

  term definition; 220 (Q9.14)

  thread dumps, as analysis tool; 220 (Q9.14)

    (code example); 221 (Q9.14)

debugging

See also event-handling; exceptions

_g terminated files used for; 268 (Q11.13)

main method as useful tool for; 78 (Q3.1)

redraw failures due to repaint method;
175 (Q8.4)

declaring

arrays; 66 (Q2.19)

exceptions; 70 (Q2.22)

deep copying

term definition and code example; 32 (Q1.28)

default keyword

as reserved keyword; 46 (Q2.4)

defining

Exception subclasses; 70 (Q2.22)

dependencies

object-oriented facilities role in reducing;
2 (Q1.1)

deselecting list items

AWT notification in JDK 1.1; 164 (Q7.9)

design patterns

flyweight, *See* inner classes

destroying

applets

managed by applet context; 108 (Q4.16)

destroy method in Applet class

invoked by applet context; 94 (Q4.3),
107 (Q4.16)

sleep not recommended; 224 (Q9.17)

when invoked, (table); 108 (Q4.16)

destroy method in Process class

interacting with native platform processes,
(table); 258 (Q11.2)

frames; 144 (Q6.7)

peers; 126 (Q5.10)

windows

in JDK 1.0.2; 144 (Q6.7)

in JDK 1.1; 167 (Q7.11)

dialogs

Dialog class

positioning methods inherited from Window
class; 127 (Q5.11)

events associated with, (table); 136 (Q6.2)

windows, frames and; 127–131 (Q5.11–Q5.16)

directories

package relationship to; 102 (Q4.9)

disassembler

for Java class files, javap as; 79 (Q3.3)

displaying

images; 180 (Q8.9)

web pages from applets; 113 (Q4.21)

dispose method

destroying frames with; 144 (Q6.7)

DNS (Domain Name Service)

creating InetAddress instance from IP
address lacking DNS entry; 245 (Q10.18)

required in JDK 1.0.2 IP address use;
254 (Q10.27)

do keyword

as reserved keyword; 46 (Q2.4)

document base

term definition and relation to location of applet
files; 101 (Q4.9)

doLayout method (JDK 1.1)

invoked by validate; 122 (Q5.5)

double

Class instance corresponding to, (table);
63 (Q2.17)

converting from string; 230 (Q10.4)

Double class

converting string to numerical value
(code example); 230 (Q10.4)

(table); 230 (Q10.4)

double keyword

as reserved keyword; 46 (Q2.4)

Double(String) constructor

extracting numerical values from applet
parameters; 110 (Q4.19)

literal, (table); 50 (Q2.8)

random numbers; 260 (Q11.4)

suffix on numerical literals, (table); 50 (Q2.8)

drawing

See also AWT (Abstract Window Toolkit)

AWT components; 173–179 (Q8.1–Q8.8)

(chapter); 173–200 (Q8.1–Q8.24)

clipping rectangle in JDK 1.0.2; 192 (Q8.20)

drawImage method

copying images in JDK 1.0.2, (code example); 193 (Q8.21)

drawing image subareas; 198 (Q8.24)

as trigger for image loading, (table);
182 (Q8.11)

pulling image data across the network;
179 (Q8.9)

purpose and characteristics; 185 (Q8.13)

drawRect method

drawing outlines, (code example);
124 (Q5.8)

drawString method

drawing text over background images;
187 (Q8.15)

drawing (*continued*)

images; 179–191 (Q8.9–Q8.19)

checking the status of; 185 (Q8.13)

offscreen; 189 (Q8 .18)

(code example); 190 (Q8 .18)

subareas; 198 (Q8.24)

(code example); 199 (Q8.24)

JDK 1.0.2; 192–194 (Q8.20–Q8.21)

JDK 1.1; 195–200 (Q8.22–Q8.24)

on frames and avoiding borders; 128 (Q5.12)

outlines around component groups; 124 (Q5.8)

text over background images; 187 (Q8.15)

`update` relationship with `paint` and `repaint`; 176 (Q8.5)

XOR drawing mode; 178 (Q8.8)

dynamic

allocation of arrays; 65 (Q2.19)

binding; 23 (Q1.18)

component layout; 121 (Q5.5)

font attributes; 133 (Q5.21)

inspection of public methods, fields, and constructors; 60 (Q2.16)

method invocation; 62 (Q2.17)

caution advised; 64 (Q2.17)

user interface changes; 122 (Q5.6)

E

else keyword

as reserved keyword; 46 (Q2.4)

encapsulation

access modifiers used for; 37 (Q1.32)

of code in classes; 64 (Q2.18)

method signature as tool for; 5 (Q1.3)

as object-orientation benefit; 1 (Q1.1)

end-of-stream marker

testing for; 248 (Q10.22)

enumerations

`Enumeration` interface

stepping through object collection with; 258 (Q11.3)

(code example); 259 (Q11.3)

lack of `enum` in Java, class constant as workaround; 45 (Q2.3)

eof (end of file)

as line terminator; 225 (Q10.1)

equals method

overloaded in hypothetical `String2` class; 18 (Q1.15)

overridden in `String` class; 18 (Q1.15)

error(s)

in class format as symptom of MIME type mismatch; 116 (Q4.24)

communicated by exceptions; 68 (Q2.22)

`Error` class characteristics; 74 (Q2.25)

in image loading

rendering and tracking, (code example); 186 (Q8.13)

`ImageTracker` methods, (table); 184 (Q8.12)

monitored by `MediaTracker`; 183 (Q8.12)

in integer conversion; 41 (Q2.1)

from reading string input with binary methods; 229 (Q10.3)

signaling with `beep`; 132 (Q5.19)

static reference to nonstatic variable, error; 57 (Q2.14)

`System.err` for error output; 227 (Q10.2)

event(s)

See also exceptions (concepts); key themes

action events

information in, (table); 137 (Q6.2)

JDK 1.0.2; 141 (Q6.5)

JDK 1.1, handling; 161 (Q7.7)

(table); 161 (Q7.7)

registering listener for; 161 (Q7.7)

term definition; 141 (Q6.5)

action key events

in JDK 1.0.2; 142 (Q6.6)

in JDK 1.1; 169 (Q7.13)

adapter classes

strategies for using; 158 (Q7.4)

(table); 158 (Q7.4)

class hierarchy in JDK 1.1, (table); 152 (Q7.1)

component resizing notification; 168 (Q7.12)

delivered first to peer; 137 (Q6.2)

`EventObject` class

information carried by; 151 (Q7.1)

public methods, (table); 154 (Q7.1)

`Event` class

information carried by; 135 (Q6.1)

`modifiers` field values for mouse clicks, (table); 148 (Q6.11)

`public int` class variables; 143 (Q6.6)

event classes

listeners, methods, and, JDK 1.1; 151–161 (Q7.1–Q7.6)

public methods in each, (table); 154 (Q7.2)

event handling

applet handles events sent by AWT; 107 (Q4.16), 108 (Q4.16)

event(s) (*continued*)

  event handling (*continued*)

    JDK 1.0.2 methods; 139 (Q6.4)

    JDK 1.0.2 model; 138 (Q6.3)

    JDK 1.1 model; 152 (Q7.2)

    sleep not recommended; 224 (Q9.17)

  event listeners

    JDK 1.1 event model use of; 152 (Q7.2)

    types of; 156 (Q7.3)

  event model

    ability to use JDK 1.0.2 event model inside
      JDK 1.1; 160 (Q7.6)

    JDK 1.1 versus JDK 1.0.2; 160 (Q7.5),
      160 (Q7.6)

  event propagation; 160 (Q7.5)

  event types

    information in, (table); 136 (Q6.2)

    Scrollbar class, (table); 147 (Q6.10)

  focus events

    information in, (table); 136 (Q6.2)

  JDK 1.0.2, (chapter); 135–150 (Q6.1–Q6.11)

  JDK 1.1, (chapter); 151–171 (Q7.1–7.14)

  keyboard events

    handling, JDK 1.1; 169 (Q7.13)

    information in, (table); 136 (Q6.2)

  low-level; 167–171 (Q7.11–Q7.14)

  low-level versus semantic; 164 (Q7.9)

  menu item events

    in JDK 1.0.2, (code example); 145 (Q6.8)

    in JDK 1.1; 163 (Q7.8)

  methods for handling events

    in JDK 1.0.2, (table); 140 (Q6.4)

    in JDK 1.1, (table); 157 (Q7.3)

  modifiers field values for mouse clicks,
    (table); 148 (Q6.11)

  mouse events

    determining button selection

      in JDK 1.0.2; 148 (Q6.11)

      in JDK 1.1; 171 (Q7.14)

    information in, (table); 136 (Q6.2)

  semantic; 161–167 (Q7.7–Q7.10)

    term definition; 164 (Q7.9)

  window events

    information in, (table); 136 (Q6.2)

  window exposure as trigger for paint;
    177 (Q8.6)

  window resizing notification; 168 (Q7.12)

examples (code)

  accept method run in separate thread;
    250 (Q10.24)

examples (code) (*continued*)

  accessing URL header information;
    239 (Q10.10)

  action events

    ActionEvent class; 163 (Q7.8)

    ActionListener class; 162 (Q7.7)

  addImage method

    adding images to tracking group with;
      183 (Q8.12)

  adding components to containers; 123 (Q5.7)

  animations

    preparing for; 195 (Q8.22)

    triggering; 196 (Q8.22)

  anonymous inner classes; 156 (Q7.2)

  applets

    AppletContext interface; 264 (Q11.8)

  assignment of listeners; 163 (Q7.8)

  audio clip termination; 263 (Q11.7)

  AWT (Abstract Window Toolkit) container
    management; 211 (Q9.8)

  broadcast datagram packets; 254 (Q10.27)

  buffer

    BufferedReader class; 228 (Q10.2)

  buffering, double; 190 (Q8.18)

  buttons, adding and removing from panel;
    123 (Q5.6)

  bytes, Byte class; 231 (Q10.4)

  catching events; 162 (Q7.7)

  class(es), inner; 162 (Q7.7)

  clipping rectangle

    image copying use; 193 (Q8.21)

    JDK 1.0.2; 192 (Q8.20)

    JDK 1.1; 197 (Q8.23)

  component(s), ComponentListener;
    168 (Q7.12)

  copying

    deep; 32 (Q1.28)

    images; 193 (Q8.21), 199 (Q8.24)

  creating, broadcast datagram packets;
    254 (Q10.27)

  data, DataInputStream class; 228 (Q10.2)

  datagram

    DatagramSocket class; 252 (Q10.26),
      253 (Q10.26)

    packets; 254 (Q10.27)

  double, Double class; 230 (Q10.4)

  drawImage method

    copying images; 193 (Q8.21)

  drawing

    drawRect method; 124 (Q5.8)

    images; 190 (Q8 .18), 199 (Q8.24)

examples (code) (*continued*)

enumerations, looping through; 259 (Q11.3)

errors, image loading and rendering; 186 (Q8.13)

events, menu item; 145 (Q6.8)

exec method
platform-dependent method; 234 (Q10.6)
starting native environment processes with; 233 (Q10.6)

flipping images; 199 (Q8.24)

floating point, Float class; 230 (Q10.4)

floating point, float type; 260 (Q11.4)

generating random numbers; 260 (Q11.4)

getInsets method; 124 (Q5.8)

getLocalHost method; 245 (Q10.17)

GET request (http protocol), sending data to CGI program with; 241 (Q10.12)

grabPixels method; 191 (Q8.19)

header (URL) information, accessing; 239 (Q10.10)

images
copying; 193 (Q8.21)
drawing; 190 (Q8.18), 199 (Q8.24)
flipping; 199 (Q8.24)
loading; 186 (Q8.13)
rendering; 186 (Q8.13)
tracking; 183 (Q8.12)

inner class
event handling simplification with; 162 (Q7.7)
term definition; 153 (Q7.2)

input, enhancing System.in capabilities; 228 (Q10.2)

inset values, insets method in JDK 1.0.2; 124 (Q5.8)

integers
classes; 110 (Q4.19)
Integer class; 230 (Q10.4)

IOException class, URL connection handling of; 236 (Q10.8)

Java language, java.prof file; 267 (Q11.12)

JDK 1.0.2
code encapsulation in; 64 (Q2.18)
exec methods; 234 (Q10.6)
reading from remote files; 237 (Q10.9)

JDK 1.1
abstract class locks; 214 (Q9.9)
AWT container management; 211 (Q9.8)
class literal; 213 (Q9.9)

keys, event handling; 170 (Q7.13)

line(s), length; 226 (Q10.1)

examples (code) (*continued*)

list(s), List class; 165 (Q7.9)

listeners, assigning; 163 (Q7.8)

loading, images; 186 (Q8.13)

long, Long class; 230 (Q10.4)

MalformedURLException, thrown by URL(String) constructor; 236 (Q10.8)

method(s), synchronized; 211 (Q9.8)

modifiers field; 171 (Q7.14)

mouse
MouseAdapter class; 158 (Q7.4)
MouseMotionListener interface; 153 (Q7.2)

opening, openStream method; 237 (Q10.9)

overriding, handleEvent; 141 (Q6.4), 146 (Q6.9), 147 (Q6.10)

packets, datagram; 254 (Q10.27)

panels, adding and removing buttons from; 123 (Q5.6)

performance, java.prof files; 267 (Q11.12)

playing sounds, playback; 263 (Q11.7)

posting
POST request (http protocol); 242 (Q10.12)
postEvent method; 138 (Q6.3)

radix, specifying in string-to-number conversion methods; 232 (Q10.4)

random numbers, generating; 260 (Q11.4)

reading
readLine method; 226 (Q10.1)
remote files; 237 (Q10.9)

rendering images; 186 (Q8.13)
transparent images; 188 (Q8.16)

scrolling, ScrollPane class; 166 (Q7.10)

short, Short class; 231 (Q10.4)

strategies
reading from remote files; 237 (Q10.9)
stopping threads; 206 (Q9.4)

termination, audio clips; 263 (Q11.7)

thread dumps; 221 (Q9.14)

threads, stopping; 206 (Q9.4)

time, audio clip playback; 263 (Q11.7)

tracking
image loading and rendering; 186 (Q8.13)
images; 183 (Q8.12)

UnknownHostException, thrown by getByName; 244 (Q10.16)

while loop as condition variable mechanism; 216 (Q9.11)

windows, windowClosing method in Window-Listener class; 167 (Q7.11)

workarounds, clipping rectangle; 192 (Q8.20)

examples (files)

ActionEvent11Example.html; 162 (Q7.7)

ActionEventExample.html; 142 (Q6.5)

ActionKey11Example.html; 170 (Q7.13)

ActionKeyExample.html; 143 (Q6.6)

AppGetImageExample.html; 181 (Q8.10)

AppletAndApplicationExample.html;
    95 (Q4.3)

AppletMenuExample.html; 106 (Q4.14)

AppletSizeExample.html; 104 (Q4.12)

AwtPeerExample.html; 126 (Q5.10)

Beep11Example.html; 132 (Q5.19)

BlockAWTThreadExample.html; 224 (Q9.17)

BorderedPanelExample.html; 124 (Q5.8)

BroadcastExample.html; 254 (Q10.27)

BusyRepaintExample.html; 176 (Q8.4)

ButtonCanvasExample.html; 118 (Q5.1)

ChangeCursor11Example.html; 107 (Q4.15)

ChangeCursorExample.html; 107 (Q4.15)

ChangingFontsExample.html; 133 (Q5.21)

ClassClassExample.html; 60 (Q2.16)

CloneExample.html; 32 (Q1.28)

CloseFrameExample.html; 144 (Q6.7)

ConditionVariableExample.html; 217 (Q9.11)

CopyImageSubarea11Example.html;
    200 (Q8.24)

CopyImageSubareaExample.html; 194 (Q8.21)

CreateButtonsExample.html; 123 (Q5.6)

CreateThreadExample.html; 204 (Q9.2)

DatagramExample.html; 253 (Q10.26)

DeadlockExample.html; 221 (Q9.14)

DetectSocketClosureExample.html;
    248 (Q10.22)

EnumerationExample.html; 259 (Q11.3)

EventListener11Example.html; 156 (Q7.2)

ExceptionExample.html; 70 (Q2.22)

FailedDrawImageExample.html; 186 (Q8.13)

FlushImageExample.html; 187 (Q8.14)

FlushOutputExample.html; 233 (Q10.5)

FocusExample.html; 132 (Q5.17)

ForNameExample.html; 87 (Q3.7)

GetFrameExample.html; 130 (Q5.14)

GetHeaderExample.html; 239 (Q10.10)

GetMethod11Example.html; 61 (Q2.16)

GrabPixelsExample.html; 191 (Q8.19)

HowToStopThreadExample.html; 207 (Q9.4)

http://java.sun.com/applets/applets/Animator/
    example3.html; 96 (Q4.4)

InetAddressExample.html; 244 (Q10.16)

InitializeObjectArrayExample.html;
    67 (Q2.20)

examples (files) (*continued*)

InitStartStopExample.html; 109 (Q4.18)

InstanceofExample.html; 30 (Q1.26)

InstantiateInterfaceExample.html; 27 (Q1.22)

InterappletExample.html; 112 (Q4.20)

InvokeMethodDynamically11Example.html;
    64 (Q2.17)

JoinExample.html; 218 (Q9.12)

KeywordExample.html; 46 (Q2.4)

LinkedListExample.html; 57 (Q2.13)

ListEvent11Example.html; 165 (Q7.9)

ListEventExample.html; 146 (Q6.9)

LocalHostExample.html; 245 (Q10.17)

MainExample.html; 78 (Q3.1)

MatchBackgroundExample.html; 105 (Q4.13)

MemoryImageExample.html; 189 (Q8.17)

MenuItemEvent11Example.html; 164 (Q7.8)

MenuItemEventExample.html; 146 (Q6.8)

MethodTable11Example.html; 65 (Q2.18)

MultiButtonMouse11Example.html;
    171 (Q7.14)

MultiButtonMouseExample.html; 149 (Q6.11)

NonblockingServer11Example.html;
    250 (Q10.24)

NonblockingServerExample.html;
    250 (Q10.24)

NumericalParametersExample.html;
    111 (Q4.19)

OffscreenImageExample.html; 190 (Q8.18)

OverrideMethodExample.html; 17 (Q1.14)

PaintExample.html; 174 (Q8.1)

PlaceFrame11Example.html; 128 (Q5.11)

PlaceFrameExample.html; 128 (Q5.11)

PlayAndStopExample.html; 262 (Q11.5)

PostExample.html; 242 (Q10.12)

ProcessOutput11Example.html; 235 (Q10.6)

ProcessOutputExample.html; 235 (Q10.6)

ProfileExample.html; 268 (Q11.12)

PropagateEvent11Example.html; 160 (Q7.5)

RandomExample.html; 261 (Q11.4)

ReadFromURLAppletExample.html;
    238 (Q10.9)

ReadFromURLExample.html; 238 (Q10.9)

ReadIntExample.html; 230 (Q10.3)

ReadLine11Example.html; 226 (Q10.1)

ReadLineExample.html; 226 (Q10.1)

ReadNumber11Example.html; 232 (Q10.4)

ReadNumberExample.html; 232 (Q10.4)

RepaintExample.html; 175 (Q8.3)

ResetClip11Example.html; 198 (Q8.23)

ScrollbarExample.html; 148 (Q6.10)

examples (files) (*continued*)

ScrollPane11Example.html; 167 (Q7.10)

SimpleTimer.html; 78 (Q3.1)

SleepExample.html; 208 (Q9.5)

SlowPaintExample.html; 174 (Q8.2)

Socket11Example.html; 246 (Q10.19)

SocketExample.html; 246 (Q10.19)

SocketWithoutNetwork11Example.html; 247 (Q10.20)

SocketWithoutNetworkExample.html; 247 (Q10.20)

StandardInputOutput11Example.html; 229 (Q10.2)

StandardInputOutputExample.html; 229 (Q10.2)

StopExample.html; 205 (Q9.3)

StringReplaceExample.html; 256 (Q11.1)

SubgraphicsExample.html; 193 (Q8.20)

SuperExample.html; 22 (Q1.17)

SynchronizationExample.html; 212 (Q9.8)

SystemThreadsExample.html; 223 (Q9.16)

TextOnImageExample.html; 187 (Q8.15)

TrackErrorImageExample.html; 185 (Q8.12), 186 (Q8.13)

TrackImageExample.html; 185 (Q8.12)

TransparentComponent11Example.html; 178 (Q8.7)

TransparentImageExample.html; 188 (Q8.16)

UnsignedByteExample.html; 45 (Q2.2)

UpdateExample.html; 177 (Q8.5)

URLConnectionExample.java; 236 (Q10.8)

VariableExample.html; 8 (Q1.6)

WaitNotifyExample.html; 215 (Q9.10)

WindowExample.html; 129 (Q5.13)

WindowResizeEvent11Example.html; 168 (Q7.12)

XORDrawingExample.html; 179 (Q8.8)

exceptions (classes)

`ArrayIndexOutOfBoundsException`
meaning of; 69 (Q2.22)

`ClassCastException`
caused by illegal downward cast; 52 (Q2.9)

`Exception` class
automatic import of; 35 (Q1.31)
characteristics; 74 (Q2.25)
checked exceptions and; 72 (Q2.24)
error condition information in; 68 (Q2.22)
`throw` statement relationship to; 69 (Q2.22)

`IllegalArgumentException`
meaning of; 69 (Q2.22)
thrown by `invoke`; 63 (Q2.17)

exceptions (classes) (*continued*)

`InterruptedException`; 70 (Q2.23)
thrown by `sleep`; 207 (Q9.5)

`InvocationTargetException`
thrown by `invoke`; 63 (Q2.17)

`NoSuchMethodException`
thrown by `getMethods`; 63 (Q2.17)

`NullPointerException`
meaning of; 68 (Q2.22)

`RuntimeException`
subclassing, to define unchecked exceptions; 75 (Q2.26)

`UnknownHostException`
thrown by `getByName`, (code example); 244 (Q10.16)

exceptions (concepts); 68–76 (Q2.22–Q2.26)
See also event(s)
catching; 69 (Q2.22)
checked
advantages of; 71 (Q2.24)
handling; 70 (Q2.23)
as part of API contract; 75 (Q2.26)
term definition; 70 (Q2.23)
unchecked exceptions compared with, (table); 72 (Q2.24)
declaring; 70 (Q2.22)
handling, mechanisms for; 69 (Q2.22)
match required when overriding; 16 (Q1.14)
runtime, characteristics; 73 (Q2.25)
security, applets versus applications; 243 (Q10.15)
term definition and characteristics; 68 (Q2.22)
throwing; 70 (Q2.22)

exec method
as platform-dependent method, (code examples); 234 (Q10.6)
process execution with; 257 (Q11.2)
starting native environment processes with, (code example); 233 (Q10.6)

execution
of applets, requirments for; 92 (Q4.1)
executables named with _g
debugging use of; 268 (Q11.13)
stack, private for each thread; 202 (Q9.1)
suspending execution
of threads, methods for, (table); 218 (Q9.12)
of threads, until another finishes; 217 (Q9.12)

exit
`exit` method
terminating applications; 144 (Q6.7)

exit (*continued*)

    `exitValue` method

        interacting with native platform processes, (table); 258 (Q11.2)

    exit status,relation to exceptions and return value; 72 (Q2.24)

expressions

    array creation; 66 (Q2.19)

extends keyword

    extending superclasses with; 13 (Q1.11)

    interface implementation use; 26 (Q1.21)

    as reserved keyword; 46 (Q2.4)

    subclassing as extension; 13 (Q1.11)

    superinterfaces declared with; 29 (Q1.25)

F

F suffix

    See also floating point; numbers

    reasons for use; 49 (Q2.8)

factories

    for objects, class viewed as; 2 (Q1.2)

fairness

    See also performance; scheduling

    among threads, with `yield`; 218 (Q9.13)

    not guaranteed by `wait` and `notifyAll`/`notify` service; 214 (Q9.10)

fetching

    documents, simulating browser actions in an application; 243 (Q10.14)

field(s)

    See also object-oriented concepts

    access modifiers; 36 (Q1.32)

    `Class` class information available JDK 1.1; 59 (Q2.15)

    `Field` class

        inspecting fields with; 60 (Q2.16)

        changing value of field; 62 (Q2.17)

    as part of class declaration; 3 (Q1.2)

    public

        in `Event` class, (table); 135 (Q6.1)

        within nonpublic classes; 38 (Q1.34)

    static compared with nonstatic; 6 (Q1.5)

    term definition, (table); 8 (Q1.6)

file(s)

    class files

        applet, specified in URL; 101 (Q4.9)

        as applet components; 99 (Q4.8)

        `javap` as disassembler for; 79 (Q3.3)

        maximum identifier size; 48 (Q2.6)

file(s) (*continued*)

    data files

        as applet components; 99 (Q4.8)

    `File` class

        operating system access; 257 (Q11.2)

    `FileDialog` class

        user file access with; 130 (Q5.14)

    `FileInputStream` class

        as subclass of `InputStream` class; 13 (Q1.11)

    file I/O, handled by `java.io` package; 257 (Q11.2)

    media files, as applet components; 99 (Q4.8)

    remote files

        accessing images in; 179 (Q8.10), 181 (Q8.10)

        reading from, with URL; 236 (Q10.9)

    URL-specified files

        writing to from applets, restrictions and workarounds; 243 (Q10.13)

filters

    `FilterInputStream` class

        reading from remote files with; 237 (Q10.9)

final keyword

    characteristics and use; 24 (Q1.19)

    class constant defined with; 45 (Q2.3)

    as reserved keyword; 46 (Q2.4)

    static binding declared with; 23 (Q1.18)

finalization

    `finalize` method

        when invoked; 85 (Q3.6)

    limitations and dependencies; 84 (Q3.6)

finally keyword

    as reserved keyword; 46 (Q2.4)

firewalls

    See also networks

    handling; 248 (Q10.23)

    SOCKS, handling; 249 (Q10.23)

flipping

    images, (code example); 199 (Q8.24)

floating point

    See also numbers

    classes

        converting strings to; 110 (Q4.19)

        (code example); 111 (Q4.19)

    constants, reasons for f suffix; 49 (Q2.8)

    `double`

        random numbers; 260 (Q11.4)

        as reserved keyword; 46 (Q2.4)

file(s) (*continued*)
  float
    Class instance corresponding to, (table);
      63 (Q2.17)
    random numbers, (code example);
      260 (Q11.4)
    reading from string; 230 (Q10.4)
    as reserved keyword; 46 (Q2.4)
  Float class
    converting string to numerical value
      (code example); 230 (Q10.4)
      (table); 230 (Q10.4)
  float literal, F suffix required; 51 (Q2.8)
  Float(String) constructor
    extracting numerical values from applet
      parameters; 110 (Q4.19)
  suffixes on numerical literals, (table); 50 (Q2.8)
FlowLayout class; 119 (Q5.2)
flushing
  automatic occurences, PrintStream versus
    PrintWriter; 232 (Q10.5)
  cached images; 186 (Q8.14)
  flush method; 186 (Q8.14), 232 (Q10.5)
  output
    buffers, migrating from JDK 1.0.2 to JDK
      1.1 issues; 228 (Q10.2)
    streams; 232 (Q10.5)
flyweight design pattern
  See inner classes
focus
  focus events
    information in, (table); 136 (Q6.2)
  FocusAdapter class
    strategies for use of; 158 (Q7.4)
  FocusEvent class
    position in JDK 1.1 class hierarchy, (table);
      152 (Q7.1)
    public methods, (table); 154 (Q7.2)
  FocusListener interface
    methods, (table); 157 (Q7.3)
  setting; 131 (Q5.17)
fonts
  attributes, dynamically changing; 133 (Q5.21)
  determining availability; 133 (Q5.20)
for keyword
  as reserved keyword; 46 (Q2.4)
forName method
  objects returned from, guidelines for use;
    85 (Q3.7)
  obtaining Class instance with; 59 (Q2.15)
  obtaining class objects with; 213 (Q9.9)

frame(s)
  See also AWT (Abstract Window Toolkit);
    windows
  adding applets to; 115 (Q4.23)
  as applet menu workarounds; 105 (Q4.14)
  closing frames
    correcting problems with; 143 (Q6.7)
    correcting problems with, JDK 1.0.2;
      144 (Q6.7)
    correcting problems with, JDK 1.1;
      167 (Q7.11)
  controlling frames, with showDocument
    (table); 113 (Q4.21)
  destroying; 144 (Q6.7)
  drawing on, border considerations; 128 (Q5.12)
  Frame class
    as applet menu workaround; 105 (Q4.14)
    events associated with, (table); 136 (Q6.2)
    instance containing current component;
      129 (Q5.14)
    menu containment hierarchy rooted in;
      145 (Q6.8)
    positioning methods inherited from Window
      class; 127 (Q5.11)
    setting cursors in; 106 (Q4.15)
    window creation use; 129 (Q5.13)
  required for main in Applet subclass;
    94 (Q4.3)
  term definition; 94 (Q4.3), 128 (Q5.12)
  windows, dialogs and; 127–131 (Q5.11–Q5.16)
frameworks
  See also AWT (Abstract Window Toolkit)
  component integration, supported by reflection;
    62 (Q2.17)
fully qualified class names
  term definition; 34 (Q1.30)
function(s)
  See also methods
    See also keys
  pointers, creating the equivalent of; 64 (Q2.18)
function keys
  event handling
    in JDK 1.0.2; 142 (Q6.6)
    in JDK 1.1; 169 (Q7.13)

G

_g terminated files
  See also debugging
  debugging use; 268 (Q11.13)

garbage collection
  JDK algorithm, characteristics of; 83 (Q3.5)
Gaussian distribution
  See also numbers
  generating random numbers from; 260 (Q11.4)
generating
  random numbers; 259 (Q11.4)
    (code example); 260 (Q11.4)
  sounds, not supported; 265 (Q11.10)
get... methods
  getActionCommand method
    return values, (table); 154 (Q7.2)
  getAdjustable method
    return values, (table); 154 (Q7.2)
  getAdjustmentType method
    return values, (table); 154 (Q7.2)
  getApplet method
    inter-applet communcation with;
      111 (Q4.20)
  getAudio methods
    playing sounds in an applet; 261 (Q11.5)
  getByName method
    creating InetAddress instance with;
      244 (Q10.16)
      without DNS; 245 (Q10.18)
    creating instances with, cautions; 9 (Q1.7)
  getChild method
    return values, (table); 154 (Q7.2)
  getClass method
    obtaining Class instance with; 59 (Q2.15)
    obtaining class objects with; 213 (Q9.9)
  getClickCount method
    return values, (table); 155 (Q7.2)
  getClip method
    (table); 197 (Q8.23)
  getClipBounds method
    (table); 197 (Q8.23)
  getConstructors method
    accessing constructors with; 60 (Q2.16)
  getContainer method
    return values, (table); 154 (Q7.2)
  getErrorsAny method
    (table); 184 (Q8.12)
  getErrorsId method
    (table); 184 (Q8.12)
  getErrorStream method
    connecting native process with Java applica-
      tion, (table); 233 (Q10.6)
    interacting with native platform processes,
      (table); 258 (Q11.2)

get... methods (*continued*)
  getFields method
    accessing fields with; 60 (Q2.16)
  getFontList method
    determining available fonts with;
      133 (Q5.20)
  getGraphics method
    return values, (table); 155 (Q7.2)
  getHeader method
    return values, reasons for null value;
      238 (Q10.10)
  getHeight method
    as trigger for image loading, (table);
      182 (Q8.11)
  getID method
    return values, (table); 154 (Q7.2)
  getImage method
    establishing image source pointers;
      179 (Q8.9), 180 (Q8.10)
  getInputStream method
    connecting native process with Java applica-
      tion, (table); 233 (Q10.6)
    interacting with native platform processes,
      (table); 258 (Q11.2)
  getInsets method
    drawing on frames, use to avoid borders;
      128 (Q5.12)
    outline drawing, (code example); 124 (Q5.8)
    setting inset values with; 119 (Q5.3)
  getItem method
    return values, (table); 154 (Q7.2)
  getItemSelectable method
    return values, (table); 154 (Q7.2)
  getKeyChar method
    return values, (table); 155 (Q7.2)
  getKeyCode method
    return values, (table); 155 (Q7.2)
  getLocalHost method
    accessing local host with; 244 (Q10.17)
      (code example); 245 (Q10.17)
  getMethods method
    accessing methods with; 60 (Q2.16)
  getModifiers method
    return values, (table); 154 (Q7.2), 155 (Q7.2)
  getOutputStream method
    connecting native process with Java applica-
      tion, (table); 233 (Q10.6)
    interacting with native platform processes,
      (table); 258 (Q11.2)
    restrictions on use; 239 (Q10.11)
      overcoming; 240 (Q10.11)

get... methods (*continued*)
  getParameter method
    parsing values returned by; 110 (Q4.19)
  getPoint method
    return values, (table); 155 (Q7.2)
  getProperty method
    as trigger for image loading, (table);
      182 (Q8.11)
  getSize method
    obtaining applet size with; 103 (Q4.11)
  getSource method
    as EventObject accessor; 152 (Q7.1)
    return values, (table); 154 (Q7.2)
  getStateChange method
    return values, (table); 154 (Q7.2)
  getValue method
    return values, (table); 154 (Q7.2)
  getWhen method
    return values, (table); 155 (Q7.2)
  getWidth method
    as trigger for image loading, (table);
      182 (Q8.11)
  getWindow method
    return values, (table); 155 (Q7.2)
  getX method
    return values, (table); 155 (Q7.2)
  getY method
    return values, (table); 155 (Q7.2)
GET request (http protocol)
  POST request compared with; 241 (Q10.12)
  sending data to CGI program with;
    240 (Q10.12)
    (code example); 241 (Q10.12)
GIF image
  transparent, loading over background image;
    187 (Q8.16)
gotFocus method
  as JDK 1.0.2 event-handling method, return
    values, (table); 140 (Q6.4)
goto keyword
  not allowed in Java; 46 (Q2.4)
  as reserved keyword; 46 (Q2.4)
grabPixels method
  as trigger for image loading, (table);
    182 (Q8.11)
  as synchronous method, implications of;
    191 (Q8.19)
    (code example); 191 (Q8.19)
Graphics class
  clipRect method
    JDK 1.0.2; 192 (Q8.20)

Graphics class (*continued*)
  drawImage method
    drawing image subareas; 198 (Q8.24)
    purpose and characteristics; 185 (Q8.13)
  drawString method
    drawing text over background images;
      187 (Q8.15)
  methods that trigger image loading, (table);
    182 (Q8.11)
GridBagLayout class; 119 (Q5.2)
GridLayout class; 119 (Q5.2)

H

handleEvent method
  See also event(s)
  in event handling, JDK 1.0.2 algorithm;
    139 (Q6.3)
  as JDK 1.0.2 general purpose event-handling
    method; 139 (Q6.4)
    (table); 140 (Q6.4)
hasMoreElements method; 259 (Q11.3)
header (URL) information
  accessing with getHeader; 238 (Q10.10)
  (code example); 239 (Q10.10)
heap
  management by JDK; 83 (Q3.5)
height
  applet, determining; 103 (Q4.11)
  height attribute (APPLET tag)
    characteristics; 96 (Q4.4)
    from JDK README file; 98 (Q4.7)
hexadecimal values
  See also numbers
  string to numeric value conversions, JDK 1.1;
    231 (Q10.4)
hiding
  term definition; 20 (Q1.17)
hierarchy
  class
    interface independence from; 29 (Q1.24)
    JDK 1.1 AWT events, (table); 152 (Q7.1)
  containment
    events propagated up, JDK 1.0.2; 138 (Q6.3)
    inheritance hierarchy compared with;
      118 (Q5.1)
    menu, Frame class as root of; 145 (Q6.8)
    as strict tree structure; 123 (Q5.7)
  interitance, containment hierarchy compared
    with; 118 (Q5.1)

host

See also network(s)

address, specifying for server socket listening; 250 (Q10.25)

local, accessing; 244 (Q10.17)

remote, detecting input stream termination by; 248 (Q10.22)

HotJava

development experience, as example of checked exception advantages; 73 (Q2.24)

hspace attribute (APPLET tag)

characteristics; 96 (Q4.4)

from JDK README file; 99 (Q4.7)

HTML (Hypertext Markup Language)

APPLET tag; 92 (Q4.1)

attributes of; 95 (Q4.4)

syntax; 98 (Q4.7)

http protocol

GET request, sending data to CGI program with; 240 (Q10.12)

`HttpURLConnection` class, overcoming URL output stream restrictions in; 240 (Q10.11)

POST request, sending data to CGI program with; 240 (Q10.12)

servers

applet delivery by; 115 (Q4.24)

applet delivery role; 92 (Q4.1)

`URLConnection` class representation of; 235 (Q10.7)

I

I/O

basic; 225–235 (Q10.1–Q10.6)

input, output, and network, (chapter); 225–254 (Q10.1–10.27)

ICMP (Internet Control Message Protocol)

messages, native methods required to; 247 (Q10.21)

id field

in JDK 1.0.2, meaning of, (table); 135 (Q6.1)

identifiers

capitalization conventions; 47 (Q2.5)

maximum size in class file; 48 (Q2.6)

if keyword

as reserved keyword; 46 (Q2.4)

IllegalArgumentException class

meaning of; 69 (Q2.22)

images

See also media

accessing pixel data; 190 (Q8.19)

background

drawing text over; 187 (Q8.15)

setting; 104 (Q4.12)

copying, JDK 1.0.2, (code example); 193 (Q8.21)

creating, from raw image data; 188 (Q8.17)

displaying, steps in; 180 (Q8.9)

drawing; 179–191 (Q8.9–Q8.19)

checking the status of; 185 (Q8.13)

offscreen; 189 (Q8.18)

(code example); 190 (Q8.18)

subareas; 198 (Q8.24)

(code example); 199 (Q8.24)

flipping, (code example); 199 (Q8.24)

flushing; 186 (Q8.14)

forcing reload, with `flush` method; 186 (Q8.14)

`Image` class

methods that trigger image loading, (table); 182 (Q8.11)

purpose of; 179 (Q8.9)

`ImageObserver` interface

tracking image loading and rendering; 185 (Q8.13)

`imageUpdate` method

tracking images with; 185 (Q8.13)

loading; 179–191 (Q8.9–Q8.19)

into applets; 179 (Q8.9)

into applications; 180 (Q8.10)

`MediaTracker` methods, (table); 184 (Q8.12)

methods that trigger, (table); 182 (Q8.11)

strategies for; 181 (Q8.11)

tracking errors in, (code example); 186 (Q8.13)

rendering, tracking errors in, (code example); 186 (Q8.13)

tracking

(code example); 183 (Q8.12)

`MediaTracker` use; 183 (Q8.12)

transparent, loading over background image; 187 (Q8.16)

immutable

characteristic of `String` class; 255 (Q11.1)

windows, creating nonresizable; 131 (Q5.16)

implements keyword

as reserved keyword; 46 (Q2.4)

import keyword
  as reserved keyword; 46 (Q2.4)
importing
  classes and interfaces, advantages of;
      34 (Q1.30)
  import declaration, required for simple class
      name use; 34 (Q1.30)
  subpackages, requirements for; 35 (Q1.30)
InetAddress class
  creating instance from IP address;
      245 (Q10.18)
  creating instances of, with getByName;
      244 (Q10.16)
inheritance
  See also object-oriented concepts
  hierarchy
      containment hierarchy compared with;
          118 (Q5.1)
      events, JDK 1.1; 151 (Q7.1)
  multiple, interfaces used for; 29 (Q1.25)
  overriding relationship to; 16 (Q1.14)
  super keyword relationship to; 20 (Q1.17)
  term definition, characteristics and; 14 (Q1.12)
  virtual methods used with; 22 (Q1.18)
initialization(s)
  of applet, managed by applet context;
      108 (Q4.16)
  of arrays; 66 (Q2.19), 66 (Q2.20)
  chain of, via super keyword; 20 (Q1.17)
  init method
      as constructor replacement in applets;
          109 (Q4.17)
      invoked by applet context; 107 (Q4.16)
      setting background color in; 104 (Q4.12)
      sleep not recommended; 224 (Q9.17)
      when invoked, (table); 108 (Q4.16)
  term definition; 87 (Q3.8)
inner class
  creating function pointer equivalents with;
      64 (Q2.18)
  event handling simplification with, (code exam-
      ple); 162 (Q7.7)
  term definition; 65 (Q2.18)
      uses, and benefits, (code example);
          153 (Q7.2)
input
  See also buffer(ing); data; event(s); file(s);
      key themes; keys; mouse; output;
      standard I/O; stream(s)
  basic; 225–235 (Q10.1–Q10.6)

input (*continued*)
  enhancing System.in capabilities, with
      DataInputStream, (code example);
      228 (Q10.2)
  file input, handled by java.io package;
      257 (Q11.2)
  input, output, and network, (chapter); 225–254
      (Q10.1–10.27)
  InputEvent class
      position in JDK 1.1 class hierarchy, (table);
          152 (Q7.1)
      public methods, (table); 155 (Q7.2)
  InputStream class
      as example of abstract method use; 10 (Q1.8)
      read, exceptions thrown by; 72 (Q2.24)
  reading, one line at a time; 225 (Q10.1)
  streams
      detecting termination by remote host;
          248 (Q10.22)
      Java, connecting process output streams to;
          233 (Q10.6)
      process, connecting Java output streams to;
          233 (Q10.6)
insert method
  (table); 256 (Q11.1)
inset values
  getInsets method
      drawing on frames, use to avoid borders;
          128 (Q5.12)
      JDK 1.1; 119 (Q5.3)
      outline drawing use, (code example);
          124 (Q5.8)
  insets method
      JDK 1.0.2; 119 (Q5.3)
  setting; 119 (Q5.3)
  term definitions; 119 (Q5.3)
inspecting
  public methods, fields, and constructors at run
      time; 60 (Q2.16)
installing
  applet components; 99 (Q4.8)
  applets; 95–103 (Q4.4–Q4.10)
instance(s)
  See also class(es); object-oriented concepts;
      objects
  classes compared with, (table); 3 (Q1.2)
  creating; 8 (Q1.7)
      of class type returned by forName;
          86 (Q3.7)
      at run time; 62 (Q2.17)

instance(s) (*continued*)
  information, obtaining with object references;
    11 (Q1.10)
  instance variables
    array components compared with;
      67 (Q2.20)
    class variables compared with; 6 (Q1.5)
    definition of; 57 (Q2.14)
    static reference to nonstatic variable, error;
      57 (Q2.14)
  methods, class methods compared with;
    7 (Q1.6)
  as objects; 3 (Q1.2)
  term definition; 2 (Q1.1)
instanceof keyword
  characteristics and uses; 30 (Q1.26)
  as reserved keyword; 46 (Q2.4)
integers
  converting from strings, (code example);
    110 (Q4.19)
  `int`
    `Class` instance corresponding to, (table);
      63 (Q2.17)
    `Integer` class compared with; 41 (Q2.1)
    literal, (table); 50 (Q2.8)
    random numbers; 260 (Q11.4)
    reading from string; 230 (Q10.4)
  `int` keyword
    as reserved keyword; 46 (Q2.4)
  `Integer` class
    converting strings to numerical values
      (code example); 230 (Q10.4)
      (table); 230 (Q10.4)
    `int` data type, compared with; 41 (Q2.1)
  `long`, random numbers; 260 (Q11.4)
interactions
  applet, as part of standard Java Applet API;
    112 (Q4.20)
  as applet capability; 92 (Q4.1)
  thread; 208–221 (Q9.6–Q9.14)
    difficulties with; 202 (Q9.1)
    synchronization contrasted with;
      214 (Q9.10)
interface(s)
  See also object-oriented concepts
  abstract classes and; 25–32 (Q1.20–Q1.28)
  abstract classes compared with; 27 (Q1.24)
    (table); 28 (Q1.24)
  access modifiers; 36 (Q1.32)
  `Class` class information available; 58 (Q2.15)

interface(s) (*continued*)
  classes, interfaces, and packages, (chapter);
    1–40 (Q1.1–Q1.34)
  components, positioning control of; 118 (Q5.2)
  concrete classes compared with; 28 (Q1.24)
  instantiation prohibition; 27 (Q1.22)
  `interface` keyword
    as reserved keyword; 46 (Q2.4)
  loopback, term definition; 246 (Q10.20)
  as part of class declaration; 3 (Q1.2)
  public, nonpublic class implementations,
    access impact; 38 (Q1.34)
  as reference type; 41 (Q2.1)
  term definition and characteristics; 25 (Q1.20)
  variables, object references as value of;
    12 (Q1.10)
interleaved execution
  as multithreading issue; 208 (Q9.6)
Internet
  See also applet(s); networks
  addresses; 244–245 (Q10.16–Q10.18)
interpretation
  of Java bytecodes, by JDK; 81 (Q3.4)
InterruptedExecution class
  as checked exception in `sleep`; 70 (Q2.23)
  thrown by
    `sleep`; 207 (Q9.5)
    `wait`, (code example); 216 (Q9.11)
    `waitForId`; 184 (Q8.12)
invalidate method
  container layout management by; 121 (Q5.5)
  when invoked, (table); 122 (Q5.5)
invocation
  `InvocationTargetException` class
    thrown by `invoke`; 63 (Q2.17)
  `invoke` method
    invoking methods with; 63 (Q2.17)
  of `main`, to start applications; 77 (Q3.1)
  of methods
    activation contrasted with; 4 (Q1.3)
    arguments passed by value, implications of;
      54 (Q2.12)
    from names, at run time; 61 (Q2.17)
IOException class
  thrown by `read`; 72 (Q2.24)
  URL connection handling of, (code example);
    236 (Q10.8)
IP (Internet Protocol)
  See also networks
  address, specifying for server socket listening;
    250 (Q10.25)

IP (Internet Protocol) (*continued*)

address 127.0.0.1, standalone machine socket communication; 246 (Q10.20)

creating an InetAddress instance from; 245 (Q10.18)

headers, native methods required to manipulate; 247 (Q10.21)

local host, accessing; 244 (Q10.17)

is... methods

isActionKey method
return values, (table); 155 (Q7.2)

isAltDown method
return values, (table); 155 (Q7.2)

isConsumed method
return values, (table); 155 (Q7.2)

isControlDown method
return values, (table); 155 (Q7.2)

isErrorAny method
(table); 184 (Q8.12)

isErrorID method
(table); 184 (Q8.12)

isMetaDown method
return values, (table); 155 (Q7.2)

isPopupTrigger method
return values, (table); 155 (Q7.2)

isShiftDown method
return values, (table); 155 (Q7.2)

isTemporary method
return values, (table); 154 (Q7.2)

items

ItemEvent class
position in JDK 1.1 class hierarchy, (table); 152 (Q7.1)
public methods, (table); 154 (Q7.2)
semantic event handling by; 165 (Q7.9)

ItemListener interface
methods, (table); 157 (Q7.3)
semantic event handling by; 165 (Q7.9)

ItemSelectable interface
characteristics and use; 161 (Q7.7)
semantic event handling by; 165 (Q7.9)

menu items
catching events from, JDK 1.1; 163 (Q7.8)
MenuItem action events
in JDK 1.0.2, (table); 142 (Q6.5)
in JDK 1.1, (table); 161 (Q7.7)

iterators

extracting elements with; 258 (Q11.3)

J

Java language

See also compilation; Java Virtual Machine (JVM); key themes; loading; platform-dependent issues; security

(chapter); 41–75 (Q2.1–Q2.26)

data types, accessing information about; 58 (Q2.15)

java.applet.Applet class
main applet class file as subclass of; 100 (Q4.8)

java.awt.peer package
peer interface definitions contained in; 125 (Q5.9)

java.io package
as C/C++ standard I/O library analogue; 227 (Q10.2)
File class, operating system access; 257 (Q11.2)
file I/O handled by; 257 (Q11.2)

java.lang package
automatic import of; 35 (Q1.31)
classes in; 255–261 (Q11.1–Q11.4)
operating system access; 257 (Q11.2)

java.net package
operating system access; 257 (Q11.2)

java.prof file
creation and use; 266 (Q11.12)
(code example); 267 (Q11.12)

java.util package
classes in; 255–261 (Q11.1–Q11.4)
EventObject class, as root of event class hierarchy; 151 (Q7.1)
Random class; 259 (Q11.4)

JavaBeans, reflection API support of; 62 (Q2.17)

javac compiler, optimization problems with; 87 (Q3.8)

javap program
as class file disassembler; 79 (Q3.3)
Java Virtual Machine instructions, (example); 80 (Q3.3)

JavaScript, Java compared with; 265 (Q11.11)

Java Media Framework, planned capabilities; 263 (Q11.7)

Java Virtual Machine (JVM)

See also Java language; key themes; platform-dependent issues; security

(chapter); 77–90 (Q3.1–Q3.9)

Java Virtual Machine (JVM) (*continued*)
  deadlock handling; 220 (Q9.14)
  platform independence model role;
      269 (Q11.14)
  platform-dependent implementation issues,
      thread scheduling; 222 (Q9.15)
  threads
    scheduling options; 219 (Q9.13)
    synchronization, monitors as mechanism for;
        211 (Q9.8)
JDK 1.0.2; 250 (Q10.25)
  See also key themes
  abstract class locks; 213 (Q9.9)
  automatic output flushing; 232 (Q10.5)
  bugs
    broadcast packets; 254 (Q10.27)
    loopback interface; 246 (Q10.20)
  Class class information available; 58 (Q2.15)
  code encapsulation in, (example); 64 (Q2.18)
  Component class method name changes in JDK
      1.1, (table); 127 (Q5.11)
  drawing; 192–194 (Q8.20–Q8.21)
  event handling
    (chapter); 135–150 (Q6.1–Q6.11)
    Event class, information carried by;
        135 (Q6.1)
  event model; 138 (Q6.3)
    return values; 158 (Q7.3)
  garbage collection algorithm; 83 (Q3.5)
  inset values; 119 (Q5.3)
    for drawing on frames; 128 (Q5.12)
    for outline drawing; 124 (Q5.8)
  JDK 1.1 features not available
    resetting clipping rectangle; 192 (Q8.20),
        196 (Q8.23)
    transparency; 177 (Q8.7)
    window resizing notification; 168 (Q7.12)
  layout manager interface; 118 (Q5.2)
  obtaining applet size; 103 (Q4.11)
  octal strings to numeric value conversions;
      231 (Q10.4)
  popup window creation; 129 (Q5.13)
  reading from remote files, (code example);
      237 (Q10.9)
  reading lines; 225 (Q10.1)
  readLine, DataInputSream replaced by
      readLine in BufferedReader;
      230 (Q10.3)
  setting cursors in; 106 (Q4.15)

JDK 1.0.2 (*continued*)
  starting the Java Virtual Machine; 77 (Q3.1)
  string output methods; 227 (Q10.2)
  versus JDK 1.1
    Class class information available;
        58 (Q2.15)
    event model compatibility; 160 (Q7.6)
  window closing problem solutions; 144 (Q6.7)
  window positioning; 127 (Q5.11)
JDK 1.1; 128 (Q5.12), 250 (Q10.25)
  See also key themes
  abstract class locks; 213 (Q9.9)
    (code example); 214 (Q9.9)
  automatic output flushing; 232 (Q10.5)
  AWT container management, synchronization
      use by (code example); 211 (Q9.8)
  Byte class
    parsing routines; 110 (Q4.19)
  Class class information available; 59 (Q2.15)
    inspecting public methods, fields, and
        constructors at run time; 60 (Q2.16)
  class literal, accessing class objects from,
      (code example); 213 (Q9.9)
  code encapsulation in, inner class use for;
      65 (Q2.18)
  Component class method name changes from
      JDK 1.0.2, (table); 127 (Q5.11)
  creating broadcast datagram packets;
      253 (Q10.27)
  drawing; 195–200 (Q8.22–Q8.24)
  event handling
    (chapter); 151–171 (Q7.1–7.14)
    EventObject class, information carried by;
        151 (Q7.1)
  event model; 152 (Q7.2)
    return values; 158 (Q7.3)
  event propagation; 160 (Q7.5)
  features not available in JDK 1.0.2
    inner classes; 64 (Q2.18), 153 (Q7.2),
        162 (Q7.7)
    resetting clipping rectangle; 192 (Q8.20),
        196 (Q8.23)
    transparency; 177 (Q8.7)
    window resizing notification; 168 (Q7.12)
  garbage collection algorithm, characteristics of;
      83 (Q3.5)
  hexadecimal strings to numeric value conver-
      sions; 231 (Q10.4)
  input handling; 228 (Q10.2)

JDK 1.1 (*continued*)

inset values; 119 (Q5.3)

in drawing on frames; 128 (Q5.12)

in outline drawing; 124 (Q5.8)

layout manager interface; 118 (Q5.2)

`LayoutManager` interface

extensions; 118 (Q5.2)

listener interfaces and methods, (table);

157 (Q7.3)

obtaining applet size; 103 (Q4.11)

octal strings to numeric value conversions;

231 (Q10.4)

popup window creation; 129 (Q5.13)

reading from remote files; 237 (Q10.9)

reading lines; 225 (Q10.1)

`readLine` method

`BufferedReader` replaces `readLine` in

`DataInputSream`; 230 (Q10.3)

reflection API, characteristics; 61 (Q2.17)

`reverse` method

(table); 256 (Q11.1)

scrolling control, with `ScrollPane` class;

148 (Q6.10)

setting cursors in; 106 (Q4.15)

`Short` class

parsing routines; 110 (Q4.19)

starting the Java Virtual Machine; 77 (Q3.1)

string output methods; 227 (Q10.2)

string to numeric value conversions, (table);

231 (Q10.4)

transparent background workaround in;

104 (Q4.13)

Unicode input handling; 226 (Q10.1)

versus JDK 1.0.2

`Class` class information available;

59 (Q2.15)

event model compatibility; 160 (Q7.6)

window closing problem solutions;

167 (Q7.11)

window positioning; 127 (Q5.11)

JIT compilers

See just-in-time (JIT) compilers

join method

thread execution suspension, (table);

218 (Q9.12)

thread serialization use of; 217 (Q9.12)

just-in-time (JIT) compilers

characteristics; 82 (Q3.4)

speed impact of; 88 (Q3.9)

JVM

See Java Virtual Machine (JVM)

K

key themes

See also question relationships and themes

action events, *See*

accessing

creating

debugging

destroying

drawing

loading

overloading

overriding

reading

setting

writing

AWT, *See*

browser

component(s)

containers

frame(s)

menu(s)

windows

data, *See*

applets

array(s)

bytes

list(s)

numbers

stacks

string(s)

event-handling, *See*

event(s)

exceptions (concepts)

listeners

model, event

input/output, *See*

buffer(ing)

files

input

output

standard I/O

stream(s)

Java, *See*

compilation

JVM

loading

platform-dependent issues

security

JDK 1.0.2

JDK 1.1
media, *See*
  audio
  images
  video
network, *See*
  applets
  Internet
  IP (Internet Protocol)
  packets
  servers
  socket(s)
  URL (Uniform Resource Locator)
  web pages
  WWW (World Wide Web)
object-oriented concepts, *See*
  class(es)
  constructors
  field(s)
  inheritance
  instance(s)
  interface(s)
  member(s)
  method(s)
  object(s)
  package(s)
  peers
  references
programs, *See*
  applets
  applications
threads, *See*
  deadlock
  performance
  synchronization
  wait/notify
keys
  key events
    handling, JDK 1.0.2; 142 (Q6.6)
    handling, JDK 1.1; 169 (Q7.13)
    handling, JDK 1.1, (code example);
      170 (Q7.13)
    information in, (table); 136 (Q6.2)
  key field, in JDK 1.0.2, meaning of, (table);
    135 (Q6.1)
  KeyAdapter class
    strategies for use of; 158 (Q7.4)
  keyDown method
    as JDK 1.0.2 event-handling method, (table);
      140 (Q6.4)

keys *(continued)*
  KeyEvent class
    constants in, (table); 169 (Q7.13)
    position in JDK 1.1 class hierarchy, (table);
      152 (Q7.1)
    public methods, (table); 155 (Q7.2)
  KeyListener interface; 169 (Q7.13)
    methods, (table); 157 (Q7.3)
  keyUp method
    as JDK 1.0.2 event-handling method, (table);
      140 (Q6.4)
  meta, status testing; 149 (Q6.11)
  navigation, event handling; 169 (Q7.13)
keyword(s)
  const, not allowed in Java; 46 (Q2.4)
  goto, not allowed in Java; 46 (Q2.4)
  reserved, list of; 46 (Q2.4)
  static, class variables defined with; 7 (Q1.5)
  void; 4 (Q1.3)
killing
  See destroying

L

Label class
  opaque nature of; 187 (Q8.15)
layout manager
  container management by; 118 (Q5.2)
  defining; 119 (Q5.2)
  layout method (JDK 1.0.2), container layout
    management; 122 (Q5.5)
  LayoutManager interface
    characteristics and JDK 1.1 extensions;
      118 (Q5.2)
length
  identifiers, maximum size; 48 (Q2.6)
  length field, array size contained in;
    68 (Q2.21)
life cycle
  applet life cycle
    managed by applet context and AWT;
      107 (Q4.16)
    methods, precautions against sleep use in;
      224 (Q9.17)
    peers, disjoined from AWT component life
      cycle; 126 (Q5.10)
    thread; 205 (Q9.3)
lightweight
  components, JDK 1.1 support for; 178 (Q8.7)

line(s)

See also input; output; streams

length, calculating with readLine, (code example); 226 (Q10.1)

LineNumberReader class, Unicode input handling; 226 (Q10.1)

reading; 225 (Q10.1)

terminators, readLine handling of; 225 (Q10.1)

linking

term definition; 87 (Q3.8)

list(s)

See also data

item selection/deselection notification, JDK 1.1; 164 (Q7.9)

items, selection/deselection events; 146 (Q6.9)

linked, creating in Java; 55 (Q2.13)

List class

action events

in JDK 1.0.2, (table); 142 (Q6.5)

in JDK 1.1, (table); 161 (Q7.7)

catching item events from, (code example); 165 (Q7.9)

events associated with, (table); 137 (Q6.2)

listeners

See also event(s)

assigning, (code example); 163 (Q7.8)

event

classes, methods, and, JDK 1.1; 151–161 (Q7.1–Q7.6)

JDK 1.1 event model use of; 152 (Q7.2)

types of; 156 (Q7.3)

interfaces and methods, JDK 1.1, (table); 157 (Q7.3)

registering, JDK 1.1; 167 (Q7.11)

literals

See also char; constants; numbers; strings

in Java

examples of, (table); 50 (Q2.8)

suffixes on, (table); 50 (Q2.8)

long outside int range, L suffix required; 51 (Q2.8)

term definition; 49 (Q2.8)

loading

applets into applications; 114 (Q4.23)

images; 179–191 (Q8.9–Q8.19)

ImageTracker methods, (table); 184 (Q8.12)

into applets; 179 (Q8.9)

loading (*continued*)

images (*continued*)

into applications; 180 (Q8.10)

methods that trigger, (table); 182 (Q8.11)

strategies for; 181 (Q8.11)

tracking errors in, (code example); 186 (Q8.13)

loader class

processes managed by; 87 (Q3.8)

term definition; 86 (Q3.7)

term definition; 87 (Q3.8)

web pages, image handling issues; 182 (Q8.11)

local

host IP address, accessing; 244 (Q10.17)

variables, definition of; 57 (Q2.14)

locating

applet class files; 101 (Q4.9)

reusable custom classes; 102 (Q4.10)

locks

for abstract classes; 213 (Q9.9)

for mutual exclusion; 210 (Q9.7)

not needed for join; 218 (Q9.12)

released when thread terminates; 205 (Q9.3)

synchronization, impact on container layout management; 122 (Q5.5)

logical-and (&) operator

preventing sign extension of byte value with; 44 (Q2.2)

long

See also integers; numbers

Class instance corresponding to, (table); 63 (Q2.17)

Long class

converting strings to numerical values (code example); 230 (Q10.4)

(table); 230 (Q10.4)

long keyword

as reserved keyword; 46 (Q2.4)

reading from string; 230 (Q10.4)

suffixes on, (table); 50 (Q2.8)

loopback interface

term definition; 246 (Q10.20)

loops

exiting from multiple layers of; 46 (Q2.4)

lostFocus method

as JDK 1.0.2 event-handling method, (table); 140 (Q6.4)

low-level events; 167–171 (Q7.11–Q7.14)

M

machine language

Java Virtual Machine, bytecodes as; 78 (Q3.2)

main method

for applications that can run as applets, (example); 94 (Q4.3)

invocation, by Java Virtual Machine; 77 (Q3.1)

required for combined applet/applications; 93 (Q4.3)

MalformedURLException class

thrown by URL(String) constructor, (code example); 236 (Q10.8)

managing

name spaces, package support for; 33 (Q1.29)

system resources; 84 (Q3.6)

mark-and-sweep

garbage collection algorithm; 83 (Q3.5)

matching

backgrounds, as transparency solution; 104 (Q4.13)

Math class

random method; 259 (Q11.4)

max methods

as example of overloading; 15 (Q1.13)

media

See also audio; images; key themes; video

files, as applet components; 99 (Q4.8)

MediaTracker class

image loading manager; 183 (Q8.11)

methods, (table); 184 (Q8.12)

methods that trigger image loading, (table); 182 (Q8.11)

tracking images with; 183 (Q8.12)

streams, Java Media Framework planned capabilities; 263 (Q11.7)

mediation

as wait and notifyAll/notify service characteristic; 214 (Q9.10)

member(s)

See also object-oriented concepts

access modifiers; 36 (Q1.32)

term definition, (table); 8 (Q1.6)

MemoryImageSource class

animation

control with, JDK 1.1; 195 (Q8.22)

methods, (table); 195 (Q8.22)

creating images with, JDK 1.0.2; 188 (Q8.17)

menu(s)

See also AWT (Abstract Window Toolkit); events

on applets, workaround for; 105 (Q4.14)

menu items

catching events from, JDK 1.1; 163 (Q7.8)

MenuItem class action events, JDK 1.0.2, (table); 142 (Q6.5)

MenuItem class action events, JDK 1.1, (table); 161 (Q7.7)

MenuComponent class

component-like behavior; 144 (Q6.8)

event handling, compared with Component, (table); 145 (Q6.8)

MenuItem class

events associated with, (table); 137 (Q6.2)

Quit/Close command

correcting problems with

in JDK 1.0.2; 143 (Q6.7)

in JDK 1.1; 167 (Q7.11)

metaDown method

meta key status testing; 149 (Q6.11)

method(s)

See also object-oriented concepts

abstract, term definition; 9 (Q1.8)

access modifiers; 36 (Q1.32)

API contract components; 75 (Q2.26)

applet methods

invoked by applet context; 107 (Q4.16)

invoked by AWT; 107 (Q4.16)

class methods

instance methods compared with; 7 (Q1.6)

method overriding not permitted with; 23 (Q1.18)

static reference to nonstatic variable, error; 57 (Q2.14)

Class class information available, JDK 1.1; 59 (Q2.15)

creating instances by invoking; 9 (Q1.7)

event classes

JDK 1.1, (table); 154 (Q7.2)

listeners, and, JDK 1.1; 151–161 (Q7.1–Q7.6)

event handling, JDK 1.0.2; 139 (Q6.4)

final, characteristics and use; 24 (Q1.19)

instance methods

class methods compared with; 7 (Q1.6)

interface methods

class implementation requirements; 26 (Q1.21)

method(s) (*continued*)
  invocation
    arguments passed by value; 54 (Q2.12)
    conversion, as trigger for `byte` to `int`
        promotion; 43 (Q2.2)
    exception handling compared with;
        68 (Q2.22)
    from names, at run time; 61 (Q2.17)
    `Method` class, inspecting methods with;
        60 (Q2.16)
  objects, and classes; 1–12 (Q1.1–Q1.10)
  obtaining `Class` instance for the class of;
      59 (Q2.15)
  output behavior, exceptions as part of;
      72 (Q2.24)
  overloaded methods
    signatures as differentiator among;
        15 (Q1.13)
  overriding, with `super` keyword; 21 (Q1.17)
  public methods
    access at run time; 60 (Q2.16)
    within nonpublic classes, accessibility
        issues; 38 (Q1.34)
  `read`, advantages as abstract method; 10 (Q1.8)
  signatures, components of; 6 (Q1.4)
  `static`, `final` keywords used to declare;
      23 (Q1.18)
  `synchronized`, (code example); 211 (Q9.8)
  term definition; 2 (Q1.1)
    characteristics and; 4 (Q1.3)
  tracing execution of; 267 (Q11.12)
  variables and; 53–65 (Q2.11–Q2.18)
  virtual, characteristics and use; 22 (Q1.18)
  vocabulary of methods as interface
      specification; 27 (Q1.22)
MIME type
  class file requirements; 116 (Q4.24)
miscellaneous topics
  (chapter); 255–269 (Q11.1–Q11.14)
model
  colors, default, (table); 188 (Q8.17)
  event model
    in JDK 1.0.2; 138 (Q6.3)
    in JDK 1.1; 152 (Q7.2)
    JDK 1.1 versus JDK 1.0.2; 160 (Q7.5),
        160 (Q7.6)
  semantic model
    semantic events defined in terms of;
        164 (Q7.9)

modifiers
  access modifiers
    class members and interfaces; 36 (Q1.32)
    packages and; 33–40 (Q1.29–Q1.34)
    as part of class declaration; 3 (Q1.2)
  `modifiers` field
    in `Event` class, JDK 1.0.2, meaning of,
        (table); 135 (Q6.1)
    in `Event` class, mouse button selection
        with, (table); 148 (Q6.11)
    in `MouseEvent` class, mouse button selec-
        tion with, (code example); 171 (Q7.14)
  by subclassing, term definition; 13 (Q1.11)
modification
  of behavior, by subclasses; 13 (Q1.11)
  of field values, at run time; 62 (Q2.17)
modularity
  program modularity
    package support for; 33 (Q1.29)
monitors
  locks, recursive access to; 210 (Q9.7)
  not needed for `join`; 218 (Q9.12)
  scope definition; 211 (Q9.8)
  `synchronized` keyword relationship with;
      212 (Q9.8)
  term definition; 209 (Q9.7)
Motif
  impact on AWT peers
    requirement of top-level window;
        126 (Q5.10)
mouse
  clicks, button selection
    in JDK 1.0.2; 148 (Q6.11)
    in JDK 1.1; 171 (Q7.14)
  events, information in, (table); 136 (Q6.2)
  location, not controlled by application;
      132 (Q5.18)
  `MouseAdapter` class
    strategies for use of; 158 (Q7.4)
    (code examples); 158 (Q7.4)
  `mouseDown` method
    as JDK 1.0.2 event-handling method, (table);
        140 (Q6.4)
  `mouseDrag` method
    as JDK 1.0.2 event-handling method, (table);
        140 (Q6.4)
  `mouseEnter` method
    as JDK 1.0.2 event-handling method, (table);
        140 (Q6.4)

mouse (*continued*)

MouseEvent class

position in JDK 1.1 class hierarchy, (table);
152 (Q7.1)

public methods, (table); 155 (Q7.2)

modifiers field, button selection use;
171 (Q7.14)

mouseExit method

as JDK 1.0.2 event-handling method, (table);
140 (Q6.4)

MouseListener interface

methods, (table); 157 (Q7.3)

MouseMotionAdapter class

strategies for use of; 158 (Q7.4)

MouseMotionListener interface

implementing event listener, (code example);
153 (Q7.2)

methods, (table); 157 (Q7.3)

mouseMove method

as JDK 1.0.2 event-handling method, (table);
140 (Q6.4)

mouseUp method

as JDK 1.0.2 event-handling method, (table);
140 (Q6.4)

move method (JDK 1.0.2)

positioning windows with; 127 (Q5.11)

multiprocessors

multithreading value for; 202 (Q9.1)

multihomed machines

See also networks

specifying server socket address for listening;
250 (Q10.25)

multimedia

Java Media Framework planned capabilities;
263 (Q11.7)

multiple inheritance

interfaces use for; 28 (Q1.24), 29 (Q1.25)

multithreading

relationship to operating system resource
management; 202 (Q9.1)

mutex

See lock, mutual exclusion

N

name(s)

applet names

inter-applet communication with;
111 (Q4.20)

Class class information available; 58 (Q2.15)

name(s) (*continued*)

class names

fully qualified

term definition; 34 (Q1.30)

simple

automatic import of all java.lang
classes; 35 (Q1.31)

sources of; 36 (Q1.31)

term definition; 34 (Q1.30)

simple versus fully qualified; 34 (Q1.30)

identifier names

capitalization conventions; 47 (Q2.5)

invoking methods from run-time names;
61 (Q2.17)

method name, as part of signature; 6 (Q1.4)

name attribute (APPLET tag)

characteristics; 96 (Q4.4)

JDK README file; 98 (Q4.7)

name spaces

package use for managing; 33 (Q1.29)

native

process, connecting to Java application;
233 (Q10.6)

native keyword

nonmatch permittted in method overriding;
19 (Q1.16)

as reserved keyword; 49 (Q2.4)

methods, required for

ping program; 247

raw sockets; 247

operating system calls, accessing; 257 (Q11.2)

peers

need eliminated in lightweight components;
178 (Q8.7)

tool kit, inset value handling; 120 (Q5.3)

navigation keys

event handling; 169 (Q7.13)

network(s)

See also applets; client; Internet; IP (Internet
Protocol); key themes; packets; servers;
socket(s); URL (Uniform Resource
Locator); WWW (World WIde Web)

code, loopback interface use for testing;
246 (Q10.20)

connection, managing with URLConnection;
235 (Q10.7)

firewalls, handling; 248 (Q10.23)

input, output, and network, (chapter); 225–254
(Q10.1–10.27)

loading images into applets; 179 (Q8.9)

socket communication without; 246 (Q10.20)

new
  new keyword
    in array creation expressions; 66 (Q2.19)
    creating instances with; 9 (Q1.7)
    as reserved keyword; 46 (Q2.4)
  newInstance method
    creating instances with; 9 (Q1.7)
    invoking on objects returned by forName;
      86 (Q3.7)
  newline, as line terminator; 225 (Q10.1)
  newline-return, as line terminator; 225 (Q10.1)
  newPixels method; 195 (Q8.22)
next... methods
  nextDouble method
    return value, (table); 260 (Q11.4)
  nextElement method; 259 (Q11.3)
  nextFloat method
    return value, (table); 260 (Q11.4)
  nextGaussian method
    return value, (table); 260 (Q11.4)
  nextInt method
    return value, (table); 260 (Q11.4)
  nextLong method
    return value, (table); 260 (Q11.4)
nonresizable
  windows, creating; 131 (Q5.16)
notification
  See also wait/notify
  of component resizing; 168 (Q7.12)
  of list item selection/deselection
    in JDK 1.0.2; 146 (Q6.9)
    in JDK 1.1; 164 (Q7.9)
null
  null keyword
    as reserved keyword; 49 (Q2.4)
  as return value from getHeader; 238 (Q10.10)
NullPointerException class
  meaning of; 69 (Q2.22)
numbers
  See also data; F suffix; floating point; Gaussian
      distribution; hexadecimal values; long;
      octal values
  applet parameters, reading; 110 (Q4.19)
  conversion, byte to int promotion; 43 (Q2.2)
  literals, suffixes on, (table); 50 (Q2.8)
  Number class
    as example of abstract method use; 10 (Q1.8)
  NumberFormatException class
    thrown by string conversion methods;
      231 (Q10.4)

numbers (*continued*)
  random numbers, generating; 259 (Q11.4)
  reading
    from binary; 229 (Q10.3)
    from string; 230 (Q10.4)

O

object(s)
  See also object-oriented concepts
  arrays as; 65 (Q2.19)
  class relationship with; 2 (Q1.2)
  classes, and methods; 1–12 (Q1.1–Q1.10)
  numbers as objects, classes for; 230 (Q10.4)
  object attribute (APPLET tag)
    characteristics, from JDK README file;
      99 (Q4.7)
  Object class
    automatic import of; 35 (Q1.31)
    as interface superclass; 29 (Q1.25)
    multithreading operations handled by;
      257 (Q11.2)
  object references
    casting criteria; 51 (Q2.9)
    operations on, (table); 12 (Q1.10)
    pointer comparison to; 55 (Q2.13)
    term definition and characteristics;
      11 (Q1.10)
  object types
    reference types comprised of; 41 (Q2.1)
    runtime checking, instanceof operator
      use for; 30 (Q1.26)
  object-orientation
    encapsulation characteristics and benefits;
      1 (Q1.1)
    superclass-subclass relationship importance;
      13 (Q1.11)
  pointers compared with; 53 (Q2.11)
  term definition; 1 (Q1.1)
object-oriented concepts
  See also key themes
  See class(es); constructors; field(s); inheritance;
      instance(s); interface(s); member(s);
      method(s); object(s); package(s); peers;
      references;
observers
  Observable class
    Observer interface compared with;
      28 (Q1.24)

observers (*continued*)

Observer interface

Observable class compared with; 28 (Q1.24)

octal values

See also numbers

string to numeric value conversions, JDK 1.1; 231 (Q10.4)

opening

openConnection method

connecting to URL with; 236 (Q10.8)

openStream method

reading from remote files, (code example); 237 (Q10.9)

operating system

calls, accessing; 257 (Q11.2)

events, as platform-dependent features not accessible in Java; 224 (Q9.18)

operations

on object references, (table); 12 (Q1.10)

operator(s)

cast operator

reference and primitive type use of; 52 (Q2.9)

logical-and (&) operator

preventing sign extension of byte value with; 44 (Q2.2)

overloading

restricted in Java; 48 (Q2.7)

plus (+) operator

See + (plus) operator

right shift (>>>) operator

preventing sign extension of byte values with; 44 (Q2.2)

optimization

See performance

options

compiler

-prof for profiling; 266 (Q11.12)

outlines

drawing around component groups; 124 (Q5.8)

output

See also buffer(ing); events; files; input; key themes; standard I/O; stream(s)

basic; 225–235 (Q10.1–Q10.6)

file, handled byjava.io package; 257 (Q11.2)

flushing output

migrating from JDK 1.0.2 to JDK 1.1; 228 (Q10.2)

input, output, and network, (chapter); 225–254 (Q10.1–10.27)

output (*continued*)

output streams

flushing; 232 (Q10.5)

connecting output sream

from Java to process input stream; 233 (Q10.6)

from process to Java input stream; 233 (Q10.6)

writing to output stream despite URL connection restrictions; 240 (Q10.11)

standard output; 227 (Q10.2)

string output methods

PrintStream class in JDK 1.0.2; 227 (Q10.2)

PrintWriter class in JDK 1.1; 227 (Q10.2) (code example), 228 (Q10.2)

overloading

operators

restricted in Java; 48 (Q2.7)

overriding

compared with; 16 (Q1.13), 17 (Q1.15) (table); 18 (Q1.15)

subclassing and; 13–24 (Q1.11–Q1.19)

term definition and characteristics; 15 (Q1.13)

overriding

See also dynamic binding

action events; 142 (Q6.5)

clone, as cloning design requirement; 31 (Q1.28)

event handling methods; 160 (Q7.5)

JDK 1.0.2 options; 139 (Q6.3)

handleEvent

implementation issues; 140 (Q6.4) (code example); 141 (Q6.4)

in list event handling, (code example); 146 (Q6.9)

in scroll bar event handling, (code example); 147 (Q6.10)

methods, permitted as Java default; 23 (Q1.18)

not permitted with class methods; 23 (Q1.18)

overloading

compared with; 16 (Q1.13), 17 (Q1.15)

compared with, (table); 18 (Q1.15)

subclassing, and; 13–24 (Q1.11–Q1.19)

restrictions on; 19 (Q1.16)

new exception declarations, reasons and workaround; 75 (Q2.26)

run; 203 (Q9.2)

super keyword used for; 21 (Q1.17)

term definition and characteristics; 16 (Q1.14)

P

pack method
  peer creation triggered by; 126 (Q5.10)
  validate invoked by, (table); 122 (Q5.5)
package keyword
  as reserved keyword; 46 (Q2.4)
package(s)
  See also object-oriented concepts
  access modifiers and; 33 (Q1.29), 33–40
      (Q1.29–Q1.34)
  applet, directory correspondance; 102 (Q4.9)
  as C/C++ library analogue; 227 (Q10.2)
  classes, interfaces, and packages, (chapter);
      1–40 (Q1.1–Q1.34)
  directory relationship to; 102 (Q4.9)
  java.lang, automatic import of; 35 (Q1.31)
  package private access
      as default for classes and interfaces;
          36 (Q1.32)
      term definition; 36 (Q1.32)
  subpackages
      explicit import required; 35 (Q1.30)
  term definition and characteristics; 33 (Q1.29)
  unnamed; 34 (Q1.29)
packets
  See also networks
  datagram packets
      broadcast, creating; 253 (Q10.27)
          (code example); 254 (Q10.27)
      normal sockets compared with datagram
          sockets; 252 (Q10.26)
      sending and receiving; 251 (Q10.26)
painting
  See also AWT (Abstract Window Toolkit);
      drawing; frames; windows
  paint method
      contents; 174 (Q8.2)
      invoked
          after re-exposure; 177 (Q8.6)
          by AWT; 107 (Q4.16)
          by update; 173 (Q8.1)
      purpose; 173 (Q8.1)
      sleep not recommended; 224 (Q9.17)
      update relationship with; 176 (Q8.5)
      when invoked, (table); 108 (Q4.16)
  PaintEvent class
      position in JDK 1.1 class hierarchy, (table);
          152 (Q7.1)
      public methods, (table); 155 (Q7.2)

panels
  adding and removing buttons from, (code
      example); 123 (Q5.6)
  drawing on frames with; 129 (Q5.12)
  Panel class
      applets as subclass of; 115 (Q4.23)
      drawing outlines with; 124 (Q5.8)
PARAM tag (HTML)
  characteristics, from JDK README file;
      99 (Q4.7)
  custom applet parameter information conveyed
      by; 96 (Q4.4)
parameters
  method parameters
      match required for method overriding;
          19 (Q1.16)
      as part of API contract; 75 (Q2.26)
      as part of method; 4 (Q1.3)
      as part of signature; 6 (Q1.4)
  numeric parameters
      reading with applet; 110 (Q4.19)
  paramString method
      return values, (table); 154 (Q7.2)
parsing
  parseByte method
      extracting integer values from applet param-
          eters; 110 (Q4.19)
  parseInt method
      extracting integer values from applet param-
          eters; 110 (Q4.19)
  parseLong method
      extracting integer values from applet param-
          eters; 110 (Q4.19)
  parseShort method
      extracting integer values from applet param-
          eters; 110 (Q4.19)
  values returned by getParameter;
      110 (Q4.19)
partially conservative mark-and-sweep
  as JDK garbage collection algorithm; 83 (Q3.5)
passing arguments
  by value, as Java method invocation mode;
      54 (Q2.12)
pattern
  for objects, class viewed as; 2 (Q1.2)
pausing
  threads, with sleep; 207 (Q9.5)
peers
  See also object-oriented concepts
  components, containers and; 117–126
      (Q5.1–Q5.10)

peers (*continued*)
   creating and destroying; 126 (Q5.10)
   event priorities; 137 (Q6.2)
   peerless, lightweight components,
      characteristics and advantages; 178 (Q8.7)
   precautions in using; 125 (Q5.9)
   term definition; 125 (Q5.9)
performance; 109 (Q4.18)
   See also threads
   double buffering, impact on image drawing;
      189 (Q8.18)
   `final` class advantages for; 24 (Q1.19)
   `java.prof` files
      creation and use; 266 (Q11.12)
      (code example); 267 (Q11.12)
   multithreading, impact on; 202 (Q9.1)
   optimizing redrawing by overriding `update`;
      176 (Q8.5)
   `paint` method efficiency
      importance of; 174 (Q8.1)
      ways to enhance; 174 (Q8.2)
   platform-dependent performance due to thread
      scheduling; 222 (Q9.15)
   profile, obtaining; 266 (Q11.12)
   redrawing efficiency, strategies for; 175 (Q8.4)
   speed, Java compared with C and C++; 88
      (Q3.9)
   web page loading
      image handling impact; 182 (Q8.11)
ping program
   native methods required for implementing;
      247 (Q10.21)
pixels
   creating images from; 188 (Q8.17)
   pixel values, accesssing; 190 (Q8.19)
   `PixelGrabber` class
      accessing pixel values with; 190 (Q8.19)
      methods that trigger image loading, (table);
         182 (Q8.11)
platform-dependent issues
   automatic versus hand-done layouts;
      121 (Q5.4)
   `exec` as platform-dependent method;
      234 (Q10.6)
   native environment process, connecting to Java
      applications; 233 (Q10.6)
   native tool kit, inset value handling; 120 (Q5.3)
   operating system calls; 257 (Q11.2)
   peers as on-screen AWT component counter-
      parts; 125 (Q5.9)
   playing sounds in an application; 263 (Q11.8)

platform-dependent issues (*continued*)
   threads
      priorities; 222 (Q9.15)
      time-slicing; 222 (Q9.15)
playing sounds
   See also audio; images; painting
   in applets; 261 (Q11.5)
      `play` method; 261 (Q11.5)
      simultaneous play of multiple clips;
         262 (Q11.6)
   playback, completion, estimating, (code exam-
      ple); 263 (Q11.7)
plus (+) operator
   See + (plus) operator
pointers
   See also object(s), references
   function, creating the equivalent of; 64 (Q2.18)
   objects compared with; 53 (Q2.11)
   references compared with; 53 (Q2.11),
      55 (Q2.13)
polymorphism
   characteristics, (table); 14 (Q1.11)
   term definition; 13 (Q1.11)
   virtual methods use with; 22 (Q1.18)
popup windows
   creating; 129 (Q5.13)
port number
   not required by datagram socket; 252 (Q10.26)
   specified at socket creation time; 245 (Q10.19)
positioning
   components
      layout manager handling; 118 (Q5.2)
      precautions about; 120 (Q5.4)
   windows; 127 (Q5.11)
posting
   POST request (http protocol)
      GET request compared with; 241 (Q10.12)
      as mechanism for writing to remote files
         from applets; 243 (Q10.13)
      sending data to CGI program with;
         240 (Q10.12)
      (code example); 242 (Q10.12)
   `postEvent` method
      event handling, (code example); 138 (Q6.3)
precautions
   `grabPixels` use; 191 (Q8.19)
prepareImage method
   as trigger for image loading, (table);
      182 (Q8.11)
preprocessor macros
   reasons for omission; 49 (Q2.7)

primitive data types
See also types
advantages of; 42 (Q2.1)
Class instances for
obtaining; 62 (Q2.17)
(table); 63 (Q2.17)
reference types versus; 41 (Q2.1)
printing
print method
printing to standard output and error;
227 (Q10.2)
println method
printing to standard output and error;
227 (Q10.2)
PrintStream class
automatic output flushing; 232 (Q10.5)
printing to standard output and error;
227 (Q10.2)
PrintWriter class
as Unicode-savvy PrintStream replacement; 227 (Q10.2)
automatic output flushing with; 232 (Q10.5)
to standard output and error; 227 (Q10.2)
priorities
peer events; 137 (Q6.2)
thread, scheduling considerations; 219 (Q9.13)
private access
See also access; security
private keyword
as reserved keyword; 46 (Q2.4)
restricting access for class members;
36 (Q1.32)
process(es)
native environment, connecting to Java applications; 233 (Q10.6)
Process class
accessing operating system calls with;
257 (Q11.2)
connecting native process with Java application, (table); 233 (Q10.6)
exec methods return an instance of;
257 (Q11.2)
methods, (table); 258 (Q11.2)
starting, with exec; 257 (Q11.2)
terminating, with destroy; 258 (Q11.2)
threads as form of; 201 (Q9.1)
program structure
applet; 107–111 (Q4.16–Q4.19)

programming
See also API (Application Programming
Interface); applets; applications;
AWT (Abstract Window Toolkit)
style
access modifiers use for encapsulation;
37 (Q1.32)
capitalization in identifiers; 47 (Q2.5)
classes versus structures; 53 (Q2.10)
name reuse precautions; 33 (Q1.29)
operator overloading prohibition, reasons
for; 48 (Q2.7)
system resource management; 84 (Q3.6)
promotion
of byte values to int; 43 (Q2.2)
propagating
event listeners; 160 (Q7.5)
events
JDK 1.1 versus JDK 1.0.2; 160 (Q7.5)
menu component limitations; 145 (Q6.8)
protected access
See also access; security
impact on classes and subclasses; 37 (Q1.33)
protected keyword
as reserved keyword; 46 (Q2.4)
restricting access for class members;
36 (Q1.32)
protocols
See also networks; sockets; URLs
internet, URLConnection use of; 235 (Q10.7)
public access
See also access
public int class variables, used in event
handling; 143 (Q6.6)
public keyword
interfaces not required to include; 27 (Q1.23)
marking public access for classes, interfaces,
and class members; 36 (Q1.32)
as reserved keyword; 46 (Q2.4)

Q

queries
http GET request use; 240 (Q10.12)
question relationships and themes
See also key themes
Question 1.1
Referenced by Q2.10, Q2.11
object(s); 1

question relationships and themes (*continued*)

Question 1.2
Referenced by Q1.1, Q1.2, Q1.3, Q1.6,
Q1.13, Q1.20, Q1.25, Q1.29, Q2.10,
Q2.11, Q3.1
class(es); 2
Question 1.3
Referenced by Q1.1, Q1.2, Q1.6, Q1.13,
Q2.10, Q3.1
method(s); 4
Question 1.4
Referenced by Q1.13, Q1.14, Q1.16
signatures; 6
Question 1.5
Referenced by Q1.12
class and instance variable comparison; 6
Question 1.6
Referenced by Q1.3, Q1.12, Q9.5, Q10.16
class and instance method comparison; 7
Question 1.7
Referenced by Q1.1, Q1.2, Q1.22
creating instances; 8
Question 1.8
Referenced by Q1.9, Q1.23
abstract methods; 9
Question 1.9
Referenced by Q1.21, Q1.24
abstract classes; 10
Question 1.10
Referenced by Q1.7, Q1.18, Q2.11, Q2.13,
Q3.5
object references; 11
Question 1.11
Referenced by Q1.9, Q1.17, Q1.25
subclasses; 13
superclasses; 13
Question 1.12
Referenced by Q1.2, Q1.11, Q1.13, Q1.14,
Q1.17, Q1.18, Q1.25
inheritance; 14
Question 1.13
Referenced by Q1.4, Q1.15, Q1.16
overloading; 15
Question 1.14
Referenced by Q1.3, Q1.4, Q1.13, Q1.15,
Q1.16, Q1.18
overriding; 16
Question 1.15
Referenced by Q1.16
overloading and overriding comparison; 17

question relationships and themes (*continued*)

Question 1.16
Referenced by Q1.14, Q1.15
overriding restrictions; 19
Question 1.17
Referenced by Q1.14, Q6.4
`super` keyword uses; 20
Question 1.18
Referenced by Q1.19, Q1.34
virtual methods; 22
Question 1.19
Referenced by Q1.18
`final` keyword; 24
Question 1.20
Referenced by Q1.2, Q1.21, Q1.23, Q1.24,
Q1.25, Q1.29, Q7.2, Q11.3
interfaces; 25
Question 1.21
Referenced by Q1.20, Q1.22, Q9.2
interfaces, implementation; 26
Question 1.22
Referenced by Q1.21
interfaces, instantiation prohibition; 27
Question 1.24
Referenced by Q1.20
interface and abstract class comparison; 27
Question 1.25
Referenced by Q1.11, Q1.24
multiple inheritance, interfaces used for; 29
Question 1.26
Referenced by Q1.18
assignment compatibility testing; 30
`instanceof` keyword; 30
Question 1.27
Referenced by Q1.28, Q1.32
`clone` method error messages; 31
Question 1.28
Referenced by Q1.27
cloning, designing class for; 31
Question 1.29
Referenced by Q1.30, Q1.31, Q1.32, Q1.33,
Q1.34
package(s); 33
Question 1.30
Referenced by Q1.29, Q1.31
names, simple versus fully qualified; 34
Question 1.31
Referenced by Q1.30
package(s), `java.lang`, automatic import
of; 35

question relationships and themes (*continued*)

Question 1.32
Referenced by Q1.2, Q1.23, Q1.28, Q1.29, Q1.33, Q1.34
access modifiers, class members and interfaces; 36

Question 1.33
Referenced by Q1.27, Q1.28, Q1.32
access control, `protected` access implications; 37

Question 1.34
access, for public members within nonpublic class; 38

Question 2.1
Referenced by Q2.2, Q2.3, Q2.11
`Integer` class and `int` data type comparison; 41

Question 2.2
`byte` type; 43

Question 2.3
enumerated types workaround; 45

Question 2.4
`goto`, not allowed in Java; 46
keywords, reserved, list of; 46

Question 2.5
case sensitivity and capitalization conventions; 47

Question 2.6
identifiers, maximum size; 48

Question 2.7
operator overloading prohibition, reasons for; 48

Question 2.8
Referenced by Q1.10
floating point; 49

Question 2.9
Referenced by Q1.16, Q2.8, Q3.7
casting, reference not class; 51
class casting, object reference casting as workaround for; 51

Question 2.10
Referenced by Q1.3
C-like data structures, creating in Java; 52

Question 2.11
Referenced by Q2.13, Q2.20, Q3.5
object and pointer comparison; 53

Question 2.12
Referenced by Q2.11, Q2.13
pass by value; 54

question relationships and themes (*continued*)

Question 2.13
Referenced by Q2.11
creating linked lists; 55

Question 2.14
class method, static reference to nonstatic variable, error; 57

Question 2.15
Referenced by Q1.7
classes, accessing information about; 58

Question 2.16
Referenced by Q2.17
inspecting public methods, fields, and constructors at run time; 60

Question 2.17
method(s), invocation from names at run time; 61

Question 2.18
encapsulating code in classes; 64
inner classes, creating function pointer equivalents with; 64

Question 2.19
arrays, dynamic allocation of; 65

Question 2.20
Referenced by Q2.19
arrays, initializing; 66

Question 2.21
arrays, size determination; 68

Question 2.22
Referenced by Q2.17, Q2.23, Q2.24, Q2.25
exception handling, mechanisms for; 69

Question 2.23
Referenced by Q2.17, Q2.22, Q2.24, Q2.25, Q8.19, Q9.5, Q9.9, Q10.8, Q10.16
checked exceptions, handling; 70

Question 2.24
Referenced by Q1.4, Q2.23, Q2.25, Q2.26, Q10.8
checked exceptions, advantages of; 71

Question 2.25
Referenced by Q2.24, Q2.26
runtime exceptions; 73

Question 2.26
Referenced by Q1.14, Q2.25
API (application programming interface); 75

Question 3.1
Referenced by Q4.2, Q4.3
invoking applications; 77

Question 3.2
Referenced by Q3.3, Q3.4
bytecodes; 78

question relationships and themes (*continued*)

Question 3.3
Referenced by Q3.2, Q3.4, Q3.9
Java language, `javap` as class file disassembler; 79
Question 3.4
bytecodes, JDK interpretation of; 81
Question 3.5
Referenced by Q1.7
garbage collection, JDK algorithm; 83
Question 3.6
finalization, limitations and dependencies; 84
Question 3.7
Referenced by Q1.7
`forName` method; 85
Question 3.8
verification, optimization as source of problems with; 87
Question 3.9
Referenced by Q11.12
performance, speed, Java compared with C and C++; 88
Question 4.1
Referenced by Q11.11
applets; 91
web pages; 91
Question 4.2
Referenced by Q9.16, Q11.8, Q11.11
applets, applications compared with; 92
Question 4.3
Referenced by Q4.2
applets, writing applications that can run as; 93
Question 4.4
Referenced by Q4.6, Q11.11
HTML (Hypertext Markup Language), APPLET tag; 95
Question 4.5
applets, multiple, inclusion on web pages; 97
Question 4.6
applets, including information for non–Java-enabled browsers; 97
Question 4.7
Referenced by Q4.1, Q4.4, Q4.6, Q4.20
HTML (Hypertext Markup Language), APPLET tag, syntax and component description; 98

question relationships and themes (*continued*)

Question 4.8
Referenced by Q4.9, Q4.10
installing applet components; 99
Question 4.9
Referenced by Q4.8, Q4.10
applet class files, specified in URL; 101
Question 4.10
Referenced by Q4.8, Q4.9
applet class file location; 102
Question 4.11
applet size, determining; 103
Question 4.12
Referenced by Q8.9, Q8.10
applet background color, setting; 104
Question 4.13
Referenced by Q4.12, Q8.7
transparent applet background, setting; 104
Question 4.14
menus on applets, workaround for; 105
Question 4.15
Referenced by Q5.14
cursors, setting; 106
Question 4.16
Referenced by Q4.2, Q4.3, Q4.17, Q4.18, Q9.16, Q9.17
applet context; 107
Question 4.17
Referenced by Q4.3, Q4.16, Q4.18
`init` method, as constructor replacement in applets; 109
Question 4.18
Referenced by Q4.3, Q4.16, Q4.17
web pages, applet behavior when focus leaves; 109
Question 4.19
Referenced by Q10.4
reading numeric applet parameters; 110
Question 4.20
Referenced by Q4.3, Q4.5, Q4.22
communication among applets on the same web page; 111
Question 4.21
activating web pages from applets; 112
Question 4.22
communication among applets on different web pages; 114
Question 4.23
loading applets into applications; 114

question relationships and themes (*continued*)

Question 4.24
Referenced by Q4.1
http servers, applet delivery; 115

Question 5.1
Referenced by Q1.9, Q1.14, Q4.11, Q4.12,
Q4.23, Q5.2, Q5.3, Q5.5, Q5.7, Q6.3,
Q6.8, Q8.1
component(s), Component class,
characteristics; 117
containers, Container class, characteristics;
117

Question 5.2
Referenced by Q4.23, Q5.1, Q5.3, Q5.5,
Q5.11
component(s), methods for positioning; 118
containers, layout manager handling of; 118

Question 5.3
Referenced by Q5.2
setting inset values; 119

Question 5.4
Referenced by Q5.2
positioning components, precautions about;
120

Question 5.5
Referenced by Q5.2, Q5.6
container management by validate and
invalidate; 121

Question 5.6
Referenced by Q5.5
AWT (Abstract Window Toolkit), dynami-
cally adding components; 122

Question 5.7
Referenced by Q5.5, Q5.6
containment hierarchy, as strict tree structure; 123

Question 5.8
Referenced by Q5.3
drawing outlines around compnent groups;
124

Question 5.9
Referenced by Q5.10, Q6.2, Q6.3, Q8.7
platform-dependent issues, peers as on-
screen AWT component counterparts;
125

Question 5.10
Referenced by Q5.9
peers, creating and destroying; 126

Question 5.11
positioning windows; 127

question relationships and themes (*continued*)

Question 5.12
Referenced by Q5.3, Q5.11
drawing on frames, border considerations;
128

Question 5.13
creating borderless windows; 129

Question 5.14
Referenced by Q4.15, Q5.13
Frame class, determining instance contain-
ing current component; 129
FileDialog class, user file access with; 130

Question 5.15
accessing files; 130

Question 5.16
creating nonresizable windows; 131

Question 5.17
requestFocus method; 131

Question 5.18
mouse location, not controlled by application; 132

Question 5.19
beep method, signaling errors with; 132

Question 5.20
Referenced by Q5.21
fonts, determining available; 133

Question 5.21
Referenced by Q5.20
fonts, dynamically changing attributes; 133

Question 6.1
Referenced by Q6.6
event handling, JDK 1.0.2, Event class; 135

Question 6.2
Referenced by Q6.3, Q6.6, Q6.9, Q6.10
event types, JDK 1.0.2; 136

Question 6.3
Referenced by Q6.2, Q6.4, Q6.5, Q6.6, Q6.8,
Q7.3, Q7.6
event handling, JDK 1.0.2 model; 138

Question 6.4
Referenced by Q6.3, Q6.5, Q6.6, Q6.8, Q6.9,
Q6.10, Q7.6, Q9.17
event handling, JDK 1.0.2 methods; 139

Question 6.5
Referenced by Q6.4, Q6.8, Q6.9, Q7.7
action events, JDK 1.0.2; 141

Question 6.6
Referenced by Q5.17, Q6.5
key events, handling, JDK 1.0.2; 142

question relationships and themes (*continued*)

Question 6.7
Referenced by Q7.11
closing frames, correcting problems with;
143

Question 6.8
Referenced by Q4.14, Q6.5, Q7.8
MenuComponent class, component-like
behavior; 144

Question 6.9
list items, selection/deselection events; 146

Question 6.10
Referenced by Q7.10, Q7.14
scroll bar events, JDK 1.0.2; 147

Question 6.11
mouse clicks, button selection in JDK 1.0.2;
148

Question 7.1
Referenced by Q7.3
event handling, JDK 1.1, EventObject
class; 151

Question 7.2
Referenced by Q2.18, Q7.3, Q7.4, Q7.7
event handling, JDK 1.1 event model; 152

Question 7.3
Referenced by Q7.2, Q7.4, Q7.7, Q9.17
event listeners, types of; 156

Question 7.4
Referenced by Q7.3
events, adapter classes, strategies for using;
158

Question 7.5
event model, JDK 1.1 versus JDK 1.0.2; 160

Question 7.6
event model compatibility, JDK 1.1 with
JDK 1.0.2; 160

Question 7.7
Referenced by Q6.5, Q7.8
action event handling, JDK 1.1; 161

Question 7.8
Referenced by Q4.14, Q6.8
catching menu item events, JDK 1.1; 163

Question 7.9
Referenced by Q6.9
selecting/deselecting list items, JDK 1.1
notification of; 164

Question 7.10
Referenced by Q6.10
ScrollPane class, scrolling control with,
JDK 1.1; 165

question relationships and themes (*continued*)

Question 7.11
Referenced by Q7.12
closing windows, correcting problems with,
JDK 1.1; 167

Question 7.13
Referenced by Q5.17, Q6.6
key event handling, JDK 1.1; 169

Question 7.14
Referenced by Q6.11
mouse clicks, button selection in JDK 1.1;
171

Question 8.1
Referenced by Q4.16, Q8.3, Q8.5, Q8.6,
Q9.17
paint method, purpose; 173

Question 8.2
Referenced by Q8.1, Q8.5
paint method, parts in; 174

Question 8.3
Referenced by Q8.1, Q8.5, Q8.6
redrawing components; 174

Question 8.4
Referenced by Q8.3, Q8.6
redrawing, efficiency strategies; 175

Question 8.5
Referenced by Q1.14, Q4.16, Q8.1, Q8.5,
Q8.6, Q8.18, Q9.17
update method; 176

Question 8.6
Referenced by Q8.1
applet re-exposure, actions taken by AWT;
177

Question 8.7
transparency, JDK 1.1 support for; 177
lightweight component, JDK 1.1 support for;
178

Question 8.8
drawing, XOR drawing mode; 178

Question 8.9
Referenced by Q4.12
loading images into applets; 179
displaying images, steps in; 180

Question 8.10
Referenced by Q8.12
loading images into applications; 180
remote files, accessing images in; 181

Question 8.11
Referenced by Q8.12, Q11.5
loading images, strategies for; 181

question relationships and themes (*continued*)

Question 8.12
Referenced by Q8.11
tracking images, `MediaTracker` use; 183

Question 8.13
Referenced by Q8.12
drawing images, checking the status of; 185

Question 8.14
Referenced by Q8.15, Q8.22
flushing cached images; 186

Question 8.15
Referenced by Q8.9, Q8.14, Q8.16
drawing text over background images; 187

Question 8.16
Referenced by Q8.15
transparent images, loading over background image; 187

Question 8.17
Referenced by Q8.19, Q8.22
creating images from raw image data; 188

Question 8.18
Referenced by Q8.2, Q8.5
drawing offscreen images; 189

Question 8.19
accessing image data; 190

Question 8.20
Referenced by Q8.21, Q8.23
clipping rectangle, handling, JDK 1.0.2; 192

Question 8.21
Referenced by Q8.24
copying images, JDK 1.0.2; 193

Question 8.22
Referenced by Q8.17
animations, controlling; 195

Question 8.23
Referenced by Q8.20
resetting clipping rectangle; 196

Question 8.24
Referenced by Q8.21
copying image subareas; 198

Question 9.1
Referenced by Q9.2
sharing data among threads; 201

Question 9.2
Referenced by Q4.18, Q9.1, Q9.3, Q9.4
creating threads; 203

Question 9.3
Referenced by Q4.18, Q9.2, Q9.4
restarting threads; 204
stopping threads; 204

question relationships and themes (*continued*)

Question 9.4
Referenced by Q8.4, Q9.3, Q9.16, Q9.3, Q9.12
stopping threads; 205

Question 9.5
pausing threads, with `sleep`; 207

Question 9.6
Referenced by Q9.1;
thread synchronization, importance of; 208

Question 9.7
Referenced by Q9.1, Q9.3, Q9.6, Q9.8, Q9.9, Q9.14
monitors, term definition; 209
wait-notify service, monitor use with; 209

Question 9.8
Referenced by Q9.1, Q9.6, Q9.7, Q9.8, Q9.9, Q9.14
synchronization, `synchronized` keyword, monitor relationship with; 212

Question 9.9
synchronization of class objects; 212

Question 9.10
Referenced by Q9.3, Q9.5, Q9.7, Q9.11, Q9.12
thread cooperation; 214

Question 9.11
Referenced by Q9.10
condition variables, obtaining effect of; 215

Question 9.12
thread serialization, `join` use; 217

Question 9.13
Referenced by Q8.4, Q9.15
`yield` method, characteristics and use; 218

Question 9.14
deadlocks, detection, solution, and prevention; 220

Question 9.15
Referenced by Q8.4, Q9.13
thread scheduling, platform-dependent issues; 222

Question 9.16
Referenced by Q1.21, Q8.19, Q9.4, Q9.17
applet thread interaction with system threads; 223

Question 9.17
Referenced by Q8.1, Q9.16
browser, applet thread interaction issues; 223

Question 9.18
threads, operating system events not accessible to; 224

question relationships and themes (*continued*)

Question 10.1
Referenced by Q10.2, Q10.3, Q10.9
reading one line at a time; 225

Question 10.2
Referenced by Q10.5, Q10.6, Q10.9
standard error, System.err characteristics
and use; 227
standard input, System.out characteristics
and use; 227
standard output, System.in characteristics
and use; 227

Question 10.3
Referenced by Q10.1, Q10.2, Q10.19
reading binary input; 229

Question 10.4
Referenced by Q1.7, Q4.19, Q10.2
numbers, reading from string; 230

Question 10.5
flushing output streams; 232

Question 10.6
Referenced by Q10.9, Q11.2;
process streams, connecting to Java streams;
233

Question 10.7
URL comparison with URLConnection; 235

Question 10.8
Referenced by Q10.12
URL (Uniform Resource Locator),
connecting to; 236

Question 10.9
Referenced by Q10.8, Q10.14
reading from remote files via URL; 236

Question 10.10
accessing URL header information; 238

Question 10.11
CGI (Common Gateway Interface) scripts,
connecting to; 239

Question 10.12
Referenced by Q10.11, Q10.13
CGI programs, sending data to; 240

Question 10.13
Referenced by Q10.13
writing to URL-specified files from applets;
243

Question 10.14
Referenced by Q4.21
applications, fetching documents in; 243

Question 10.15
security model, applets versus applications;
243

question relationships and themes (*continued*)

Question 10.16
Referenced by Q1.7, Q10.17, Q10.18
creating InetAddress instances; 244

Question 10.17
accessing local host IP address; 244

Question 10.18
Referenced by Q10.27
creating an instance from an IP address; 245

Question 10.19
Referenced by Q10.20, Q10.22, Q10.23,
Q10.24, Q10.25, Q10.26
creating sockets; 245

Question 10.20
Referenced by Q10.18
127.0.0.1 (IP address), as loopback interface;
246
loopback interface use for testing network
connections; 246

Question 10.21
ICMP messages, native methods required;
247
ping program, native methods required; 247
raw sockets, native methods required; 247

Question 10.22
sockets, input stream, detecting termination
by remote host; 248

Question 10.23
firewalls, handling; 248

Question 10.24
Referenced by Q10.25
creating nonblocking server sockets; 249

Question 10.25
IP address, specifying for server socket listening; 250

Question 10.26
Referenced by Q10.27
datagram packets, sending and receiving;
251

Question 10.27
Referenced by Q10.18
creating broadcast datagram packets; 253

Question 11.1
Referenced by Q2.7
string(s), immutable; 255
string(s), editable; 256

Question 11.2
accessing operating system calls; 257

Question 11.3
iterators, extracting elements with; 258

question relationships and themes (*continued*)
Question 11.4
generating random numbers; 259
Question 11.5
Referenced by Q11.6, Q11.7
playing sounds, in an applets; 261
Question 11.6
Referenced by Q11.5, Q11.7
audio, simultaneous play of mulitple clips;
262
Question 11.7
Referenced by Q11.5, Q11.6
audio clip termination; 263
Question 11.8
Referenced by Q4.3
playing sounds in an application; 263
Question 11.9
audio formats; 264
Question 11.10
generating sound; 265
Question 11.11
Java language and JavaScript comparison;
265
Question 11.12
Referenced by Q3.9
performance profile, obtaining; 266
Question 11.13
debugging, _g terminated files use for; 268
Question 11.14
platform independence model; 269
Quit command
correcting problems with; 143 (Q6.7)
JDK 1.1; 167 (Q7.11)

R

radix
specifying in string-to-number conversion
methods; 231 (Q10.4)
(code example); 232 (Q10.4)
random numbers
generating; 259 (Q11.4)
(code example); 260 (Q11.4)
Random class; 259 (Q11.4)
random method; 259 (Q11.4)
re-exposure
component, actions taken by AWT; 177 (Q8.6)
readability
as reason for prohibiting operator overloading;
48 (Q2.7)

reading
See also input; output; streams
binary input; 229 (Q10.3)
input, one line at a time; 225 (Q10.1)
numeric applet parameters; 110 (Q4.19)
read method
advantages as abstract method; 10 (Q1.8)
exceptions thrown by; 72 (Q2.24)
...Reader classes, for text-oriented input, in
JDK 1.1; 226 (Q10.1), 227 (Q10.1)
readFloat method
reading binary input with; 229 (Q10.3)
readLine method
in BufferedReader class; 226 (Q10.1)
in LineNumberReader class, (code
example); 226 (Q10.1)
reading lines with, JDK 1.0.2; 225 (Q10.1)
reading lines with, JDK 1.1; 225 (Q10.1)
from remote files
(code example); 237 (Q10.9)
URL use; 236 (Q10.9)
from URL input streams; 239 (Q10.11)
recursion
in acquiring monitor locks; 210 (Q9.7)
redrawing
components, repaint method use; 174 (Q8.3)
efficiency strategies; 175 (Q8.4)
references
See also object-oriented concepts
as array contents; 66 (Q2.20)
initializing; 67 (Q2.20)
object references
casting criteria; 51 (Q2.9)
inheritance and polymorphism impact on;
23 (Q1.18)
operations on, (table); 12 (Q1.10)
passed by value in method invocation;
54 (Q2.12)
pointer comparison to; 55 (Q2.13)
term definition and characteristics;
11 (Q1.10)
pointers compared with; 53 (Q2.11)
primitive types compared with reference types;
41 (Q2.1)
reflection API (JDK 1.1)
characteristics of; 61 (Q2.17)
registering
action event listener; 161 (Q7.7)
listeners, JDK 1.1; 167 (Q7.11)
relocating
components, notification of; 168 (Q7.12)

remote files
  reading from, URL use; 236 (Q10.9)
remove method
  `invalidate` invoked by, (table); 122 (Q5.5)
  peer destruction triggered by; 126 (Q5.10)
rendering
  connecting image source with format for, as
      Image purpose; 179 (Q8.9)
  image, tracking progress of; 185 (Q8.13)
  images, tracking errors in, (code example);
      186 (Q8.13)
  on-screen, applet, AWT control of; 107 (Q4.16)
  transparent images; 187 (Q8.16)
      (code example); 188 (Q8.16)
repaint method
  invocation of; 174 (Q8.3)
  purpose; 174 (Q8.3)
  redraw failure issues; 175 (Q8.4)
  `update` relationship with; 176 (Q8.5)
replace method
  copy actions of; 255 (Q11.1)
  (table); 256 (Q11.1)
requestFocus method
  setting focus for component; 131 (Q5.17)
reserved keywords
  list of; 46 (Q2.4)
resetting
  clipping rectangle; 196 (Q8.23)
reshape method (JDK 1.0.2)
  positioning windows with; 127 (Q5.11)
resizing
  See also AWT (Abstract Window Toolkit)
  automatic handling of; 121 (Q5.4)
  components, notification of; 168 (Q7.12)
  `resize` method (JDK 1.0.2), positioning
      windows with; 127 (Q5.11)
resources
  applet resources
    installing; 99 (Q4.8)
    location of; 101 (Q4.9)
  shared, managing thread access to; 202 (Q9.1)
  system, managing; 84 (Q3.6)
  URL-specified, connecting to; 235 (Q10.7)
restarting
  animations; 109 (Q4.18)
  threads; 204 (Q9.3), 205 (Q9.4)
resuming
  applet activities; 109 (Q4.18)
  `resume` method
    as method to avoid; 206 (Q9.4)

return
  return keyword
    as reserved keyword; 46 (Q2.4)
  return type
    match required for method overriding;
        6 (Q14)
    as part of API contract; 75 (Q2.26)
    as part of method; 4 (Q1.3)
  return values, relationship to exceptions;
      72 (Q2.24)
reuse
  inheritance role in; 14 (Q1.12)
  reusable classes, applet, location recommen-
      dations; 102 (Q4.10)
reversing
  colors, with XOR drawing mode; 178 (Q8.8)
  `reverse` method
    (table); 256 (Q11.1)
right shift (>>>) operator
  preventing sign extension of `byte` values with;
      44 (Q2.2)
robustness
  checked exceptions contribution to; 71 (Q2.24)
  `grabPixels` usage precautions; 191 (Q8.19)
running
  applet, managed by applet context; 108 (Q4.16)
  run method
    Applet class use; 26 (Q1.21)
    overriding; 203 (Q9.2)
  `Runnable` interface
    advantages; 204 (Q9.2)
    `Applet` class use; 26 (Q1.21)
    automatic import of; 35 (Q1.31)
    thread implementation of; 203 (Q9.2)
  runnable state
    relevant to thread scheduling; 219 (Q9.13)
runtime
  checking of object types, `instanceof` operator
      use for; 30 (Q1.26)
  exceptions, characteristics; 73 (Q2.25)
  `Runtime` class
    accessing operating system calls with;
        257 (Q11.2)
    connecting native environment processes to
        Java applications; 233 (Q10.6)
  `RuntimeException` class
    subclassing, to define unchecked exceptions;
        75 (Q2.26)
    as unchecked expection, (table); 72 (Q2.24)

S

safety

See also accessing; protection; security
object reference impact on; 12 (Q1.10)
term definition; 12 (Q1.10)
type, `int` and `Integer` conversion support for;
    43 (Q2.1)

scheduling

thread execution, yield use; 218 (Q9.13)

scope

monitor, defining; 211 (Q9.8)

scrolling

events, information in, (table); 137 (Q6.2)
`paint` invocation triggered by; 177 (Q8.6)
as performance analyzer; 174 (Q8.2)
scroll bar control of; 147 (Q6.10)
    with `ScrollPane` class; 166 (Q7.10)
`Scrollbar` class; 147 (Q6.10)
    events associated with, (table); 137 (Q6.2)
`ScrollPane` class
    (code example); 166 (Q7.10)
    scrolling control with, JDK 1.1; 148 (Q6.10),
        165 (Q7.10)

security

See also access; http://java.sun.com/sfaq/; Java
    Virtual Machine (JVM); protection
applet security, as strong differentiator between
    applications and applets; 93 (Q4.2)
exceptions, applets versus applications;
    243 (Q10.15)
`final` class advantages for; 24 (Q1.19)
firewall handling; 248 (Q10.23)
object reference impact on; 12 (Q1.10)
policy, applet context as manager of; 92 (Q4.1)
term definition; 12 (Q1.10)

selecting

list items
    JDK 1.1 notification of; 164 (Q7.9)
    event handling; 146 (Q6.9)

semantic events; 161–167 (Q7.7–Q7.10)
See also events; exceptions
term definition; 164 (Q7.9)

sending

data to CGI program; 240 (Q10.12)

serialization

of threads, by `join` method; 217 (Q9.12)

servers

See also client; network(s)
connecting to; 239 (Q10.11)

servers *(continued)*

creating `ServerSocket` instances;
    245 (Q10.19)
datagram handling; 253 (Q10.26)
GET request effect; 240 (Q10.12)
http server
    applet delivery by; 115 (Q4.24)
    applet delivery role; 92 (Q4.1)
`ServerSocket` class
    creating instances of; 245 (Q10.19)
    specifying address for listening;
        250 (Q10.25)
sockets
    nonblocking, creating; 249 (Q10.24)

set... methods

`setAnimated` method; 195 (Q8.22)
`setBackground` method; 104 (Q4.12)
`setBounds` method
    as JDK 1.1 name for JDK 1.0.2 `reshape`,
        (table); 127 (Q5.11)
    positioning windows with; 127 (Q5.11)
`setCharAt` method
    (table); 256 (Q11.1)
`setClip` method
    resetting clipping rectangle with;
        196 (Q8.23)
`setCursor` method
    setting applet cursors with, JDK 1.1;
        107 (Q4.15)
`setFullBufferUpdates` method;
    195 (Q8.22)
`setLength` method
    (table); 256 (Q11.1)
`setLocation` method
    as JDK 1.1 name for JDK 1.0.2 `move`,
        (table); 127 (Q5.11)
    positioning windows with; 127 (Q5.11)
`setResizable` method
    creating nonresizable windows with;
        131 (Q5.16)
`setSize` method
    as JDK 1.1 name for JDK 1.0.2 `resize`,
        (table); 127 (Q5.11)
    positioning windows with; 127 (Q5.11)
`setSocketImplFactory` method
    firewall handling; 248 (Q10.23)

setting

background color; 104 (Q4.12)
cursors; 106 (Q4.15)
focus on component; 131 (Q5.17)
inset values; 119 (Q5.3)

shallow copying
term definition; 32 (Q1.28)
shared data
among threads, issues; 201 (Q9.1)
synchronization importance; 208 (Q9.6)
short
Short class
converting strings to numerical values
(code example); 231 (Q10.4)
(table); 231 (Q10.4)
short keyword
as reserved keyword; 46 (Q2.4)
short primitive type
Class instance corresponding to, (table);
63 (Q2.17)
reading from string; 231 (Q10.4)
showing
show method
peer creation triggered by; 126 (Q5.10)
validate invoked by, (table); 122 (Q5.5)
showDocument method
selecting URLs with; 112 (Q4.21)
showing state, paint method used for;
174 (Q8.2)
sign extension
preventing, in byte value; 43 (Q2.2)
signaling
errors; 132 (Q5.19)
signatures
characteristics; 6 (Q1.4)
term definition; 6 (Q1.4), 15 (Q1.13)
signed applets
as solution to problem of cross-page applet
communication; 114 (Q4.22)
simple class names
See also accessing; class(es)
automatic import of java.lang package;
35 (Q1.31)
sources of; 36 (Q1.31)
term definition; 34 (Q1.30)
size
applet, determining; 103 (Q4.11)
array
determining; 68 (Q2.21)
dynamic specification of; 65 (Q2.19)
fixed after creation; 65 (Q2.19)
identifier, maximum size in class file; 48 (Q2.6)
size method
obtaining applet size with; 103 (Q4.11)
windows, creating nonresizable; 131 (Q5.16)

sleep method
See also threads
pausing threads with; 207 (Q9.5)
as redrawing efficiency enhancer; 176 (Q8.4)
thread execution suspension, (table);
218 (Q9.12)
sliders
controlling; 147 (Q6.10)
socket(s); 245–254 (Q10.19–Q10.27)
See also networks
characteristics and use; 245 (Q10.19)
creating; 245 (Q10.19)
datagram sockets
characteristics and use; 251 (Q10.26)
input stream, detecting termination by remote
host; 248 (Q10.22)
raw sockets
native methods required for; 247 (Q10.21)
server
creating nonblocking; 249 (Q10.24)
specifying address for listening;
250 (Q10.25)
Socket class
characteristics; 249 (Q10.23)
creating instances of; 245 (Q10.19)
firewall handling; 248 (Q10.23)
socket operations handled by; 257 (Q11.2)
SocketImpl class
firewall handling; 248 (Q10.23)
SocketImplFactory class
firewall handling; 249 (Q10.23)
SOCKS firewalls, handling; 249 (Q10.23)
standalone machine use; 246 (Q10.20)
Solaris
See also operating systems
starting the Java Virtual Machine; 77 (Q3.1)
thread scheduling on; 219 (Q9.13)
sounds
See audio
SoX program
converting audio formats with; 265 (Q11.9)
speed
Java compared with C and C++; 88 (Q3.9)
stacks
See also data
implemented in Java, (code example);
56 (Q2.13)
Stack class
creating stack with; 56 (Q2.13)

standard I/O
  See also input; output
  error, System.err characteristics and use;
      227 (Q10.2)
  input, System.out characteristics and use;
      227 (Q10.2)
  output, System.in characteristics and use;
      227 (Q10.2)
starting
  animations; 109 (Q4.18)
  applications, by invocation of main; 77 (Q3.1)
  Java Virtual Machine; 77 (Q3.1)
  processes, with exec; 257 (Q11.2)
  start method
    invoked by applet context; 107 (Q4.16)
    invoked when browser moves to applet web
        page; 109 (Q4.18)
    sleep not recommended; 224 (Q9.17)
    starting threads with; 203 (Q9.2)
    when invoked, (table); 108 (Q4.16)
  threads; 203 (Q9.2)
state
  inconsistent
    single drawing thread as mechanism for
      · avoiding; 175 (Q8.3)
  showing, paint method; 174 (Q8.2)
  thread, relevant to thread scheduling;
      219 (Q9.13)
static
  See also class(es); constants; dynamic
  binding, term definition; 23 (Q1.18)
  static keyword
    class constant defined with; 45 (Q2.3)
    class methods
      declared with; 8 (Q1.6)
      static reference to nonstatic variable, error;
          57 (Q2.14)
    class variables defined with; 7 (Q1.5)
    as reserved keyword; 46 (Q2.4)
  static synchronized methods
    class object synchronization with;
        212 (Q9.9)
status
  image drawing, checking; 185 (Q8.13)
  image loading, ImageTracker methods,
      (table); 184 (Q8.12)
  status... methods, as triggers for image
      loading, (table); 182 (Q8.11)
stopping
  animations; 109 (Q4.18)
  applet, managed by applet context; 108 (Q4.16)

stopping (*continued*)
  stop method; 204 (Q9.3)
    caution advised; 206 (Q9.4)
    invoked by applet context; 107 (Q4.16)
    invoked when browser leaves applet web
        page; 109 (Q4.18)
    sleep not recommended; 224 (Q9.17)
    stopping audio clips; 262 (Q11.5)
    when invoked, (table); 108 (Q4.16)
  threads; 204 (Q9.3)
    safe strategies for, (code example);
        206 (Q9.4)
strategies
  accessing operating system calls; 257 (Q11.2)
  applet thread interaction with system threads;
      223 (Q9.16)
  assigning listeners; 163 (Q7.8)
  class design, for cloning support; 32 (Q1.28)
  condition variables; 216 (Q9.11)
  converting strings to numerical values;
      230 (Q10.4)
  deadlock analysis; 221 (Q9.14)
  event adapter use; 158 (Q7.4)
  event handling
    JDK 1.0.2; 140 (Q6.4)
    JDK 1.1; 156 (Q7.3)
  event model
    JDK 1.0.2; 138 (Q6.3)
    JDK 1.1; 152 (Q7.2)
  loading images; 181 (Q8.11)
  monitor locks; 210 (Q9.7)
  multithreading synchronization; 208 (Q9.6)
  platform independence
    thread scheduling issues; 222 (Q9.15)
    yield method; 219 (Q9.13)
  reading from remote files, (code example);
      237 (Q10.9)
  receiving data from server; 246 (Q10.19)
  redrawing efficiency; 175 (Q8.4)
  restarting threads; 205 (Q9.3), 205 (Q9.4)
  serialization, of threads; 217 (Q9.12)
  stopping threads, safe methods for, (code exam-
      ple); 206 (Q9.4)
  thread blocking avoidance, when not to sleep;
      224 (Q9.17)
  threads, shared resource management;
      202 (Q9.1)
  writing to URL-specified files from applets,
      restrictions and workarounds;
      243 (Q10.13)

stream(s)
  See also files; input; output
  byte, Unicode differences; 226 (Q10.1)
  input, detecting termination by remote host;
      248 (Q10.22)
  media, Java Media Framework planned
      capabilities; 263 (Q11.7)
  output
    flushing; 232 (Q10.5)
    writing to, overcoming URL connection
        restrictions; 240 (Q10.11)
  process input and output, connecting to Java
      streams; 233 (Q10.6)
  sockets as; 246 (Q10.19)
  transferring data from remote files; 237 (Q10.9)
  URL; 239 (Q10.11)
string(s)
  See also data
  concatenation, plus (+) operator; 49 (Q2.7)
    printing use of; 227 (Q10.2)
  converting to numeric values; 230 (Q10.4)
  editable, handling; 256 (Q11.1)
  immutable, handling; 255 (Q11.1)
  input, errors from binary `read` methods;
      229 (Q10.3)
  `length` method
    as example of method; 4 (Q1.3)
  output, `PrintStream` methods for;
      227 (Q10.2)
  `String` class
    automatic import of; 35 (Q1.31)
    converting strings to numeric values;
        110 (Q4.19)
    as example of class; 2 (Q1.2)
    as `final` class, advantages of; 24 (Q1.19)
    methods, (table); 256 (Q11.1)
    read-only string handling with; 255 (Q11.1)
  string literal, (table); 50 (Q2.8)
  `StringBuffer` class
    editable string handling with; 256 (Q11.1)
structures
  C-like, creating in Java; 52 (Q2.10)
  `struct` declaration (C)
    class declaration compared to; 3 (Q1.2)
    emulating in Java; 52 (Q2.10)
  fields in, compared with instance variables;
      7 (Q1.5)
subareas
  image subarea
    copying, JDK 1.0.2; 193 (Q8.21)
    copying, JDK 1.1; 198 (Q8.24)

subclass(es)
  of `Exception` classes; 70 (Q2.22)
  overloading, and overriding; 13–24
      (Q1.11–Q1.19)
  not permitted with `final` classes; 24 (Q1.19)
  `protected` access implications; 37 (Q1.33)
  term definition, characteristics and; 13 (Q1.11)
subpackages
  explicit import requirements; 35 (Q1.30)
subroutines(s)
  See methods
substring methods
  as example of overloading; 16 (Q1.13)
super
  `super` keyword
    overriding not permitted for methods
        declared with; 23 (Q1.18)
    as reserved keyword; 46 (Q2.4)
    uses of; 20 (Q1.17)
  superclass
    access, `super` versus inheritance; 20 (Q1.17)
    `Class` class information about; 58 (Q2.15)
    default superclass constructor; 21 (Q1.17)
    specification, as part of class declaration;
        3 (Q1.2)
    term definition; 13 (Q1.11)
  superinterfaces, multiple permitted; 29 (Q1.25)
suspend
  `suspend` method
    as method to avoid; 206 (Q9.4)
  threads
    `InterruptedExecution` use by methods
        that can; 184 (Q8.12)
    methods that can, (table); 218 (Q9.12)
    until another finishes; 217 (Q9.12)
switch keyword
  as reserved keyword; 46 (Q2.4)
synchronization
  See also threads
  of class objects; 212 (Q9.9)
  monitor use for; 209 (Q9.7)
  `synchronized` keyword
    characteristics and use; 210 (Q9.8)
    monitor relationship with; 212 (Q9.8)
    monitor scope definition through; 211 (Q9.8)
    as reserved keyword; 46 (Q2.4)
    as synchronization mechanism; 209 (Q9.6)
  threads
    cooperation contrasted with; 214 (Q9.10)
    importance of; 208 (Q9.6)
    `join` use; 217 (Q9.12)

syntax
APPLET tag (HTML); 98 (Q4.7)
class declaration; 3 (Q1.2)
method declaration; 4 (Q1.3)

system
resources, managing; 84 (Q3.6)
System class, automatic import of; 35 (Q1.31)
threads, versus user threads; 222–224
(Q9.15–Q9.18)

T

target field
in JDK 1.0.2, meaning of, (table); 135 (Q6.1)
TCP (Transmission Control Protocol)
as protocol underlying normal sockets;
252 (Q10.26)
termination
of applications; 144 (Q6.7)
of audio clips, estimating, (code example);
263 (Q11.7)
of input stream by remote host, detecting;
248 (Q10.22)
line terminators, readLine handling of;
225 (Q10.1)
of processes, with destroy; 258 (Q11.2)
testing
class files, javap program use for; 88 (Q3.8)
multiple main methods as useful tool for;
78 (Q3.1)
text
drawing over background images; 187 (Q8.15)
event handling for, JDK 1.0.2; 139 (Q6.3)
TextEvent class
position in JDK 1.1 class hierarchy, (table);
152 (Q7.1)
public methods, (table); 154 (Q7.2)
TextField class
events associated with, (table); 137 (Q6.2)
action events
JDK 1.0.2, (table); 142 (Q6.5)
JDK 1.1, (table); 161 (Q7.7)
TextListener interface
methods, (table); 157 (Q7.3)
this
field, obtaining Class instance with;
59 (Q2.15)
instance reference, term definition, characteristics and; 7 (Q1.6)

this (*continued*)
this keyword
as implicit instance variable specifier;
57 (Q2.14)
as reserved keyword; 46 (Q2.4)
threads
See also key themes
advantages and dangers; 202 (Q9.1)
applet, interaction with
browser threads; 223 (Q9.17)
system threads; 223 (Q9.16)
AWT, applet blocking prevention; 224 (Q9.17)
blocking, prevention strategies; 224 (Q9.17)
(chapter); 201–224 (Q9.1–Q9.18)
cooperation, wait and notifyAll/notify
use; 214 (Q9.10)
creating; 203 (Q9.2)
controlling, and; 201–208 (Q9.1–Q9.5)
deadlocks, detection, solution, and prevention;
220 (Q9.14)
interactions among; 208–221 (Q9.6–Q9.14)
killing, as stop effect; 205 (Q9.3)
life cycle; 205 (Q9.3)
notifyAll effect on; 215 (Q9.10)
operating system events not accessible to;
224 (Q9.18)
pausing threads with sleep; 207 (Q9.5)
as performance enhancer in paint method;
174 (Q8.2)
priorities
as platform dependent JVM implementation;
222 (Q9.15)
scheduling considerations; 219 (Q9.13)
restarting; 204 (Q9.3), 205 (Q9.4)
running applets as, Runnable interface use for;
26 (Q1.21)
serialization, join use; 217 (Q9.12)
single AWT drawing thread, as consistency
mechanism; 175 (Q8.3)
starting; 203 (Q9.2)
states, relevant to thread scheduling;
219 (Q9.13)
stopping; 204 (Q9.3)
safe strategies for, (code example);
206 (Q9.4)
suspension of
InterruptedExecution use by methods
that can; 184 (Q8.12)
methods that can, (table); 218 (Q9.12)
until another finishes; 217 (Q9.12)

threads (*continued*)

synchronization

importance of; 208 (Q9.6)

monitor use for; 209 (Q9.7)

term definition; 201 (Q9.1)

Thread class

automatic import of; 35 (Q1.31)

creating threads from; 203 (Q9.2)

multithreading operations handled by; 257 (Q11.2)

sleep, checked exceptions for; 70 (Q2.23)

user threads versus system threads; 222–224 (Q9.15–Q9.18)

as source of platform-dependent behavior; 222 (Q9.15)

yield use; 218 (Q9.13)

throwing

throw keyword

as reserved keyword; 46 (Q2.4)

throw statement

methods compared with, (table); 69 (Q2.22)

Throwable class

class hierarchy; 73 (Q2.25)

exceptions as subclasses of; 69 (Q2.22)

thrower, term definition; 68 (Q2.22)

throwing

checked exceptions, disadvantages of; 70 (Q2.23)

exceptions; 70 (Q2.22)

throws clause

declaring exceptions with; 70 (Q2.22)

throws keyword

as reserved keyword; 46 (Q2.4)

time; 174 (Q8.1)

audio clip playboack, (code example); 263 (Q11.7)

as finalization factor; 85 (Q3.6)

image loading, strategies; 181 (Q8.11)

time-slicing

as platform dependent JVM implementation; 222 (Q9.15)

thread wait; 207 (Q9.5)

title bar

inset values use withn; 120 (Q5.3)

to... methods

toLowerCase method

(table); 256 (Q11.1)

toString method

return values, (table); 154 (Q7.2)

toUpperCase method

(table); 256 (Q11.1)

tracking

image loading and rendering; 185 (Q8.13)

errors, (code example); 186 (Q8.13)

images

(code example); 183 (Q8.12)

MediaTracker use; 183 (Q8.12)

mouse, design issues; 132 (Q5.18)

transient keyword

as reserved keyword; 46 (Q2.4)

transparency

background, creation issues and problems; 104 (Q4.13)

images, loading over background image; 187 (Q8.16)

JDK 1.1 support for; 177 (Q8.7)

trees

containment structures as; 123 (Q5.7)

implementing in Java; 56 (Q2.13)

trim method

(table); 256 (Q11.1)

try keyword

as reserved keyword; 46 (Q2.4)

try-catch block

catching checked exceptons with; 70 (Q2.23)

typedefs

reasons for omission; 49 (Q2.7)

types

enum

class constant use as workaround; 45 (Q2.3)

term definition; 45 (Q2.3)

event

component resizing notification, JDK 1.1; 168 (Q7.12)

JDK 1.0.2, information in, (table); 136 (Q6.2)

key types and bit mask variables that are not, (table); 143 (Q6.6), 169 (Q7.13)

of event listeners; 156 (Q7.3)

primitive

advantages of; 42 (Q2.1)

reference types versus; 41 (Q2.1)

reference

object-orientation and open-ended characteristics of; 42 (Q2.1)

primitive types versus; 41 (Q2.1)

safety, int and Integer conversion support for; 43 (Q2.1)

<type>Value methods, converting strings to numerical values with; 230 (Q10.4)

U

UDP (User Datagram Protocol)
as protocol underlying datagram sockets; 252 (Q10.26)

Unicode
characters, identifier size impact; 48 (Q2.6)
input, readLine difficiencies; 226 (Q10.1)
text-oriented classes, as JDK 1.1 replacement for byte-oriented classes; 227 (Q10.2)

UNIX
See also operating systems
ping program, native methods required for implementing; 247 (Q10.21)

UnknownHostException class
thrown by getByName, (code example); 244 (Q10.16)

unsigned values
treating all 8 bits of byte value as; 43 (Q2.2)

update method
invocation of; 176 (Q8.5)
by AWT; 107 (Q4.16)
overriding example using; 16 (Q1.14)
paint invoked by; 173 (Q8.1)
purpose; 176 (Q8.5)
sleep not recommended; 224 (Q9.17)
when invoked, (table); 108 (Q4.16)

URL (Uniform Resource Locator)
See also networks
accessing remote images with; 181 (Q8.10)
applet class files, specifying; 101 (Q4.9)
connections; 235–243 (Q10.7–Q10.15), 236 (Q10.8)
external, access attempts, security exception differences between applications and applets; 243 (Q10.15)
reading from remote files with; 236 (Q10.9)
selecting from an applet; 112 (Q4.21)
URL class
URLConnection class compared with; 235 (Q10.7)
URLConnection class
GET request use; 241 (Q10.12)
URL class compared with; 235 (Q10.7)
writing to URL-specified files, restrictions and workarounds; 243 (Q10.13)

user interface
adding applets to panels; 115 (Q4.23)
applets; 103–107 (Q4.11–Q4.15)
dynamically changing; 122 (Q5.6)

user interface (*continued*)
elements, AWT Component class; 117 (Q5.1)
file access dialogs, FileDialog class use for; 130 (Q5.15)
groups of, AWT Container class; 117 (Q5.1)
native-platform toolkit components, AWT use; 125 (Q5.9)

user threads
versus system threads; 222–224 (Q9.15–Q9.18)

UTF-8 format
identifier size impact; 48 (Q2.6)

Unicode
input, JDK 1.1 handling of; 226 (Q10.1)

V

validate method
container layout management by; 121 (Q5.5)
when invoked, (table); 122 (Q5.5)

valueOf method
converting strings to numerical values; 231 (Q10.4)
creating instances with; 9 (Q1.7)

values
primitive types; 42 (Q2.1)
unsigned, treating byte value as; 43 (Q2.2)

variables
accessing superclass, with super keyword; 22 (Q1.17)
array type, object references as value of; 12 (Q1.10)
class variables
definition of; 57 (Q2.14)
instance variables compared with; 6 (Q1.5)
object references as value of; 12 (Q1.10)
condition, obtaining effect of; 215 (Q9.11)
final, characteristics and use; 24 (Q1.19)
instance
array components compared with; 67 (Q2.20)
class variables compared with; 6 (Q1.5)
definition of; 57 (Q2.14)
local
definition of; 57 (Q2.14)
fields distinguished from; 8 (Q1.6)
methods and; 53–65 (Q2.11–Q2.18)
nameless, array objects as; 67 (Q2.20)

Vector class
creating linked lists, (example); 56 (Q2.13)
dynamically extensible array use; 66 (Q2.19)

verification
characteristics of; 87 (Q3.8)
circumstances where omissible; 88 (Q3.8)
optimization as source of problems with;
87 (Q3.8)
VerifyError class
for errors detected during verification;
87 (Q3.8)

video
See also media
Java Media Framework planned capabilities;
263 (Q11.7)

virtual machine
See also JVMS
(chapter); 77–90 (Q3.1–Q3.9)
instruction set, javap as tool for learning;
79 (Q3.3)
starting; 77 (Q3.1)

virtual methods
See also binding
characteristics and use; 22 (Q1.18)

void keyword
Class instance corresponding to, (table);
63 (Q2.17)
Class instance required for use with
java.lang.reflect classes; 63 (Q2.17)
as reserved keyword; 46 (Q2.4)

volatile keyword
as reserved keyword; 46 (Q2.4)

vspace attribute (APPLET tag)
characteristics; 96 (Q4.4)
from JDK README file; 99 (Q4.7)

W

wait/notify
See also threads
notify method
actions and contraints, (table); 215 (Q9.10)
monitor use; 210 (Q9.7)
obtaining condition variable effect with;
215 (Q9.11)
thread cooperation use of; 214 (Q9.10)
notifyAll method
actions and contraints, (table); 215 (Q9.10)
monitor use; 210 (Q9.7)
obtaining condition variable effect with;
215 (Q9.11)
thread cooperation use of; 214 (Q9.10)

wait/notify (*continued*)
threads
states relevant to thread scheduling;
219 (Q9.13)
serialization of; 217 (Q9.12)
sleep use; 207 (Q9.5)
wait methods
actions and contraints, (table); 215 (Q9.10)
interacting with native process, (table);
258 (Q11.2)
join compared with; 218 (Q9.12)
monitor use; 210 (Q9.7)
as methods that trigger image loading,
(table); 182 (Q8.11)
obtaining condition variable effect with;
215 (Q9.11)
(table); 184 (Q8.12)
thread cooperation use of; 214 (Q9.10)
thread execution suspension, (table);
218 (Q9.12)
as thread pause control mechanism;
208 (Q9.5)
wait-notify service, monitor use with;
209 (Q9.7)

warnings
against hand-done layouts; 121 (Q5.4)
applet thread interaction with system threads;
223 (Q9.16)
key types and bit masks that are not event types,
(table); 143 (Q6.6)
layout manager definition, difficulties;
119 (Q5.2)
methods to avoid
resume; 206 (Q9.4)
suspend; 206 (Q9.4)
output issues, migrating from JDK 1.0.2 to JDK
1.1; 228 (Q10.2)
overriding validate and layout; 122 (Q5.5)
peer object management; 125 (Q5.9)
prefer
notifyAll to notify; 217 (Q9.11)
while toif as condition variable mechanism;
216 (Q9.11)
synchronization issues
code vulnerable to unsynchronized code
actions; 212 (Q9.8)
in multithreaded applications; 208 (Q9.6)
thread blocking avoidance, when not to sleep;
224 (Q9.17)

web pages
See also networks; WWW (World Wide Web)
activating from applets; 112 (Q4.21)
applets
   behavior when browser leaves page;
      109 (Q4.18)
   behavior when browser returns to page;
      109 (Q4.18)
   as embeddable Java programs; 91 (Q4.1)
   methods for embedding; 95 (Q4.4)
   web page area transformed by; 92 (Q4.1)
class file location; 103 (Q4.10)
communication among applets on
   different pages; 114 (Q4.22)
   same page; 111 (Q4.20)
loading, image handling issues; 182 (Q8.11)
when field
in JDK 1.0.2, meaning of, (table); 135 (Q6.1)
while
loop, for condition variable effect; 215 (Q9.11)
   (code example); 216 (Q9.11)
`while` keyword
   as reserved keyword; 46 (Q2.4)
width
applet, determining; 103 (Q4.11)
width attribute (APPLET tag)
   characteristics; 96 (Q4.4)
      from JDK README file; 98 (Q4.7)
wildcards
`import` declaration use of; 35 (Q1.30)
windows
See also AWT (Abstract Window Toolkit)
adding applets to; 115 (Q4.23)
borderless, creating; 129 (Q5.13)
closing , correcting problems with
   in JDK 1.0.2; 144 (Q6.7)
   in JDK 1.1; 167 (Q7.11)
events, information in, (table); 136 (Q6.2)
frames, dialogs and; 127–131 (Q5.11–Q5.16)
hierarchy, *See* containment hierarchy
nonresizable, creating; 131 (Q5.16)
popup, creating; 129 (Q5.13)
positioning; 127 (Q5.11)
re-exposure, actions taken by AWT; 177 (Q8.6)
resizing notification; 168 (Q7.12)

windows (*continued*)
`Window` class
   creating borderless windows; 129 (Q5.13)
   event information, (table); 136 (Q6.2)
`WindowAdapter` class
   strategies for use; 158 (Q7.4)
`windowClosing` method
   (code example); 167 (Q7.11)
`WindowEvent` class
   position in JDK 1.1 class hierarchy, (table);
      152 (Q7.1)
   public methods, (table); 155 (Q7.2)
`WindowListener` interface; 167 (Q7.11)
   methods, (table); 157 (Q7.3)
Windows NT/95, time-slicing; 219 (Q9.13)
workarounds
applet menus; 105 (Q4.14)
clipping rectangle, JDK 1.0.2, (code example);
   192 (Q8.20)
transparent backgrounds; 104 (Q4.13)
writing
to URL output streams; 239 (Q10.11)
to URL-specified files from applets, restrictions
   and workarounds; 243 (Q10.13)
`...Writer` classes, as JDK 1.1 text-oriented
   output handlers; 227 (Q10.2)
WWW (World WIde Web)
See also networks; web pages
accessing, with http GET; 240 (Q10.12)

X

x field
in JDK 1.0.2, meaning of, (table); 135 (Q6.1)
XOR drawing mode
characteristics and use; 178 (Q8.8)

Y

y field
in JDK 1.0.2, meaning of, (table); 135 (Q6.1)
yield method
characteristics and use; 218 (Q9.13)
as redrawing efficiency enhancer; 176 (Q8.4)

The Addison-Wesley Java™ Series

The Java™ Programming Language
Ken Arnold and James Gosling
ISBN 0-201-63455-4

The Java™ Tutorial
Object-Oriented Programming for the Internet
Mary Campione and Kathy Walrath
ISBN 0-201-63454-6

The Java™ Class Libraries
An Annotated Reference
Patrick Chan and Rosanna Lee
ISBN 0-201-63458-9

The Java™ Language Specification
James Gosling, Bill Joy, and Guy Steele
ISBN 0-201-63451-1

The Java™ Application Programming Interface, Volume 1
Core Packages
James Gosling, Frank Yellin, and The Java Team
ISBN 0-201-63453-8

The Java™ Application Programming Interface, Volume 2
Window Toolkit and Applets
James Gosling, Frank Yellin, and The Java Team
ISBN 0-201-63459-7

JDBC™ Database Access with Java™
A Tutorial and Annotated Reference
Graham Hamilton, Rick Cattell, and Maydene Fisher
ISBN 0-201-30995-5

The Java™ FAQ
Jonni Kanerva
ISBN 0-201-63456-2

Concurrent Programming in Java™
Design Principles and Patterns
Doug Lea
ISBN 0-201-69581-2

The Java™ Virtual Machine Specification
Tim Lindholm and Frank Yellin
ISBN 0-201-63452-X

Please see our web site (http://www.awl.com/cp/javaseries.html) for more information on these and other forthcoming titles.